🙠 IN MEMORIAM 🙠

Tracy Burr Strong

(6 August 1943 - 11 May 2022)

David B. Allison and Tracy B. Strong near the Merchant's Gate in New York City's Central Park.

New Nietzsche Studies
The Journal of the Nietzsche Society

POLITICAL REDEMPTION, WORLD HISTORY AND ETERNAL RETURN, DIONYSUS AND ARIADNE — AND NIETZSCHE'S DEBTS

BOOK REVIEWS
& REVIEW ESSAYS

REDEMPTION, THE SACRED, WORLD HISTORY, THE TIME OF ETERNAL RETURN, AND NIETZSCHE'S DEBTS

ZARATHUSTRA'S CRISIS OF REDEMPTION

HEINRICH MEIER

The speech 'On the Poets'—the seventeenth chapter of the Second Part of *Thus Spoke Zarathustra*—is a conclusion and a prelude. After the critique of the famous wise man, who remains subservient to the people; of the hero of knowledge, who wants to be nothing but honest; of the self-forgetting observer, who imagines himself to be a pure mirror of the world; and of the manifoldly fragmented scholar, who does not know how to risk his life for One thing or turn it toward One thing, the final chapter of the two groups of five whose subject is the philosopher (II, 8-12 and II, 13-17) marks the end of the series of contrasts with the critique of the poet. But since Zarathustra advances the critique of the poet as a self-critique, the speech at the same time indicates the beginning of the destruction of the teaching that Zarathustra has announced as a poet and prophet. "On the Poets" contains the first encounter with a single disciple since the speech "On the Tree on the Mountain." And, like the dialogue in I, 8 with the youth who needed to be addressed nobly, the conversation in II, 17 with the unspecified disciple, who can stand for the disciple simply, signifies a turning-point in the action.[1] Zarathustra opens the conversation with a challenging assertion concerning the spirit, which in the fifth of the ten chapters figured as the decisive concept of the will to power for the "wisest ones" and their ideas: Now that he knows the body better, the spirit is to him "only as it were spirit," and what—like the spirit—is called the "permanent" is "also only a parable." The disciple shows no particular interest in the spirit. But he recalls having heard something of that kind from Zarathustra "once before." This is true at least of the statement's conclusion. In fact, the sentence about the "permanent" from the speech "On the Blessed Isles" is so present to him that he can reproduce its continuation almost word for word: "at the time you added: 'but the poets lie too much.'" The question that the disciple adds—"Yet why did you say that the poets lie too

New Nietzsche Studies, Vol. 11, Nos. 3 and 4 (Fall 2021 / Spring 2022), pp. 1–25.
© 2022 Nietzsche Society. ISSN 1091–0239.

much?"—is harshly rejected by Zarathustra. He is not among those "whom one may ask about their Why." The impression, suggested by Zarathustra's reaction, that he is refusing to provide information about his reasons because he expects unquestioning acceptance of his announcement, expects faith or obedience, turns out to be unfounded just as quickly as Zarathustra's statement to the disciple—namely, that it would overexert his memory should he wish to carry the reasons for his judgment with him, the more so as he "experienced" them "long ago"—proves to be untrue. The saying from the prologue that the disciple had memorized concerned nothing less than the "conjecture" of God, and no philosopher will forget the reasons he "experienced" in the confrontation with a question concerning him existentially, or which are most intimately connected to his answer to this question. Rather, he will so much "carry" them "with him" as to be able to give himself an account of them day and night. Zarathustra attempts to unsettle the disciple sufficiently to point him to the movement of thought: "Yet what did Zarathustra once say to you? That the poets lie too much?—But Zarathustra too is a poet./Now do you believe that he was telling the truth here? Why do you believe that?" To Zarathustra's question concerning the reasons, the disciple answers with the profession: "I believe in Zarathustra." Zarathustra shakes his head. He is still speaking to believers. Not only the political, but the pedagogical hopes, too, that he expressed in the farewell speech at the end of the First Part, have remained unfulfilled. He is getting nowhere.[2] "Belief does not make me blessed," confirms the counter-Jesus, "least of all belief in me." After the admonition to the disciples—"Perhaps he has deceived you"—has faded away without having had the desired effect, he now sharpens the tone: "But given that someone said in all seriousness that the poets lie too much: well he is right—we do lie too much." No more Perhaps. Zarathustra decisively presses ahead with the weaning from faith in him. In two rounds, on which he spends two-thirds of the speech, he demonstrates that he has on hand the reasons for his judgment. The first round of the critique of the poets leads to the exclamation: "all Gods are poets' parables, poets' deceptions!" Zarathustra repeats, comprehensibly compressed, what he had already taught in his first appearance in the city "The Motley Cow," with the difference that at that time the teacher of the overman did not group himself among the poets.[3] The repetition prepares the dramatic peak in the central verse of the chapter: "Verily, it draws us ever upward—namely to the realm of the clouds: upon these we place our motley brood and then call them Gods and overmen." To make sure that the disclosure of the "poets' deception" reaches the disciple, Zarathustra immediately adds: "For they are just light enough for these chairs!—all these Gods and overmen." And at the end of the self-critique he does not fail to indicate a break, tedium, and dissatisfaction. "Ah, how weary I am of the poets!"[4] The crisis that Zarathustra provokes with the undermining of his original teaching is noted laconically by the narrator. The disciple is angry with Zarathustra, and both keep silent. Only once before, and never again, do we learn about a disciple's, or the disciples', being angry with Zarathustra. There, Zarathustra refers to the reaction sparked among the disciples by his teaching that there is no "reward- and pay-master" for their virtue. In one case it is about the providential God, in the other it concerns the meaning-giving overman. In both, Zarathustra provokes the disciples' anger because he takes away the authority from which they expect a foothold, or because he denies the salvation in which they place their hope and which is supposed to lie outside themselves.[5]

The second round of the critique of the poets above all serves the separation of the poet from the philosopher. It is no longer addressed to the disciple, who persists in silence, but instead turns toward future things and people. Zarathustra looks back at the poets. Instead of "we" and "us" he speaks now of "they" and "them." Even the last words of the first round, "how weary I am of the poets," belong to the past: "I became weary of the poets, the old and the new: superficial ones are they all to me, and shallow seas." The crux concerns reasons and reflection, i.e., exactly that at which the examination of the disciple in the previous conversation was aimed. "They did not take their thought deep enough: therefore their feeling never sank down to the grounds./A little lust and a little boredom: that has so far been their best reflection." That the poets do not actually think deeply is determinative for Zarathustra's judgment. Everything else follows from this: That they are "not clean enough" and are eager for spectators, that they are ruled by their vanity and primp heaven and earth, or that they fall victim to self-intoxication and believe that when they feel tender emotions, "nature herself is in love with them." Their will goes to the surface, to appearance, to deception. Since their spirit lacks the foothold that would allow them to come to rest in themselves, Zarathustra sees those "penitents of the spirit," who want to be nothing but honest and consider themselves sublime because they have turned cruelty against themselves into a moral duty, as growing, ultimately, out of the poets. Zarathustra concludes the critique of the poet with a look at the very same "penitent of the spirit" with the critique of whom he began the final group of five on the philosopher.[6] The philosopher is to be confused with neither the one nor the other. Which does not mean that he may dispense with honesty. Or that he should not make use of poetry. Just as for the Socrates of the *Republic*, who banishes the poets from the city and at the end speaks as a poet himself, for Zarathustra it is obviously first and foremost a matter of determining the order of rank. Two, not One.[7]

The crisis of Zarathustra's teaching is the central theme of the fourth group of five in the Second Part. Because the crisis manifests itself in Zarathustra's relationship to the disciples, the action of the chapters that follow the speech "On the Poets" is of particular importance and the narrator's interventions have a weight that they have not had since the Prologue. In other words: after Nietzsche has Zarathustra level the most thorough critique of the poetic type, he makes the most conspicuous use of the means of poetry. With the fantastical narrative of the "conversation with the fire-dog," "On Great Events" (II, 18) presents Zarathustra's attempt to fill the disciples in on his view of revolution. The narrator prefaces Zarathustra's narrative, which comprises 29 of the 42 verses, with a no less fantastical story. It takes place on an island, on which "a fire-mountain steadily smokes" and on which "the people" believe a gate to the underworld or the entrance to hell can be found. "Toward the hour of midday," the company of a ship that was anchored there because the crew wanted to shoot rabbits on the island thought that they heard a voice saying clearly: "it is time! It is high time!" And they believed they saw Zarathustra flying "like a shadow" in the direction of the fire-mountain. We can first of all take from the story of the sailors, of whose origin we learn nothing, the fact that the people well beyond the blessed isles know and love

Zarathustra, "as the people love: that is, with love and awe together in equal parts." In addition, the narrator makes visible to us how love and awe are able, out of the metaphors that Zarathustra used in his speeches—from the great midday, to flying, to the shadow of the overman—to achieve the *realia* of a miraculous account that transports the prophet from the Orient into the realm of the supernatural. Even the call issuing from the heights, of "it is time!" draws on a speech of Zarathustra's, namely the most famous of all his speeches, "which is also called 'the Prologue.'"[8] The narrator continues with the parody: At the time when the seamen marveled at the flying Zarathustra across the "fire-island," the rumor that Zarathustra had disappeared at night caused disquiet on the blessed isles; 'but three days later the sailors' story added to this disquiet—and now all the people were saying that the devil had taken Zarathustra away." The disciples did not believe in the descent into hell. They laughed at the people's gossip, yet "in the ground of their souls they were all filled with concern and longing: therefore great was their joy when on the fifth day Zarathustra appeared among them." Zarathustra narrates to the disciples that he went over the sea to discover the secret of the "fire-dog," and that he has in fact "seen the truth naked." The truth that Zarathustra seeks to make accessible to the disciples with his curious account is that revolution, like the state, which "by all means wants to be the most important animal on earth," is indeed "much bellowing and smoke," but that "great events" are not to be expected of either. "The greatest events—those are not our loudest but our stillest hours./Not around the inventors of new noise: but around the inventors of new values does the world revolve; inaudibly it revolves." At the end of the parable, Zarathustra underlines the message for the disciples by opposing to the ash- and smoke-spewing fire-dog "another fire-dog," whose breath "exhales gold." Zarathustra's counterrevolution demands speaking "really out of the heart of the earth." From there it wants to recover not only, like Hölderlin's Hyperion, the mysteriously growing gold, but likewise the laughter.[9] Zarathustra's vision of a counterrevolution filled with gold and laughter gets through to the disciples as little as his saying of the stillest hour reaches them. They are hardly listening to him. Too great is "their desire to tell him about the sailors, the rabbits, and the flying man." The people's small events completely captivate them. Zarathustra shakes his head once more. He asks himself why "the specter" of whom the disciples told him cried, "it is time!" "*For what* is it then—high time?" The call that he once addressed to the people in the market does not cross his mind. It is no longer his call.[10]

Zarathustra's teaching has come a long way from the revolutionary demand that the overman *be* the meaning of the earth to the counterrevolutionary confidence that the heart of the earth *is* gold. The disciples have not come along with it. For them, the futurist doctrine has remained intact. Not in the sense that they were initiating the decisive reversal or would even undertake significant steps to prepare it, but rather that they rally around the faith planted by Zarathustra and cling steadfastly to it. Zarathustra's change, which was indicated by his dissatisfaction with the poets as well as his contempt for great events, has, at most, made the disciples angry, though without disturbing them in such a way as to have induced a fertile restlessness. Therefore they are unprepared for the shock that the apocalyptic prophecy in the chapter "The Soothsayer" (II, 19) triggers in Zarathustra, and the turn that he ultimately accomplishes must leave them perplexed. The prophecy comes out of nowhere. It begins with the words "and I saw," as do seven of the twenty-two chapters of the *Revelation of John*: "—and I saw a great sadness come over men. The best became weary of their works./A teaching was issued, and a belief went along with it: 'All is empty, All is alike, All was!'/And from all the hills it echoed: 'All is empty, All is alike, All was!'" The vision of general exhaustion, inversion, and futility concerns not only men, but also the fruits and fields, every wellspring, and in the end the sea, which Zarathustra had deployed as the first image of the overman: "'Ah, where is there yet a sea in which one can drown': thus resounds our lament—across shallow swamps./ Verily, we have even become too weary to die; now we are still awake and live on—in sepulchers!"[11] "Thus," the narrator reports, "Zarathustra heard a soothsayer speak." We learn nothing about place and time, occasion or context of the "prophecy," which strikes like lightning. Rather, however, that it touched Zarathustra's "heart" and "transformed" him. It affects him so greatly that he becomes "like those of whom the soothsayer had spoken." What does the prophecy show him that he did not see himself? Was he not long familiar with the historicism encountering him in it? To say nothing of egalitarianism. And had he not opposed his futurist doctrine to precisely that which is commonly called "nihilism"? Why then is he seized by the great sadness and weariness proclaimed by the soothsayer? He speaks to his disciples of the "long twilight" that threatens. "Ah, how am I to salvage my light across that!" As in the prologue to the Second Part, Zarathustra's concern appears to be for his teaching. Just as he then saw it to be "in danger" because his enemies had distorted its "image," so now he is haunted by the question of how it is to be capable of surviving the onrushing world-darkness, were the prophecy to prove true. In "The Child with the Mirror" (II, 1), Zarathustra wanted to set out for his friends like "a cry and a cheer," in order to support his teaching. Eighteen chapters later he sees that his disciples remain at the level of the camel. He has not succeeded in creating companions for himself. But are camels not sufficient to carry the teaching through a time of drought, to preserve it and pass it on? In view of a growing retinue of disciples who raise themselves up by means of the teaching, are loyal to it, and know it *verbatim*, its light should certainly be salvageable across this time. Unless with the salvation of its light, not its transmission, but the teaching itself is put in question: its adequacy, its suitability to the task set, its truth.[12]

After the prophecy Zarathustra wanders about restlessly, neither eats nor drinks for three days, loses "his speech," and finally falls into a deep sleep. Unlike the sleep at the end of the Prologue, from which he awoke with the "new truth" that in the future he should not speak to the people, but to companions, the sleep this time does not last only a few hours. In "long night-watches" the disciples sit around him and tremble, until "he should wake and talk again and convalesce from his affliction." When he awakens, he turns to his disciples, "as if from a great distance," with the narrative of a dream, and asks them to help him "guess" its meaning. For whereas he was effortlessly able to interpret the dream in "The Child with the Mirror" and to put it in the service of his desire to resume his teaching activity, he says of the dream he has now dreamed that it is still a riddle to him. In fact, the enigmatic narrative makes vivid the deep crisis into which the soothsayer has plunged Zarathustra with the saying *All is empty, All is alike, All was*. Zarathustra dreams that he has renounced all life and, as a night- and grave-watchman on the "lonely mountain-castle of death," guarded glass coffins, out of which "life that had been overcome" looks at him. With the "rustiest of all keys" he is able to open the "creakiest of all gates." He wakes a bird, whose "malicious croaking" reverberates through the long corridors. It is still "more dreadful and heart-constricting" when the cry is once again quiet and he sits alone in the "deceitful silence." Finally, three blows strike the door "like thunder-claps." Three times Zarathustra calls "Alpa!" and "Who is carrying his ashes up the mountain?" He cannot open the door with his key until "a roaring wind" tears its wings apart and casts a black coffin in front of him, which bursts open and spews forth a "thousandfold laughter." From "a thousand grimaces" it laughs and jeers and roars at Zarathustra. "Hence I was terribly frightened: it threw me down. And I screamed in horror, as I have never screamed before." Whereas Zarathustra does not yet know how to interpret the dream from which his own scream woke him, "his most beloved disciple" is immediately on the spot with an interpretation. He grasps Zarathustra by the hand and assures him, himself, and the other disciples of the teaching's brilliant victory. In order to interpret the dream in the sense of the teaching, however, the disciple must make a transposition. Life provides him with the key: 'Your life itself interprets this dream for us, O Zarathustra!" Zarathustra is not the night- and grave-watchman who renounced all life, but, on the contrary, the wind that tears open the gates of the "castles of death," and the coffin with which life enters into "all death-chambers." His laughter triumphs over the terrors of death. "And even when the long twilight comes and the weariness of death, you will not go under in our heaven, you advocate of life!" Zarathustra is the bringer of light, the mighty savior, the confidence of his disciples: "Now child's- laughter will ever well up out of coffins; now a strong wind will ever come victoriously to all weariness of death: of this you are our guarantor and soothsayer!" The disciple is able to explain that Zarathustra dreamed his "heaviest dream" through the assumption that Zarathustra dreamed the dream of his enemies, who, once they wake up, will come to him and increase his flock of disciples. The counter-Jesus seems to have reached the peak of his effectiveness.

His going-under is overcome in the disciples' faith. For them he is the way, and the truth, and the life.[13]

Does the teaching put the disciple in the position of understanding the master better than he understood himself? For, along with the interpretation of Zarathustra's "heaviest dream," the understanding of the crisis set off by the soothsayer's prophecy is also in question. Did Zarathustra not recognize that he is the true counter-soothsayer and that the prophecy is not able to harm his teaching? Or is there, in the interpretation put forth by the beloved disciple, "much ringing play," meant to drown out the circle's concern and give courage to all, master and disciples alike? Zarathustra looks at his disciples and examines their faces. But "still" he does not recognize them. When they set him "on his feet," "all at once his eye" is transformed: he understands "all that had happened," and strokes his beard. Zarathustra comprehends what the crisis of the teaching is about, how the dream is to be interpreted, and who those surrounding him are. The crisis lies behind him. He calls on the disciples to provide a good meal in common. The soothsayer is to be at his side, for he "still wants to show him a sea in which he can drown." Now that he has "recognized" them, he no longer addresses the disciples with "you friends" but as "my disciples." It is the first time in the Second Part and the third and final time in the book that he calls them "my disciples." Finally, he gazes long into the face of the disciple who interpreted the dream, and while doing so, shakes his head. Three times, in three successive chapters, the disciples have proven to be believers. Three times they have fallen back upon their belief in Zarathustra. Three times Zarathustra shakes his head. Even the beloved disciple will not be in a position to support the teaching with reasons and amend it so that it can outlast the twilight. Far from being able to recognize the futurist doctrine's birth defect, he shows himself unreceptive to the soothsayer's verdict, *All was!*, which indicates its future.[14]

All Zarathustra's paths lead to the speech "On Redemption" (II, 20). All expectations for the prophet enter into it. All questions to the philosopher are condensed in it. All lines of action connect and dissolve in One speech, which breaks the work into two unequal halves. It counts among the chapter's special features that we hear Zarathustra speak to the people, to the disciples, and to himself, and that we are specifically pointed to the different approaches to the addressees, should we not have been paying attention to it up till now.[15] Zarathustra speaks to the people, not because he has given up the resolution no longer to address his speech to the people, but because "the cripples and beggars" surround him, as, according to the old Gospels, they surrounded Jesus when they recognized him with his disciples. As Zarathustra is going "across the great bridge one day," a "hunchback" steps up to him and says: "Behold, Zarathustra! The people too learn from you and come to believe in your teaching: but in order for them to believe you completely, One more thing is needed—you must yet persuade us cripples!" Zarathustra encounters believers on all sides. But unlike the disciples, the people are not satisfied with metaphors and parables. To grasp faith, they want to hear of deeds. Their love and awe demand miracles: The cripples could be "persuaded" if the prophet were to take the infirmities from which they suffer away from them, if his teaching were to prove its truth by making the world new, if the overman were to signify redemption for everyone. Whom can Zarathustra redeem once he has gone "across the great bridge"? The people? the disciples? himself? He scorns the desire to testify to his glory through miracles. "If one takes the hunch away from the hunchback, one thereby takes away his spirit—thus the people teach." Zarathustra will not make the crooked to be straight, the lame to walk, the blind to see. He is no miracle-healer, no miracle-doer, no miracle-announcer. The appeal to what the people teach—"why should Zarathustra not also learn from the people, if the people learn from Zarathustra?"—seems in all this to be no more than a rhetorical evasion. In fact, however, Zarathustra's wisdom will have to prove that it is able to recover the reason contained in the teaching of the non-wise: There's a good side to everything. But first he embarks on a course that leads directly to the futurist teaching's smoldering core. He answers the cripples' complaint about their infirmities with the complaint about "inverse cripples,"whose infirmities the people consider to be marks of greatness and genius, men "with too little of Everything and too much of One thing." Zarathustra confesses that cripples in the ordinary sense are "what matters least" to him. What exasperates him, what fills him with revulsion, are the aberrations, instances of one-sidedness, dismemberments, the patchwork that does not integrate into a meaningful whole. The people know well about cripples in the ordinary sense. They do not know well about "inverse cripples," because they lack the idea of what man in the best case can and is to be.[16] "In deep *Unmut*,"[i] Zarathustra turns from the people to the disciples: "Verily, my friends, I walk among men as if among fragments and limbs of men." Zarathustra's anger applies not only to the men of the present, but to those of the past as well. Whether he looks around himself or looks backward, his eye "always finds the like: fragments and limbs and gruesome accidents—but no men!" Zarathustra draws on the diagnosis that he made of mankind in the center of the farewell speech in the First Part and which is supposed to constitute the futurist teaching's therapy: "Still we fight step by step with the giant Accident, and over the whole of mankind there has reigned so far only nonsense, without-sense." But only now does he express the consequence of the verdict regarding the history of mankind and the displacement of all meaning into the future: There has been no man, and there will be no man, as long as the all-important reversal, the consciously brought about great midday, the hoped-for future event, is still pending. Zarathustra goes even further. He confesses something he has not confessed in any of the previous forty-three chapters, to say nothing of the Prologue: "The *Now and Formerly* upon earth—ah! my friends—that is what I find most unbearable; and I should not know how to live if I were not also a seer of that which must come." In the speech to the sun with which the book began, Zarathustra had come to the understanding that an overflow of wisdom led him to return from solitude to men. He became a prophet out of love for man, a love that had to express itself as a demand of men and which he wanted to understand as an expression of fullness. In the "Night-Song," he convinced himself that even a God's love is to be understood in terms of a lack. And now he admits in almost as many words that the prophet's love is based on a deep dissatisfaction with men, with the world as it is, and with himself. Zarathustra did not know how to live without

---

i   *Translator's Note:* The German word *Unmut* is related to *Mut* ("courage" or "heart" in the sense of nerve or boldness), though not as its negation. Instead, *Unmut* carries a sense of anger, annoyance, and resentment, and may in fact be very *mutig* ("brave"). Because of its particular importance to the author's argument, I have decided to leave the term untranslated.

becoming a prophet. The world seemed unbearable to him without the prospect of re-creating it. He considered everything, past and present, to be in need of salvation by the future. "A seer, a willer, a creator, a future himself and a bridge to the future—and alas, also as it were a cripple by this bridge: all this is Zarathustra."[17] As a prophet who wills salvation and creates meaning, Zarathustra already belongs to the future to which he provides a bridge for others. But even with the directedness toward the future of his willing, his creating, his being, he himself—here the speech's radical turn sets in—is still "as it were" a cripple. The physician's diagnosis shows that the physician is not someone who has convalesced. His orientation toward the future proves to be dependence on the future, on the imaginary. The redemption Zarathustra promises transforms all Now and Formerly on earth into a realm of the unredeemed, Zarathustra included. The futurist teaching is rooted in indignation over reality. With the nerve of the teaching laid bare, the question concerning the teacher becomes acute: *Who is Zarathustra to us?* Zarathustra poses it for the disciples, who remain silent. He had prepared the question since the speeches "On the Rabble" (II, 6) and "On the Tarantulas" (II, 7), when he drew attention to the role of *disgust*, which he claimed to have overcome, and of *revenge*, which he characterized as a serious temptation. Then he turned, in ten speeches and songs, to a thorough self-questioning and self-clarification, whose yield first put him in the position to carry out the turn that comes to light in "On Redemption." In the last of these speeches, he incurred the anger of a believer in Zarathustra when he undermined the teaching of the overman by providing a glimpse into the poet's workshop in which it originates. Having placed the questions "Is he a poet? Or a truthful one?" in the mouths of the disciples, Zarathustra exposes the poet's share in the futurist teaching in four summarizing verses at the end of his look back. In verse 16 he takes up the assertion with which he began the speech to the disciples eight verses before: "I walk among men as among fragments of the future: that future which I envisage." He replaces the *as if* [*wie*] of verse 8 with an *as* [*als*] and thus makes use of the subtle distinction that he introduced in order to correct a "mocking speech" in the Second Part's first teaching-speech: The poet and prophet sees men *as* fragments of a future that he imagines. The futurist teaching *makes* them into fragments of the yet-to-be-created whole. Verse 17 reiterates the all-important significance of the salvific deed and recalls the saying regarding the "poets' deception": "And this is all my poetizing and striving, that I poetize into One and bring together what is fragment and riddle and gruesome accident." Verse 18 confirms and illuminates the "most unbearable thing" as the mission's real driving force: "And how could I bear to be man if man were not also a poet and riddle-guesser and the redeemer of accident." Finally, verse 19 marks the point at which the poet-prophet's verdict must encounter the soothsayer's verdict, and the futurist teaching's powerlessness becomes evident: "To redeem those of the past and to re-create all 'It was' into a 'Thus I willed it!'—that alone should I call redemption!" The attempt to re-create the past through a later meaning-giving and to redeem all that was through a future event becomes aware of its necessary failure in the face of the apocalyptic prophecy, because the event that is burdened with redemption is unable to assert its outstanding position in time against all *It was*, and instead itself falls victim to the soothsayer's *All was!*[18]

When Zarathustra came to his senses after his "heaviest dream" and grasped "all that had happened," he recognized, together with the powerlessness of the futurist teaching, its falsehood. His critique of the will to power at work in the will to truth allowed him to determine the evasive movement to which his own will to power had recourse in light of its powerlessness in the face of the *It was*: What eluded the will's direct access was subjected to it indirectly, distorted in perception, reduced in valuation. In the second half of the speech "On Redemption," Zarathustra will speak of the *spirit of revenge* in regard to this evasive movement by the will to power. It is the greatest danger for the philosopher because it does not allow the will to truth to reach its goal. The futurist teaching takes its revenge on the *It was*, against which its power fails, by relegating it to nonsense or without-sense and by promising salvation for those who do not need salvation. Who but a believer in Zarathustra could believe Socrates to be in need of redemption by Zarathustra? Since Zarathustra knows that he cannot build on believers, he has every reason to change the teaching itself so that it is able to survive the prophesied world-darkness. The disciples hear for the first time from Zarathustra that the teacher of the meaning of the earth was "still as it were" a cripple who only knew how to live with the Now and Formerly in hopes of its future overcoming. But he does not explain the significance of the spirit of revenge to them by the example of the doctrine that he presented to them earlier. He begins with the lion-wisdom of the will as "liberator and joy-bringer," which he taught them after his second return from solitude, in order now to add, supplementing and in fact completely changing everything, that the will itself is "still a prisoner" of the *It was*. "Powerless with respect to what was done" because it is not able to "break" time, the will that wants to create, not observe, is imprisoned in its inaction, "an evil spectator of all that is past." The will proves to be the opposite of a joy-bringer. "That time does not run backwards, this arouses the will's fury; 'that which was'—that is the stone which it cannot roll away." The lion-wisdom culminates in the insight of the great reversal of the will: "And so it rolls stones in fury and *Unmut*, and takes revenge on whatever does not, like itself, feel fury and *Unmut*." Zarathustra states the fatal inversion in the speech's central verse. That he speaks there not only about the will in general, but also about and to himself, is clear from everything he has said about what was "most unbearable" for him. The narrator further emphasizes the self-critical turn by attributing "deep *Unmut*" to Zarathustra, for the first and only time, immediately before the speech to the disciples.[19] *Unmut*, anger, *thymos* drives the will in the reversal. "Thus the will, the liberator, became a harmer: and upon all that can suffer it takes revenge for its inability to go backwards./This, yes this alone, is what revenge itself is: the will's ill will toward time and its 'It was.'" The will to power's ill will is sparked by that which precedes the will and at which the will's power fails—its own nature, down to every necessity, which *was*, before it *wills*. Revenge is the expression of a lack of power, an evasion and deviation of the will, which rebels in vain against necessity. Zarathustra speaks of the "great folly" which dwells in "our" will and which, heightened into the *spirit of revenge*, has been "up to now men's best reflection." He elucidates this reflection in a particular form: "where there was suffering, there was always supposed to be punishment." The revenge of the will that became aware of its powerlessness moralized the world. The suffering that aroused its *Unmut* was construed as punishment and thus made subject to justice. The justice of the moral world order, which is supposed to be ruled by an intention and to guarantee a meaning, takes the place of justice toward the world, toward life, toward the self, which the knower seeks to reach in the sense of an *adaequatio rei*. The spirit of revenge contrives a moral law to which it subjugates the innocence of becoming, or a higher will through which it can establish an order that the will is not capable of creating by its own power. On the path that Zarathustra shows to the disciples, the spirit of revenge has reached its goal by distorting willing itself into a punishment and hence reducing life to a punishment. He makes visible to his audience the consequences of such a distortion and reduction in a panopticon of judgments ultimately "preached" by "madness." He begins with a variation of Mephistopheles' maxim, which he had drawn on in characterizing the reality of the "present ones" in "On the Land of Education" (II, 14): "Everything passes away, therefore everything deserves to pass away!" And he ends with the later teaching of the will's self-redemption from willing to non-willing, returning him to the present. In the middle of the series, in the third of the five judgments intended to illustrate the justice demanded by the spirit of revenge, he draws on one of the oldest sayings of the philosophers: "Morally things are ordered according to justice and punishment. Oh, where is there redemption from the flux of things and from the punishment 'existence'?"[20] As he expressly remarks, Zarathustra had wanted to lead the disciples away from such "fable-songs" when he taught them that the will is a creator. In light of the completed lion-wisdom, the teaching of the will as a "liberator and joy-bringer" must be advanced by just one, decisive, step, which liberates the will from *Unmut* against the *It was*. Zarathustra picks up the thread from the end of the speech's first part, when, looking back at the futurist doctrine, he said: "To redeem those of the past and to re-create all 'It was' into a 'Thus I willed it!' —that alone should I call redemption!" The task is now recast: "All 'It was' is a fragment, a riddle, a gruesome accident—until the creating will says to it: 'but thus I willed it!'" The *re-creation* of the "It was," which the futurist teaching claimed to bring about through a meaning-giving event, is no longer mentioned. Those of the past, moreover, no longer need to be redeemed. What is to be redeemed is the will, from its indignation at reality and from its rebellion against necessity, from the perceptual distortion of what is and the devaluation of what was. Zarathustra corrects himself following a dash: "—Until the creating will says to it: 'But thus I will it! Thus shall I will it!'" The will becomes its own liberator when it can say Yes to becoming as a whole, can affirm what is past as past, what is present as present, presently and futurally, because the will wills ahead. All Zarathustra adds are questions that pose themselves to him and of which he can hardly expect an answer from his disciples, eight questions concerning the will: "But has it yet spoken thus? And when does that happen? Has the will been unharnessed yet from its own foolishness?" The third determination from the treatment of the will in the triad II, 11-13, the *unharnessed will*, returns. Just as, for the hero's will in the speech "On The Sublime Ones" (II, 13), the harness of cruelty against oneself, understood as a purpose, had to be removed if it was to ascend to the serenity of the over-hero, so too must the knower's will to power be unhitched from the harness that makes it incessantly pull and rush and rush and pull further, no matter which pathways, detours, digressions it might happen to end up in during the attempt to break time and to compel necessity. The will can only be unharnessed through *insight* into the foolishness that inheres in and deceives it. "Has the will yet become its own redeemer and joy-bringer? Has it unlearned the spirit of revenge and all gnashing of teeth?/And who has taught it reconciliation with time, and something higher than all reconciliation?" The will requires orientation and guidance by insight, which protects it from *Unmut* and prevents it from straying into revenge by *instructing* it to set right. But Zarathustra demands more than instruction by insight. He demands a teaching that promises "something higher" than reconciliation with time and with necessity. Knowledge of the world as it is appears insufficient to him because it does not correspond with the direction of the will itself and so does not dispel the danger of a freshly burgeoning *Unmut*. To counter this ill will, either knowledge must be undergirded by love, or the will must be converted to the belief that it is itself the ground of the acceptance of the world as it is, so that the world is in harmony with the direction of its willing. Zarathustra follows the second option. "The will that is—will to power must will something higher than all reconciliation—: yet how shall this happen? Who could also teach it to will backwards?" The will to power, which Zarathustra had constantly in mind, is mentioned by name in the speech's final verse. But the disciples learn nothing about the *doctrine* that would be suitable for unharnessing the will to power from its foolishness. In contrast, it is clear as day to all the listeners that the deed of him who taught the will to will backwards would be able to measure up to the deed of the redeemer who rolled the stone away from the tomb.[21]

Three times Zarathustra had shaken his head over something his disciples said. Now he looks at them with a "terrified eye," since he has apparently said something that he did not want to say or that has ramifications about which he does not wish to speak. The disciples could ask him about the doctrine that is capable of teaching the will to power to will backwards. A few might conclude, based on the required willing backwards, that Zarathustra is suggesting that they will not only the ascent that leads to the great midday, but also the descent that follows the great midday. One or another might finally conceive the thought that the willing backwards has for him the sense of redeeming the *Now and Formerly* on earth from the need for redemption. Yet the disciples remain mute. In fact, since Zarathustra's third head-shaking we have heard nothing more from them, nor will we ever hear them say anything else. When, with a joking remark, Zarathustra uncovers the impasse and, with a laugh, smooths over the cleft opened up by his sudden pause, the "hunchback," who has listened to the speech to the disciples with his face covered and has obviously paid attention to every change in the intonation of Zarathustra's voice, returns. "But why," he asks, "does Zarathustra speak otherwise to us than to his disciples?" Zarathustra parodies the answer that Jesus gave his disciples, not the people, to a similar question. "Unto hunchbacks one may well speak in a hunchbacked way!" By contrast, he no longer replies to the next question, so that the "hunchback," to whom the people ascribe spirit, has the last word, and "On Redemption" concludes with a question mark, the only chapter to do so: "But why does Zarathustra speak otherwise to his students than to himself?" Here ends the similarity of the redeemers.[22]

Having heard Zarathustra speak to the people, to the disciples, and especially to himself, we can conjecture how he interpreted his "heaviest dream" once "all" became clear to him. The mountain-castle of death may have pointed him toward his solitude in the mountains. There he guarded glass coffins, out of which life that had been overcome looked at him, because he wanted to redeem those of the past and all "It was." In the rustiest of all keys, with which he unlocked the gate inside the castle, he recognized the spirit of revenge, which sought to overcome the past. The bird he roused when he pushed open the gate with his meaning-giving, which relied on the future, croaked at him, "All is empty, all is alike, all was." Then the silence weighed still more dreadfully on him, connecting him with those who were made needy of redemption by his doctrine. He could not open the gate to the outside, to life, to the world, as it is, because his will to power was not unharnessed. The one who knocked three times at the gate was not a future phoenix that rises anew from the ashes of self-overcoming. What the roaring wind threw down at his feet was the futurism to which the "It was" falls victim. It brought him one more coffin in the castle of death. In the laughter that made Zarathustra scream as he had never screamed before, the fruit of the teaching harassed him, mocking his expectations and hopes. But had Zarathustra not already in the First Part claimed to be able to fly and to be beyond all tragic plays and tragic seriousness? And did he not preface his speeches with the vision of a child that deals playfully with valuations and dogmas? How, then, can Zarathustra have believed in the futurist teaching? Perhaps in this sense: The prophet-philosopher develops a conception that he considers to be the result of his nothing-but-gifting wisdom, only to learn, by way of the teaching in which he exposes himself to men, that far indeed from flying, he is in fact tied to men, whom he loves because or insofar as he wants to change them, finally becoming aware that from the beginning he has been driven by something unbearable that made him indignant and left him plotting revenge. Just as in II, 15 he no longer understands the sun's love in the sense of an exuberant fullness, but as a "thirst," so in II, 20 does he see himself as a "cripple," who does not go about his work playfully, though seriously, but rather wants to create out of a previously unacknowledged neediness. The crisis of the teaching promotes his self-knowledge. The non-unharnessed will to power was not a problem for the prophet, but it is a problem for the philosopher. Two, not One.[23]

The duality that submits to no unity persists after the peripety. Zarathustra expresses it in his way in the last two speeches that he addresses to the disciples. "On Prudence with Regard to Men" (II, 21) emphasizes the "double will" that inheres in Zarathustra's heart, and "The Stillest Hour" (II, 22) calls on an inner deliberation that allows the tension between the prophet's mission and the philosopher's path emerges in an obvious way. Zarathustra explains the double will in view of the "danger" that his glance "plunges into the heights" and his hand would like to hold on "to the depths": "To man my will fastens itself, with chains I bind myself to man, because I am swept upward, to the overman: for thither my other will wills." The overman discussed here as Zarathustra's "precipice"—designating in a paradoxical way the natural inclination of Zarathustra's will—is obviously no longer the One goal of man-kind, in which the species is supposed to overcome itself. He appears, rather, as an option of Zarathustra's, suitable for removing him from his love of men, for dissuading him from his demand of men, for leaving his teaching behind, addressed to men. After the sudden glance introduced by the opening, Zarathustra directs the disciples' attention in the further course of the speech to the "prudence with regard to men" that allowed him to persevere among men, starting with the first prudence, that of letting himself be deceived by men, up to the fourth and last prudence, of showing himself to them disguised—so that they fail to recognize him and he to recognize himself. In consequence, the overman moves back into the order of the programmatic demand. The strong presence of the overman, who appears more frequently in II, 21 than in any chapter after the Prologue,[24] nevertheless does not signify the unbroken resumption of the futurist teaching. Zarathustra will not again elevate the overman into the "meaning of the earth." Nor, after II, 20, does he encumber him with the future redemption of every Now and Formerly through the later re-creation of history. He does not burden him with the liberation of those of the past from the workings of accident, of nonsense, of without-sense. Zarathustra can adhere to the overman's demand that he move the wills of man such that he would will beyond himself, create beyond himself, and attain beyond himself, without burdening the teaching with the his-torical-eschatological expectations that in the crisis proved to be misguided, philosophically untenable. That he seeks to translate the overman into nature without such a burdening is indicated, for example, by the fact that in II, 21 he holds out to the overman the prospect of a dragon "worthy of him," an "over-dragon." Just like man, the overman requires the task that demands everything of him in order to become what he can be. But however it may be with the overman as a goal for mankind after the chapter "On Redemption," for the philosopher the return of the overman in II, 21 indicates a parallel that underscores the decisive insight: Just as the hero is only able to become an *over-hero* if he succeeds at unharnessing his will, the same goes for the most important case, that the transition of man to *overman* requires the *unharnessing of the will*: overcoming the will's foolishness in wanting to force what it does not befit the will to force.[25]

In the Second Part's farewell speech, Zarathustra does not speak of his double will. Nor does he mention the overman. Instead, he describes himself to the disciples he is leaving as "perturbed, driven away, unwillingly obedient, prepared to go," in view of a commandment he cannot escape: "Ah, my angry mistress wills it thus, she has spoken to me." And he does not neglect to establish a link to the First Part's farewell speech, in which the futurist teaching reached its peak: "Yes, once again must Zarathustra go back to his solitude: but this time the bear goes listlessly back to his cave!" He tells his disciples that the name of the "dreadful mistress" who commands him to go away is *my stillest hour*. With the highly unusual name for designating a mistress he not only bends the arc back, in the fifth speech of the final group of five, to its first speech (II, 18), in which he sought to make accessible to the disciples the fact that the greatest events are "our stillest hours," but also intimates, at the end of the Second Part, that for him thinking is the greatest event. For Zarathustra's "stillest hour" proves to be his thinking, if indeed we call thinking the inner conversation of the soul with itself, which goes on without voice.[26]   The mistress performs a service for Zarathustra reminiscent of the one performed for Socrates by the *daimonion*. An authority's commandment makes rejection, denial, refusal, more bearable for those affected by it. The appeal to the "dreadful mistress" unburdens Zarathustra, who is concerned that his disciples' hearts "not harden against the one departing so suddenly." When Zarathustra spoke for the first time of the "stillest hours," the disciples showed little interest, being too busy with narratives of miracles and other matters of faith. Now he clothes the "stillest hour," which causes him to return to solitude, in such garb as to make it capable of appearing even to them to be a great event. Although it is throughout an "it" that speaks "without voice" to an "I," the presentation Zarathustra gives of the conversation of his soul with itself is suitable for arousing the impression in the listeners that it was Zarathustra's discussion with his *mistress*—who actually has two "voices"—according to the model of a prophet's conversation with his God. The high density of borrowings from and allusions to Biblical sayings reinforces this impression. In the dialogue the role of urging the fulfillment of the mission falls to the It without voice, while the I stubbornly tries to avoid the fulfillment. One side of Zarathustra commands the sacrifice demanded by his love of men: "What do you matter, Zarathustra! Speak your word and shatter!" The other side is not at a loss for the subterfuge called upon in a similar situation by the seers, soothsayers, or messengers of God: "Ah is it *my* word? Who am I? I wait for one more worthy; I am not even worthy of being shattered by it." At the dialogue's peak the prophet and lawgiver confirms the assignment to rule: "To accomplish great things is difficult: but more difficult is to command great things./That is what is most unpardonable in you: you have the power, and you do not want to rule." To this Zarathustra's I, parodying Moses, answers the alter ego: "I lack the lion's voice for all commanding." The philosopher, whose figure attains increasingly sharp contours in the Second Part, persists to the end in his refusal: "I will not." Zarathustra closes the dramatic narrative of the great wrestling match in which, according to his own testimony, he "wept and trembled like a child," with the assurance that his No earned him a laughter that "tore open his entrails and slashed open his heart," after which the call came to him: "O Zarathustra, your fruits are ripe, but you are not ripe for your fruits!/So you must go into the solitude again: for thou shalt yet become mellow."[27]

Unlike at the end of the First Part, Zarathustra does not have to return to solitude in order to help his disciples to independently appropriate his teachings. Not the disciples' development, but Zarathustra's development, motivates the renewed farewell and postponement. The prophet declares his teachings to be "ripe," but he himself is evidently not yet "ripe" enough to stand up for them as a witness to the truth. Or he has not yet reached the age at which he would be ready to seal the mission with the sacrifice of his life.[28] The presentation that Zarathustra gives of his inner deliberation serves to spare the disciples and to justify the prophet in accordance with his mission. It is intended for the ears of believers. We have no reason to suppose that he does *not* talk to his pupils otherwise than to himself at the moment of separation.[29] In other words, we do not know whether Zarathustra goes again into solitude because he is supposed to "become mellow" for the fulfillment of the assignment to rule, or because he prefers solitude in view of his own good. It is certain that Zarathustra does not invoke any of the hopes that defined the First Part's farewell speech. Neither the promise of a chosen people that will someday grow out of the disciples, nor the expectation that the disciples, or at least some of them, would be able to attain a position toward Zarathustra's teaching that is grounded in knowledge, is mentioned. After everything the philosopher has seen and heard in the Second Part, there does not remain much for him to hope for of his pupils politically, and next to nothing philosophically. Is the refusal in which the I persisted in the dialogue with the It not therefore sufficient to explain his resolution to take leave of the blessed isles and return to the mountains? This time the narrator does not report any gift from the disciples. He also does not mention that Zarathustra is "a friend of walking alone." He concludes with the assertion that "the force of pain and the nearness of the parting" so overcame Zarathustra "that he wept loudly; and no one was able to console him." At the end of the Second Part, Zarathustra is no less torn than at its beginning. Yet his tornness points in another direction.

Translated by Justin Gottschalk

Acknowledgments

The interpretation of *Thus Spoke Zarathustra*, Chapters II, 17-22, which contain the peripety of the drama and the philosophical center of the work, is an adapted section from the author's book, *What Is Nietzsche's Zarathustra?* published by the University of Chicago Press (German original: *Was ist Nietzsches Zarathustra?: Eine philosophische Auseinandersetzung*. Munich: C. H. Beck, 2017). The page numbers in parentheses refer to the Giorgio Colli and Mazzino Montinari edition of the *Kritische Studienausgabe* (KSA), (Berlin: de Gruyter, 1980), vol. 4. [Translator's Note: In translating passages from *Thus Spoke Zarathustra*, I have consulted the translations of Walter Kaufmann (Viking, 1954), R. J. Hollingdale (Penguin, 1961) and Graham Parkes (Oxford University Press, 2008), but have not adhered to them in every particular.]

Endnotes

1. The disciples were last mentioned in II, 10, 1 (139) and before that in II, 4, 1 (117), the only two mentions of Zarathustra's disciples in the Second Part before II, 17.

2. In the center of the last part of the farewell speech Zarathustra had called to his disciples: "You say you believe in Zarathustra? But what does Zarathustra matter? You are my believers: but what do all believers matter? / You had not yet sought yourselves: then you found me. Thus do all believers; that is why all belief is worth so little." I, 22.3, 7-8 (101).

3. In "On Believers in a World Behind" Zarathustra reported that "once," before his retreat into solitude, "like all believers in a world behind," he cast his "delusion beyond man" and as a creator created, as a poet poetized, a God: "Ah, brothers, this God that I created was man's-work and -madness, *just like all Gods!*" I, 3, 7 (35), my emphasis. "There have always been many sick people among those *who poetize and long for God*; furiously they hate the knower, and that youngest among the virtues which is called: honesty." I, 3, 28 (37), my emphasis.

4. II, 17, 23-24 and 25 (164), my emphasis. The two mentions of *overmen* in the center of the chapter "On the Poets" are the only instances of the plural form in *Thus Spoke Zarathustra*.—Concerning the overmen before the gospel of Zarathustra, consider *The Gay Science* §143 (KSA 3, 490-491).

5. "When Zarathustra spoke thus, his disciple was angry with him, but he kept silent. And Zarathustra too kept silent; and his eye had turned inward, as if looking into far distances." II, 17, 26 (165). "And now you are angry with me for teaching that there is no reward- and pay-master?" II, 5, 6 (120); cf. II, 5, 39 (123).

6. II, 17, 28-30; 32; 45 (165-66) and II, 17, 18-22 (164). II, 13, 3 and 13 (150-51); cf. Footnote 3.—By means of significant references and *verbatim* borrowings in II, 17, *inter alia*, Zarathustra invokes the following ancient and modern poets: Homer (verse 12, assuming that Nietzsche is telling the truth in *The Gay Science* 84) and Aristophanes (23), Mark and Matthew (11 and 35), Shakespeare (21) and Goethe (1, 16, 22, 23 and 25; cf. II, 2, 18 [110]).

7. II, 17, 1-12; 13-25; 26; 27-42; 43-45 (163-66).

8. II, 18, 1-3 (167). See I, 7, 26 (50); I, 22.3, 11-14 (102); II, 2, 34 (112); Prologue, 5, 7 (19) as well as 26 (20).—II, 18, 1 is the first time since the title of chapter II, 2 that the blessed isles are mentioned, which here are called "Zarathustra's blessed isles."

9. II, 18, 4-6; 7-35 (168-70). On II, 18, 17-18 cf. I, 12, 16 (66). On II, 18, 31-34 see I, 22.1, 2-9 and 25 (97-99), I, 7, 10-13 and 22-26 (48-50).

10. II, 18, 36-42 (170-71).

11. II, 19, 1-9 (172). Prologue, 3, 15-16 (15). "The Soothsayer" is the only chapter that begins with a dash and in the middle of a sentence. The words "*Und ich sahe*" ("And I saw" open Chapters 5, 6, 10, 14, 15, 20, and 21 of Luther's translation of the *Revelation of John.* Beyond that, they recur often in the book's twenty-two chapters.

12. II, 19, 10-12 (172-73). II, 1, 4-10; 14; 22 (105-7).

13. II, 19, 13-14; 15-32; 33-43 (173-75). Cf. II, 11, 38 (145). See *John* 13:23 and 20:2.

14. II, 19, 44-47 (175-76). Zarathustra shakes his head three times: II, 17, 10; II, 18, 40; II, 19, 47. In II, 19 he uses two forms of address: in verse 15 "you friends"; in verse 45 "my disciples." He had previously used the form of address "my disciples" only in the farewell speech of the First Part: I, 22.1, 5 and I, 22.3, 2. *Disciple(s)* appears twenty-seven times in *Thus Spoke Zarathustra.* Twenty-six times the term refers to Zarathustra's, once to Jesus' disciples.

15. "On Redemption" is the longest chapter of the Second Part and the middle of the final group of five. Besides II, 19 before and II, 22 after it, it is the only chapter of the Second Part that ends with neither "Thus spoke Zarathustra" nor "Thus sang Zarathustra." After I, 15 (once) and II, 12 (seven times), it is the third and final chapter of the book in which the *will to power* appears (once), one of two, along with II, 13, in which the *unharnessed will* is mentioned (once each), and the only one in which the *spirit of revenge* makes its appearance (twice). II, 20, 7-12 (178-79); I, 22.2, 8 (100). Zarathustra continues in verse 13: "'And you too have often asked yourselves: 'who is Zarathustra to us? What shall we call him?' And like me you gave yourselves questions in response." In verses 14 and 15 seven pairs of questions follow. The first pair is: "Is he a promiser? Or a fulfiller?" the last: "A good one? Or an evil one?" In the middle stands the pair, "A physician? Or someone who has convalesced?" which in a draft had initially stood at the end of the series. It displaced "Is he a poet? Or a truthful one?" from the central position that this pair occupied in the draft. Cf. Matthew 16:13-20.

16. II, 20, 1-6 (177-78). Cf. Matthew 11:5 and 15:30-31. On *bridge* see Prologue, 4, 4; 11; 19 (16-17); I, 4, 22 (41); I, 5, 18 (43); I, 11, 39 (64); II, 7,7 (128).

17. II, 20, 7-12 (178-79); I, 22.2, 8 (100). Zarathustra continues in verse 13: "'And you too have often asked yourselves: 'who is Zarathustra to us? What shall we call him?' And like me you gave yourselves questions in response." In verses 14 and 15 seven pairs of questions follow. The first pair is: "Is he a promiser? Or a fulfiller?" the last: "A good one? Or an evil one?" In the middle stands the pair, "A physician? Or someone who has convalesced?" which in a draft had initially stood at the end of the series. It displaced "Is he a poet? Or a truthful one?" from the central position that this pair occupied in the draft. Cf. *Matthew* 16:13-20.

18. II, 20, 13-19 (179). II, 3, 1-5 (113). On verses 11-12 cf. II, 6, 11-13 and 17 (125). On verse 17 cf. II, 17, 22-25 (164-65) and *Genesis* 6:5-7.

19. The verse in which Zarathustra speaks twice of *Unmut* and introduces revenge into "On Redemption" is the twentieth of thirty-nine verses in his speech to the disciples and the twenty-seventh of the chapter's fifty-three verses. The *Unmut*

that the narrator ascribes to Zarathustra in verse 7 is the first instance of the term in the whole book. The double usage by Zarathustra in verse 27 is followed by two more, in III, 2.1, 16 (198) and III, 12.19, 4 (261).

20. In the young Nietzsche's translation, Anaximander's saying reads: "Whence things have their origin, thence also they have to pass away, according to necessity; for they must pay penance and be judged for their injustices, in accordance with the order of time." *Philosophy in the Tragic Age of the Greeks* 4 (KSA 1, p. 818).

21. II, 20, 20-46 (179-81). II, 2, 26 (111). II, 13, 20; 27; 35 (151-52). II, 14, 23 (154). On II, 20, 26 cf. *Luke* 24:2.

22. II, 20, 47-53 (181-82); cf. II, 12, 43-44 (149). *Matthew* 13:10-17.

23. II, 19, 17-32 (173-74).

24. In II, 21, *overman* appears six times, the same as in all of the Second Part before the undermining of the doctrine in the chapter "On the Poets" (II, 17), in which *overmen* is used twice in the plural. Before II, 21, *overman* in the singular was last mentioned in chapter II, 7, "On the Tarantulas" (once). This was preceded by five mentions in II, 4 "On the Priests" (once) and II, 2 "On the Blessed Isles" (four times). The Second Part thus contains six mentions in the singular each before and after the crisis, as well as the only two usages of the plural in the book's four parts.

25. II, 21, 1-5; 10-11 and 40-41; 31 (183-86). The *unharnessed will* occurs, as mentioned, only in II, 13 and II, 20; *over-hero* is the last word of II, 13; overman first reappears at the beginning of II, 21.—Interpreters who are convinced that the problem exposed in the chapter "On Redemption" could only be solved by the teaching of the Eternal Return have argued that it is this teaching that demands the *overman*. But the doctrine of the Eternal Return does not in itself require any overman. It requires believers.

26. II, 18, 17 (169); II, 22, 1-4 (187). Plato: *Sophist* 263e3-5. Ten times Zarathustra says of the other side in the inner conversation of his soul: "Then it spoke to me without voice" (once), "Then it spoke to me again without voice" (eight times), "Then it spoke to me again like a whisper" (once): II, 22, 10; 12; 14; 16; 18; 20; 22; 25; 30; 35 (187-89). The It without voice speaks in seventeen verses; the I replies in ten.

27. II, 22,15; 16-17; 27-29; 35; 36-38 (188-90). Cf. *Exodus* 4:10 and context. To the answer, "I lack the lion's voice for all commanding," the alter ego responds: "It is the stillest words that bring the storm. Thoughts that come on doves' feet guide the world" II, 22, 30 (189). The It without voice speaks in seventeen verses; the I replies in ten.

28. On II, 22, 37 (189) see the prologue to "On the Blessed Isles," II, 2, 1-2 (109). Cf. I, 21, 34-36 (95-96), and further, IV, 1, 1 (295).

29. Cf. II, 20, 53 (182); II, 21, 41 (186) and IV, 1, 4-5 (296).

POLITICS WITHOUT VISION

THINKING WITHOUT A BANISTER
IN THE TWENTIETH CENTURY

TRACY B. STRONG

THE SACRED QUALITY OF THE POLITICAL: NIETZSCHE, CARL SCHMITT, AND SAINT PAUL

TRACY BURR STRONG

> *Überall freilich geht diese Annahme, die ich Ihnen hier vortrage, aus von dem einen Grundsachverhalt: daß das Leben, solange es in sich selbst beruht und aus sich selbst verstanden wird, nur den ewigen Kampf jener Götter miteinander kennt, — unbildlich gesprochen: die Unvereinbarkeit und also die Unaustragbarkeit des Kampfes der letzten überhaupt möglichen Standpunkte zum Leben, die Notwendigkeit also zwischen ihnen sich zu entscheiden.*[i]
> — Max Weber

> *11] Man ruft zu mir aus Seïr: Wächter, ist die Nacht bald hin? Wächter, ist die Nacht bald hin?*
> *12] Der Wächter aber sprach: Wenn auch der Morgen kommt, so wird es doch Nacht bleiben. Wenn ihr fragen wollt, so kommt wieder und fragt.*[ii]
> — Jesaja xxi: 11–12

I

To read Carl Schmitt in the context of Paul and Hobbes is, among other things, to raise the question of the relation of significant elements of the Western tradition to the thought and political choices of Carl Schmitt. If Schmitt joined the NSDAP by *mistake*—not clear what it was, thinking it merely a more effective form of German nationalism—then it is hard to account for his remaining in the Party and his silence about it after the defeat. If he joined it by *accident*—thinking that this happened to be the best path to his advancement and for his career, then his thought will at most be only contingently related to National Socialism. This we can reject: too many people have seen links for us, again in the face of Schmitt's postwar silence,

---

[i]   Max Weber, „Wissenschaft als Beruf" — *Wissenschaftslehre* 550. [The assumption that I am offering you here is based on a fundamental fact. This is that as long as life is left to itself and is understood in its own terms, it knows only that the conflict between these gods is neverending. Or, in nonfigurative language, life is about the incompatibility of ultimate possible attitudes and hence the necessity to decide between them.]

[ii]   [One calls to me from Seir: Watchman, is the night almost gone? Watchman, is the night almost gone? The Watchman said: Even if the morning cometh, it still remains night. If you wish to inquire, then come again and inquire." (*Isaiah*, xxi, 11–12)]

New Nietzsche Studies, Vol. 11, Nos. 3 and 4 (Fall 2021 / Spring 2022), pp. 27–46.
© 2022 Nietzsche Society. ISSN 1091–0239.

for us simply to excuse or overlook.[1] We are left with the fact that reading Schmitt in the context of thinkers such as Hobbes and St. Paul raises that there are many paths to take from within what are apparently our best traditions.

I. Introduction: The Nature of Modernity for Carl Schmitt

As a preliminary, we should distinguish a "political theology" from a theology that has politics. Liberation theology,[2] as it was practiced especially in Latin American until Pope John Paul crushed it, is a theology that has a politics: as such there are many antecedents both in Protestant and Catholic thought. The "Social Gospel" teaching of such men as Walter Rauschenbusch[3] that was important around the turn of the last century in the United States is only one instance of such creeds: its proponents suggested not that the Second Coming of Christ would make everything right, but that Christ would not come until human beings had brought justice and peace to human relations.[4]

Opposed to this, it is central to any notion of *political theology* that the experience of politics requires a "theology" to be viable—that is, politics must rely on a source of authority that has the quality of being beyond question. I do not mean that people may not resist it —but that is different than questioning it. For something to be beyond question means that one must find that authority in oneself such that one can do no other than acknowledge its claims. To speak of a political theology thus means to speak of a politics in which it is held that problems cannot be resolved by universally agreed upon procedures. The justification of a policy cannot be made in person neutral terms but must and can only be made authoritatively. If the liberal dream is the rule of law and not of men, then political theology says that this is a vain dream.

So a central question of a political theology must be of the status of the authority on the basis of which decisions are taken. In the West (at least) such theological authority has typically been associated with a particular event that is authoritatively formulated, sometimes as a text whose meaning requires interpretation.[5]

1. The Fate of Authority in Modern Times: Technicity

The question of authority under conditions of modernity can only be approached on a bias—from the side as it were. For Schmitt, the political realm was, as it had been for Weber, the realm of relations between human beings, persons as opposed to roles: "*die Ordnung der menschlichen Dinge.*"[6] And persons, for Weber, made up whatever world there was that was not *entzaubert*—"demagified."[7] As Weber says, "*[g]änzlich versagt hat die Beamtenherrschaft da, wo sie mit politischen Fragen befasst wurde.*"[8] Politics has to do with persons, bureaucracy with roles.

The political realm—and thus the reality of the human—was, for Schmitt, in danger of disappearing. In modern times he saw it being replaced by two realms. One realm was the supposedly neutral space of scientific technique, in which rational and logical conclusions—neutral with regard to human beings—were attainable. "*Heute ist nichts moderner als der Kampf gegen das Politische. ... Es soll nur das organisatorish-technische und Ökonomisch-soziologische Aufgaben, aber keine politischen probleme mehr geben.*"[9] In 1929, Schmitt will lecture on Barcelona on this topic as "*Das Zeitalter der Neutralisierungen und Entpolitisierungen.*"[10] The decline or disappearance of the political is itself always for Schmitt a "political matter," as he makes clear in the preface to the second edition of *Political Theology*. If, however, the political is in danger of disappearing as a human form of life, this can only be because sovereignty as Schmitt understands it is increasingly not a constituent part of our present world. Thus in his 1938 book on Hobbes, he will write "*die Mechanisierung der Staatsvorstellung hat die Mechanisierung des anthropologischen Bildes vom Menschen vollendet.*"[11] Schmitt, with explicit reference to Max Weber, sees danger in the increasing sense of the State as "*ein grosser Betrieb.*" (PT 69/65) Increasingly this plant "*läuft jetzt von selbst [und] dadurch geht das dezisionistische und personalistische Element des bisherigen Souveränitätsbegriffes verloren.*" (PT 52/48)[12] Schmitt sees it as his role to recover that element for the contemporary period.

The Barcelona lecture was published in 1930 and was added to the 1932 edition of *The Concept of the Political*. Schmitt thought of it as part of his general argument in that book. As the political is for Schmitt the realm of that which is truly human,[13] his distress is that the West is losing touch with that which gives life human meaning. As he develops his argument in this article, the contemporary West stands at the end of a series of "central spheres of thought." "Central spheres" function here pretty much in the manner that Thomas Kuhn understood paradigms. Thus "*[i]st ein Gebiet einmal zum Zentral-gebiet geworden, so warden die Probleme der anderen Gebiete von dort aus gelöst und gelten nur noch als Probleme zweiten Ranges, deren Losung sich von selber ergibt, wenn nur die Probleme des Zentralgebiets gelöst sind.*" (BPZN 85)"[14]

There have been five "central spheres" since the Renaissance, each loosely identified with a century. As he lays it out in the Barcelona lecture, the history of the last 500 years shows a common structure, even though as the controlling force has changed, so also have what counts as evidence, as well as what was the social and political elite. Thus in the XVIth century the world was structured around an explicitly theological understanding with God and the Scriptures as foundational certainties; this was replaced in the next century by metaphysics and rational ("scientific") research and in the eighteenth by ethical humanism with its central notions of duty and virtue. In the XIXth century economics comes to dominate (although Schmitt is seen as a man of the Right he always took Marx completely seriously) and, finally, in the XX[ieth] century technicity is the ordering of the day. And this is at the core of his claim that ours is an age of "neutralisation and depoliticization": whereas all previous eras had leaders and decisionmakers—what he calls here "clercs,"—the era of technology and technological progress has no need of individual persons.[15]

Schmitt uses the French *clerc* and no doubt has in mind the 1927 book by Julien Benda, *Le trahison des clercs* [The Treason of the Intellectuals].[16] But whereas Benda had seen the clercs as mistakenly turning away from spiritual and eternal values to temporal and political activity, Schmitt, tacitly opposing Benda, sees the clerc as the person who most centrally grasps and formulates the core of a particular central sphere.[17]

The central quality of all transformations that have led to our present stage—"technicity"—is the "striving for a neutral sphere." For Europe, the attraction of a neutral sphere is that is seemed to provide a solution to the conflicts that had grown up out of quarrels over theology. It transformed the concepts elaborated "*in vielen Jahrhunderten theologischen Denkens*" into what are for Schmitt "*jetzt …*

Privatsachen." (BPZN 89)[18] However, each stage of neutralization became, in Schmitt's analysis, merely the next arena of struggle. Thus what someone like John Rawls sees as one of the most important achievements of the West—religious toleration—is for Schmitt merely the prelude to another form of conflict.

The central question now therefore is what conflicts will arise when the central sphere is technicity, which, "*eben weil sie jemand dient, ist … nicht neutral.*" (BPZN 90)[19] Here Schmitt finds himself in opposition to thinkers like Weber, Troeltsch and Rathenau, whom he reads as in despair before the "*Entzauberung der Welt.*" If one follows them, Schmitt says, one will despair, for the world will appear only as what Weber called a "*stahlhartes Gehäuse*" with no way out, not even a look.[20] This leads to quietism or despair, the most important danger now confronting Europe. This danger arises because it is Russia (i. e. the USSR) who has understood and seized technicity and made it its own in the new arena of conflict. Only in Russia does one now find a sense of a new "strong politics."

Schmitt writes somewhat chillingly in *Der Begriff des Politischen* that "*[d]adurch, dass ein Volk nicht mehr die Kraft oder den Willen hat, sich in der Sphäre des Politischen zuhalten, verschwindet das Politische nicht aus der Welt. Es verschwindet nur ein schwaches Volk.*"[21] He thus closes his Barcelona article with a truncated citation from Vergil's "Fourth Eclogue": *Ab integro nascitur ordo.* The full line is "*Magnus ab integro seclorum nascitur ordo*" which translates as "a great order of the ages is born from the renewal." Schmitt's abbreviated line means "an order is born from the renewal."[22]   The eloquent two closing paragraphs of Schmitt's article are in effect a call for the West to be equal to the need for this renewed conflict and to oppose the forces of Communism. (Here Schmitt shares concerns with Heidegger). And this is at the core of his claim that ours is an age of "neutralisation and depoliticization": whereas previous eras still had leaders and decisionmakers, the era of technology and technological progress is different in that increasingly it has no need of actual individual persons.[23]

What is wrong with technicity? The danger and problem with technicity is that it claims to have personally neutral ways of solving disputes. The "organisation technical" method is characterised by three epistemological presuppositions. The first is that one can make a clearcut conceptual separation between facts and values and that, in consequence, values were subjective, not of the world, and could be kept apart from ones analysis of social reality. This was not a denial that values were "important" but it was a denial that values were objects of knowledge.[24]

A second claim was parent to the first. It was a claim that propositions about the world could and should be made to speak for themselves—thus that propositions about the world should have a validity independent of he or she who advanced them. One could and should clearly separate the speaker from the spoken, for if one did one's work right not just empirical claims about the world but concepts themselves would stand independently of the speaker. In its simplest form, the claim was that a statement like "mass equals force times acceleration" was true independently of who said it and of when and where it was said.

The third claim derived from the first two. It held that certain forms of discourse (claims to knowledge) were responsible and responsive to the real world in ways that other forms (one might think of them as emotive, or expressive) were not.[25] In the first but not the second, the expectation was that the world would correct mistakes is an erroneous analysis.

On the basis of these presuppositions, *Technizität* seemed to provide a model of a neutral resolution to disputes and this was its attraction. These presuppositions are central to political liberalism: they ground the possibility of rational agreement. (Political liberalism does not, of course, think that all humans will behave rationally at all times; but it does think that rationality has a compelling quality such that resisting it is a sign of perversity or ignorance.)

2. The Fate of Authority in Modern Times: Aesthetic Subjectivity

Along with science, and perversely companion to it, Schmitt saw the arising of a second realm, the realm of aesthetic subjectivity. The transition to the *Technizität* sphere is made possible, Schmitt argues by an "*Ästhetisierung aller geistigen Gebiete* [aestheticization of all sectors of the spirit]." (BPZN 83) This is the epistemological basis for his critique of liberalism as a *clasa discutora*, unable to come to any decision on anything because all decisions appear the same. If the scientific realm held out a method for resolving some disputes, the aestheticization of the rest of the world—of that portion not amenable to scientific resolution—subjectivized it and held that was no way to resolve those disputes if they could not be resolved by science.

Thus liberal scienticism and romanticism come together—two sides of the same modern coin. From this we get his lapidary sentence from *The Crisis of Parliamentary Democracy*: If a liberal is asked "Christ or Barrabas, he responds with a proposal to adjourn or appoint a committee of investigation."[26]

Responding to the double bind of modern society, Schmitt argues that in such a context the recovery of the political realm must of necessity come from *outside* the liberal romantic world, that is, it cannot be justified in terms of the categories of that world. It must come, as Herbert Marcuse argued, from a state whose only "justification is its existence"[27]—or rather its practice. Justification must be ontological rather than epistemological.

a) Aesthetic Authority (*Intermezzo*)

But how can something come to have the quality of being convincingly present to us, such that it serves as an authority? I believe the model for Schmitt's approach to these questions has its origin in Kant's *Kritik der Urteilskraft*. It is here that Kant introduces the concept of "genius."[28] With this concept, Kant seeks to account for the very existence of something that has the quality of being a work of art. This account actually marks the beginning of an important shift in aesthetic theory. Generally speaking prior to the end of the XVIIIth century, examples of the aesthetic had been sought in that which existed naturally. Thus the "sublime" for instance, was generally instantiated with reference to a storm, or a sunset, or some such natural phenomenon. By the late XVIIIth century—let us say by the "storm" section of Beethoven's Third Symphony or by *D moll* sequence that marks the arrival of the Commendatore in the next to the last scene in *Don Giovanni*—the sublime was also clearly a human product. The genius-artist-creator has become part of the accepted world.[29] By introducing the idea of the genius Kant focuses on human creation, thus accomplishing a transformation that started with the XVIIth century.

The aesthetic quality is held by Kant *"von allem Zwange willkürlicher Regeln so frei scheinen."*[30] It appears as natural—that is as given in and of itself. Such is "beautiful art"—art which Kant says is both purposive and without an end. As such the origin of that which we experience as art must be without apparent foundation as it is grounded in precisely the incomprehensible.[31] So the question naturally arises as to how the work of art comes into being. Since such a work is the work of "subjective universality" (that makes a judgment of beauty without referring to any concept).[32] Somewhat later in the section Kant differentiates between the perceiver of beauty and its creator, and clearly thinks that accounting for the creation of beauty a more difficult matter. It is this that leads Kant to introduce the idea of genius.

"*Genie ist das Talent (Naturgabe), welches der Kunst die Regel giebt.*"[33] The genius has the complete freedom of incomprehensibility. "*Der Urheber eines Products, welches er seinem Genie verdankt, selbst nicht weiß, wie sich in ihm die Ideen dazu herbei finden, auch es nicht in seiner Gewalt hat, dergleichen nach Belieben oder planmäßig auszudenken und anderen in solchen Vorschrifte.*"[34] This is originality, which means for Kant that what the genius accomplishes cannot be confined to, nor explained by, any systematic understanding or procedure. In the *Anthropology*, Kant is clear that the word applies only to an "artist" and only to the artist who does something original. Later in that book he can write that "*Das Genie glänzt daher als augenblickliche, mit Intervallen sich zeigende und wieder verschwindende Erscheinung nicht mit einem willkürlich ange-zündeten und eine beliebige Zeit fortbrennenden Licht, sondern wie sprühende Funken, welche eine glückliche Anwandelung des Geistes aus der productiven Einbildungskraft auslockt.*"[35] Here it is worth noting that even Newton does not count as a genius for what he did could be set out for all to understand and thus could in principle have been discovered by others.[36]

It seems to me clear from this that the actual operation of genius remains a bit of a mystery for Kant. Thus he must ascribe it to a "happy seizure of the spirit." This mysterious quality is all the more important in that Kant thinks that a work of art (of true art) has the quality of providing grounds for others to judge and of at the same time providing the structure—as we might call it—for their mutual comprehensibility. Kant will say that "the imagination (as a productive cognitive faculty) is, namely, very powerful in creating, as it were, another nature, out of the material which the real one gives to it."[37]

I suspect that it is in response to this that Nietzsche can write in "*Vom Nutzen und Nachteil der Historie für das Leben*":

Denn da wir nun einmal die Resultate früherer Geschlechter sind, sind wir auch die Resultate ihrer Verirrungen, Leidenschaften und Irrthümer, ja Verbrechen; es ist nicht möglich sich ganz von dieser Kette zu lösen. Wenn wir jene Verirrungen verurtheilen und uns ihrer für enthoben erachten, so ist die Thatsache nicht beseitigt, dass wir aus ihnen herstammen. Wir bringen es im besten Falle zu einem Widerstreite der ererbten, angestammten Natur und unserer Erkenntniss, auch wohl zu einem Kampfe einer neuen strengen Zucht gegen das von Alters her Angezogne und Angeborne, wir pflanzen eine neue Gewöhnung, einen neuen Instinct, eine zweite Natur an, so dass die erste Natur abdorrt. Es ist ein Versuch, sich gleichsam a posteriori eine Vergangenheit zu geben, aus der man stammen möchte, im Gegensatz zu der, aus der man stammt – immer ein gefährlicher Versuch, weil es so schwer ist eine Grenze im Verneinen des Vergangenen zu finden, und weil die zweiten Naturen meistens schwächlicher als die ersten sind. Es bleibt zu häufig bei einem Erkennen des Guten, ohne es zu thun, weil man auch das Bessere kennt, ohne es thun zu können. Aber hier und da gelingt der Sieg doch, und es giebt sogar für die Kämpfenden, für die, welche sich der kritischen Historie zum Leben bedienen, einen merkwürdigen Trost: nämlich zu wissen, dass auch jene erste Natur irgend wann einmal eine zweite Natur war und dass jede siegende zweite Natur zu einer ersten wird. (HL 3 WKG III$_1$, 261)

Thus Novalis will in the last decade of the XVIIIth century define genius as "the capacity to describe imaginary objects as if they were real and to act upon them as it they were real."[38] What Kant calls genius is pretty much like what might produce what Schmitt understands as the sovereign decision on the exception.[39] (Kant's aesthetics are of course not subjectivist). Kant says that the act of genius imparts "another nature" to the world. So also the sovereign gives the rule in a condition where what to do and be is not previously defined. It is also a pretty accurate description of what happens with the creation of the Leviathan, except that for Hobbes there is apparently no single creative genius for we all make the Leviathan. Where there was nothing there is now something.

Yet what is that something? I propose that we see what happens with the creation of the Leviathan as an instance of incarnation. Here Luther's "*eingefleischt*" catches the sense of embodiment better than *Inkarnation*.

* * *

St. Paul

By declaring the exception in jurisprudence analogous to the "miracle" in theology, Schmitt reaffirms and recuperates for modern political and legal thought a secularized understanding of sovereign power analogous to the overtly theologically based understanding of the middle ages. His work calls to mind the doctrine of "Christ centered kingship" that we find in a work like Kantorowicz's *The King's Two Bodies*. It is important to note that the grounding of legal power on nonlegal sources is not unique to Schmitt, nor indeed to the Middle Ages. Whether or not theorists of the law locate sovereignty in a particular individual (be that an actual person, or an artificial one, as in Hobbes), they very often derive its authority from a source figured as "outside of," "prior to," or "beyond" the law. Thus we have God inscribing the tablets for Moses on Sinai (twice in fact); we have Rousseau's Legislator (who needs to, "*pour ainsi dire, changer la nature humaine*"). Sieyès has recourse to the *pouvoir constituant* and de Sade calls upon "Mother Nature." Bataille associates sovereignty with killing. Writing around the same time as Schmitt, Freud suggests that even the most egalitarian social arrangements cannot function without some implicit or explicit invocation of an exceptional figure: In *Totem and Taboo*, Freud invokes a primal figure; in *Group Psychology and the Analysis of the Ego* this becomes the leader; in *Moses and Monotheism*, the nation of Israel is founded by a non-Hebrew.[40]

Political theology is thus concerned not only with the appeal to a source of legitimation figured as "beyond" the law, but with the fact that the Law has the quality of seeking to annihilate or displace the lawless authority of the law's "beyond." What Schmitt shows in his critique of "normative" law is that there is necessarily a "gap" in the law such that it is in its nature incapable of addressing such lawless —anomic—situations as revolution or a general strike. It is the case that a spontaneous arising can, as Hannah Arendt argues, give rise momentarily to what Aristide Zolberg has called a "moment of madness" in which "the people" appear to take power and from which there arise various egalitarian groups (the soviets, councils etc).[41]

But such moments are fleeting and unless a sovereign acts to close this gap in the law by preserving its "spirit" against its "letter," suspending the constitution to maintain the order of law (or the existence of the state as such) nothing will be achieved.

It is thus the case that the archetype of the strategy of the exception is Paul's account of Christ as the "fulfillment of the law," the living *logos* who consigns the "old" written law to obsolescence, and who actualizes in his person the transcendent Kingdom of God. Calvin, in the *Institutes*, rails against those who would live by the Law and insists that with God we live in love. Both Schmitt and Hobbes take up the terms of Paul's or Calvin's polemic against the Mosaic law. It is thus the case that, as Hobbes himself remarks, that Jesus is the Christ is the foundation of all of Paul's thought: "Besides, this article, that Jesus is the Christ, is so fundamental, that all the rest are by St. Paul … said to be built upon it." (*De Cive* 18.9)

Paul, a Jew, found himself in struggle with not only the disciples who saw Jewishness a prerequisite to Christianity—who thus wanted to limit the extent of Christianity—but as importantly also with the very foundation of the *pax romana*. To get some idea of the revolutionary threat that Paul posed, consider the following letter from Pliny the Younger to the imperator Trajanus. Around 111 AD the emperor received a letter from Pliny endorsing the request of the citizen of Biythnia (where Pliny was governor) to form an association [*collegium*] to be a fire brigade as there had been numerous fires in the region. Aside from the fact that permission had to be gained from Rome for such a group, the emperor's response is important.

He writes:

> we must remember that it is societies like these which have been responsible for the political disturbances in your province, particularly its towns. If people assemble for a common purpose, whatever name we give them and for whatever reason, they soon turn into a brotherhood.[42]

In another letter, Pliny relays a petition from the free city of Amisos to form "benefit societies." In this case, Trajanus allowed the formation of these groups provided that the groups were "not used for riotous and unlawful assemblies, but to relieve cases of hardship among the poor."[43] In other cities, however, over which Rome had direct jurisdiction, this was not to be permitted.

Trajanus has a clear understanding of the dangers of dividing sovereignty. And the spread of the Christian churches must have over time appeared to the Roman Empire as destructive of the principle of its authority.

Instead of all things going through Rome, the Churches were in extensive and ideological communication with each other on a horizontal level. What Trajanus did not grasp is that Paul also sought to replace the universalism of the *pax romana* with a new universalism resting on the churches composing *the* Church as the mystical body of Christ.[44]

The key text here is the First Letter to the Corinthians, ch. 12, 12–27. Paul argues that just as the body [*soma*] is composed of many members [*mélé*] so also is the Church composed of many diverse elements but is still one, even as the members remain each individual. (I Cor. 12. 12 and 27: *Denn wie der Leib einer ist und doch viele Glieder hat, alle Glieder des Leibes aber, obwohl sie viele sind, doch ein Leib sind: so auch Christus. … Ihr aber seid der Leib Christi und jeder von euch ein Glied.*) Paul's description of the church would, if sketched or illustrated, look very similar to the portrait of the Leviathan that opens Hobbes' book. But this vision of the Church is universalistic for there is no principled reason why a given member cannot be of the body. It is thus a threat to the Empire and its claim to be the creator of *pax*. The Roman word *pax* tends to refer to a state of affairs achieved and preserved by arms. It is thus political and consists in separating the Roman Empire off from those who are not so pacified. However, in the well known passage from the Letter to the Galatians, Paul allows no finality in differentiation. (Gal 3.23: *Hier ist nicht Jude noch Grieche, hier ist nicht Sklave noch Freier, hier ist nicht Mann noch Frau; denn ihr seid allesamt einer in Christus Jesus.*) It is to this dismemberment that Nietzsche points in the "*Von der Erlösung*" chapter in *Zarathustra* II.

For Paul, it is precisely the resurrected Christ, the occurrence of something from beyond the realm of possibility which affects everyone, regardless of their sex, race, ethnicity and so forth, a Lacanian Real that annihilates the normal, that engenders a new universality. As Nietzsche writes: "*Paulus wusste nichts Besseres seinem Erlöser nachzusagen, als dass er den Zugang zur Unsterblichkeit für Jedermann eröffnet habe. …*" (*Morgenröte*, §72) Paul is responding to the promise that he sees instantiated in Jesus' resurrection, an Event the Truth of which can in no ways be proven but can only be believed. Just as the Real cannot be represented, language itself, Paul asserts, would diminish the promise of the resurrection (I Corinthians 1.17). It is not surprising that the Athenian philosophers refer to Paul as a *spermologos*—a babbler—Acts 17.18.

Were the Church to remain a subdivision sect of the Jews, it would not be a threat—the Jews were well known to the Romans as an odd people, but one that generally kept to itself. Thus the Church as Paul envisages it is thus an epistemological threat to the Roman Empire, but one to which the Romans will respond politically (by persecuting them—the grounds are laid out in the correspondence between Pliny and Trajanus discussed above).

All relations and authority is now to be mediated by and in Christ: to be a disciple of Christ one must hate one's family and even one's own life (Lukas 14.26). Christ and the Church function as what Schmitt called a *Grenzbegriff*.

Jesus says in Matthew 5.17: "Think not that I am come to destroy the law, or the prophets: I am not come to destroy, but to fulfill." For Paul, Christ reasserts the Law precisely and only by going beyond it. Thus Romans 13:10: "(Love is the fulfillment of the Law)."

While a number of passages oppose love and the gospel to the Law (e. g. John 1.17; II Cor 3.611: *Denn der Buchstabe tötet, aber der Geist macht lebendig*),[45] overwhelmingly the texts place the law and love into a complex relationship. What seems to me clear in Paul is what Slavoj Žižek points out: "the very act of fulfilling the Law undermines its direct authority."[46] This was also Nietzsche's position, as he writes in *Jenseits von Gut und Böse* (*Sprüche und Zwischenspiele*)

Jesus sagte zu seinen Juden: "das Gesetz war für Knechte—liebt Gott, wie ich ihn liebe, als sein Sohn! Was geht uns Söhne Gottes die Moral an!" [Jesus said to his Jews: "The law was for servants— love God as I love him, as his Son! What is morality to us sons of God!"] (BGE §164)

While the love of God fulfills the law it is by definition not covered by the law. Thus being a Christian means always living a *Grenzbegriff*—living as both exception and law. It is thus inherent in the structure of a Church that it both invokes and resists the realm that is beyond the Law. When Paul says "*So ist nun die Liebe des Gesetzes Erfüllung*," he is saying that inherent in the foundation of a Church is the opening to that which is beyond the law. The Church is the fulfillment of the Law but that fulfillment is always from beyond the Law.

How did Paul bring his vision about? In the epistles that we are relatively sure Paul wrote, he always begins them by instantiating his authority. Paul had not been a disciple; he had never known Christ. Indeed, his early career was spent in the persecution of those who followed Christ. It was on the road to Damascus that he becomes who and what is is. [Cf. I Cor 15.10: "*Aber durch Gottes Gnade bin ich, was ich bin.*"] We find a clue in the very first line of the letter to the Romans. Luther renders this as: "*Paulus, ein Knecht Christi Jesu, berufen zum Apostel, ausgesondert, zu predigen das Evangelium Gottes.*" [Paul, a servant of Jesus Christ, called to be an apostle, separated unto the gospel of God.][47] The Greek, however, gives us: "*Paulos doulos Christou Iesou, kletos apostolos aforismenos eis euanggelion Theou.*" The key is *doulos*—slave.[48] Paul, a Jew, a Roman, describes himself here by appropriating a term for precisely those who are at the bottom of the Roman world— slave. And this designation is used as the source of his authority.

Why should being a *doulos* be a claim to authority? Jacob Taubes, in *Die politische Theologie des Paulus* argues that the true founder of Christianity was Paul and not Christ.[49] In this he picks up on Nietzsche, who in *Morgenröte* §68 sees Paul as "the First Christian." Paul overcomes the law precisely because he comes to revalue what it meant to die on the cross. Instead of being shameful, that death is the prerequisite to living outside the law, thus to living beyond sin. Nietzsche will analyze this more generally in *Jenseits* and *Zur Genealogie*: slave morality consists in taking that which had designated the base and shameful and turning it into an instrument of power. Paul thus sought nothing less than to recast the entire Roman system by taking what Romans had despised and rendering it the most worthy of admiration. Slavery to the law is replaced by the transcendent slavery—*doulos*—to Christ. We find in Romans 8: 2–4:

> [2] *Denn das Gesetz des Geistes, der lebendig macht in Christus Jesus, hat dich frei gemacht von dem Gesetz der Sünde und des Todes.*

[3] *Denn was dem Gesetz unmöglich war, weil es durch das Fleisch geschwächt war, das tat Gott: er sandte seinen Sohn in der Gestalt des sündigen Fleisches und um der Sünde willen und verdammte die Sünde im Fleisch,*

[4] *damit die Gerechtigkeit, vom Gesetz gefordert, in uns erfüllt würde, die wir nun nicht nach dem Fleisch leben, sondern nach dem Geist.*[50]

This slavery is the authority by which he sets out the promise of the resurrection. It is precisely because he is a slave that he has authority as being called, as *apostolos*. The incarnation is of little importance to Paul (and likewise to Hobbes). Life after death—the resurrection—is the promise that the Law is unable to accomplish. And this inability shows the limits of the Law and why Love is the fulfillment of the law. And the question then becomes what are we to be until we pass beyond death. What is required is the Church, the assembly of those who are all similarly summoned by this call. Paul's vision of the Church is remarkably like that which we find in Hobbes. Each individual is individual and yet part of the whole. One soon finds similar sentiments in those who follow Paul. Tertullian, in his *Book of Apology Against the Heathen* will write:

> We are a body formed by our joint cognizance of Religion, by the unity of discipline, by the bond of hope. We come together in a meeting and a congregation as before God, as though we would in one body sue Him by our prayers. This violence is pleasing unto God. We pray also for Emperors, for their ministers and the powers, for the condition of the world, for the quiet of all things, for the delaying of the end.[51]

Tertullian sees the Church as had Paul, and as will Schmitt, as a *katechon*, that delays the *eschaton*. Such is the Church for Paul: how is it legitimated and against what is it defined? For Schmitt, Paul defines the Church against its enemies, which Schmitt understands as the Jews. The enemy is something "existentially other and alien" As I noted, he remarks that *"Feind ist hostis nicht inimicus im weiteren Sinne; polémios, nicht echthrós."* (BP 29 / 28) To understand this the key passage is again from Romans: *"Im Blick auf das Evangelium sind sie zwar Feinde um euretwillen; aber im Blick auf die Erwählung sind sie Geliebte um der Väter willen."*[52] The Latin Vulgate is *"secundum evangelium quidem inimici propter vos secundum electionem autem carissimi propter patres;"* The Greek is *"Kata men to euangelion echthroi di humas, kata deten eklogen agapetoi dia tous pateras."*

For Schmitt it is important that the Church be the "friend" and that it have an enemy, here the Jews who insisted on circumcision as a prerequisite for becoming Christian and hence denied the universalism that Paul was seeking. Schmitt sees the enemy as *hostes* and *polémios*. In this passage, however, Paul (and his Latin translator) refers to them as *inimici* and *echthroi*.

Thus in Schmitt's nomenclature Paul's understanding of the relation of the Church to the Jews is not what Schmitt wishes it to be. The key here is how the "enemy" is defined. For Schmitt, *inimicus* and *echthros* are enemies in a private sense (we are thus enjoined to love them by Jesus).

Hostes and *polémios* are enemies in a public sense: they are our enemies and, remarks Schmitt, we are never enjoined to love them, to welcome the Saracens' capture of Jerusalem, for instance. In Schmitt, the enemy (here the Jews) of the Church is defined politically—and thus we get an insight into Schmitt's anti-Semitism or rather his anti-Judaism.

However, Paul, in this passage, does not define the Christian relation to the Jews politically but rather defines it theologically. While it is clear that concerning the Gospel the Jews (that is those who hold Judaism to be a prerequisite for Christianity) are enemies, it is also clear that they are beloved of God. In my analysis, which leans heavily on Karl Barth and particularly on Jacob Taubes, one is to love one's enemy because since God has revealed himself as the Other in the enemy, by loving the enemy we bring ourselves into the presence of God.[53] In Romans 13:8–9 Paul basically says that the only important thing is to love your neighbor as yourself and that everything else follows as it were (including loving God). Against Schmitt, we might call this a social theology rather than a political one. What appears in Paul is that loving one's neighbour, including one's enemy, is in fact to love God. When Paul condensed the two commandments into one (Romans 13.9: *Denn was da gesagt ist: "Du sollst nicht ehebrechen; du sollst nicht töten; du sollst nicht stehlen; du sollst nicht begehren", und was da sonst an Geboten ist, das wird in diesem Wort zusammengefaßt: "Du sollst deinen Nächsten lieben wie dich selbst."*) he was establishing a social theology. Love of the neighbour was an instantiation of love of God. One is tempted to conclude that Schmitt's political theology is not a Christian political theology.[54]

Acknowledgments

This essay was originally prepared for a *Meisterkurs* on "Politische Theologie," organized at the Institut für Philosophie of the Humboldt Universität zu Berlin by and with the participation of Professor Dr. Volker Gerhardt. The other participants were Professor Dr. Enno Rudolph, Professor Dr. Angelo Bolaffi, Professor Dr. Claus Öffe. I am grateful to each for their comments as I am to the students who participated actively in the course. — TBS. [This text was written as lecture for translation into German: *Der sakrale Geist der Politik: Bemerkungen über Hobbes, Schmitt und Paulus*, a postprint appears on Tracy's Academia webpage. This excerpt, following Tracy's wish, draws on the beginning and end of Strong, "The Sacred Quality of the Political. Reflections on Hobbes, Schmitt and Saint Paul," *Politisches Denken*, Vol. 20 (2010): 245–294. — BBS]

Endnotes

1. See Volker Neumann, "Carl Schmitt: Introduction," in: Arthur Jacobson / Bernhard Schlink, eds., *Weimar: A Jurisprudence of Crisis* (Berkeley: University of California Press, 2000), 282. On the distinction of "mistake" and "accident" and the moral difference it makes, see J. L. Austin, "A Plea for Excuses," in his *Philosophical Papers* (Oxford: Clarendon, 1963).

2. See e. g., Gustavo Gutiérrez, *A Theology of Liberation: History, Politics, Salvation*, revised edition. (New York: Orbis books, 1988).

3. See Walter Rauschenbusch, *Christianity and the Social Crisis* (New York: MacMillan,1908), chapter Seven ("What To Do").

4. Heinrich Meier has argued that Schmitt has a theological politics and contrasts Schmitt to Leo Strauss' philosophical politics. See Heinrich Meier, *The Lesson of Carl Schmitt: Four Chapters on the Distinction between Political Theology and Political Philosophy*, trans. Marcus Brainard (Chicago: University of Chicago Press, 1998). I think rather that Schmitt has a political theology, that is that the way in which he thinks about politics is political and is a secularization of theological concepts. See Andrew Norris, "Carl Schmitt's Political Metaphysics: On the Secularization of 'The Outermost Sphere,'" *Theory and Event* (2000) 4, 1 (online only).

5. Alain Badiou, *Saint Paul: The Foundation of Universalism* (Stanford: Stanford University Press, 2003), refers to this as the "Christ Event," (chapter eight) by which he means the resurrection.

6. Carl Schmitt, "Das Zeitalter der Neutraliserung und Entpolitisierung" in: Schmitt, *Der Begriff des Politischen* (Berlin: Duncker & Humblot, 2002 [1932]), 95. Henceforth "BP xx" in text. English edition as *The Concept of the Political*, trans. George Schwab, with a foreword by Tracy B. Strong (Chicago: University of Chicago Press, 1996). Page numbered in text as BP xx / yy. This article is cited as BPZN.

7. Schmitt, *ibid.*, 94-95.

8. Max Weber, "Parliament und Regierung im neugeordneten Deutschland," *Gesammelte Politische Schiften* [GPS] (Tübingen: Mohr, 1971), 351.

9. Carl Schmitt, *Politische Theologie* (Berlin. Duncker & Humblot, 2004 [1922]). 68. Henceforth "PT xx" in the text. English edition as *Political Theology*, trans. George Schwab with a Foreword by Tracy B. Strong (Chicago: University of Chicago Press, 2005). Page numbers in text as PT xx (German) / yy (English): "Today nothing is more modern than the onslaught against the political ... There must be no longer be political problems, only organizational technical and economic sociological ones." (English PT 65).

10. BPZN 79–95.

11.   Carl Schmitt, *Der Leviathan in der Staatslehre des Thomas Hobbes: Sinn undFeldschlag eines politischen Symbols* (Stuttgart: Klett Cotta, 1995), 60 "… the mechanization of the conception of the State has ended by bringing about the mechanization of the anthropological understanding of human beings."

12.   "A huge industrial plant" … "runs on its own … [and] the decisionistic and personalistic element in the concept of sovereignty is lost."

13.   See Strauss, "Notes on Carl Schmitt," par. 1, in: Carl Schmitt, *The Concept of the Politcal*, 83. See footnote 5 above.

14.   "If a sphere of thought becomes central, then the problems of other spheres are solved in terms of the central sphere – they are considered secondary problems whose solution follows as a matter of course only if the problems of the central sphere are solved."

15.   This periodisation can also be found in shorter form in the 1934 preface to *Politische Theologie*, 1-2. The stages are well discussed in Henning Ottmann, "Das Zeitalter der Neutralisierungen und Ent-Totalisierungen: Carl Schmitts Theorie der Neuzeit" in: Reinhard Mehring (ed.), *Carl Schmitt. Der Begriff des Politischen. Ein Kooperativer Kommentar* (Berlin: Akademie Verlag, 2003), 156–169. See the more extensive discussion in my foreword to Schmitt, *Political Theology*.

16.   A contemporary edition is Julien Benda, *Le trahison des clercs* (Paris: Grasset, Les cahiers rouges, 2003).

17.   Jacob Taubes, *The Political Theology of Paul* (Stanford: Stanford University Press, 2004), writes that "He [Schmitt] is a clerk, and he understands his task not to be to establish the law but to interpret the law." (103)

18.   "By centuries of theological reflection …" "private matters".

19.   "Precisely because it serves all … is not neutral".

20.   Max Weber, *Die Protestantische Ethik und der Geist der Kapitalismus, in: Religionssoziologie I* (Tübingen: Mohr, 2003). The standard English translation as "iron cage" is thus misleading: not only can you not *get out* but you cannot even *see out*.

21.   BP 54: "When a people no longer has the strength or the will to hold itself to the realm of the political, the political does not thereby disappear from the world. It is only a weak people that perishes."

22.   It is worth noting both that this line served as the origins for the motto (*"novus ordo saeculorum"*) on the Great Seal of the United States as devised by Charles Thompson (an eminent Latinist), and that the following lines in Vergil speaks of the coming of a new child, which was understood by medieval Christianity to be a prophecy of the coming of Christ. The last entry in Schmitt's *Glossarium* (published in 1991) reads: *"Mit jedem neugeborenen Kind wird eine neue Welt geboren."* He goes on to hope that the child will be an *"Aggressor."*

23.   See above, note 15.

24.   See James Conant, "Must We Show What We Cannot Say" in R. Fleming and Michael Payne (eds.), *The Senses of Stanley Cavell: Bucknell Review* (1989): 242-283, esp. 252–253.

25.   See the discussion in Stanley Cavell, *Themes Out of School* (Chicago: University of Chicago Press, 1984), 36.

26.   Carl Schmitt, *The Crisis of Parliamentary Democracy*, (Cambridge: MIT, 1985), 62.

27.   Herbert Marcuse, *Negations* (Boston: Beacon Press, 1968), 31.

28.   "Genius" is one of the *topoi* of nineteenth century thought. See the account in Jochen Schmidt, *Die Geschichte des Genie Gedankens in der deutschen Literatur, Philosophie und Politik*, 1750–1945. 2 volumes (Darmstadt: Universitätsverlag Heidelberg, 1985), which covers thinkers from Klopstock and Lessing, through Kant to Schopenhauer, Nietzsche, and the twentieth century, albeit not always unconventionally. On Kant see also Giorgio Tonelli, "Kant's Early Theory of Genius (1770–1779): Part I," in: *Journal of the History of Philosophy*, vol. IV (1966): 109-131 and "Part II," in: ibid., vol. V, 209–224. Thanks to Jackob Pyetranker for calling these articles to my attention.

29. See for instance, Nietzsche, *Die Fröhliche Wissenschaft*, §105. I am indebted here to several conversations with Professor Alexander Rehding of the Harvard Music Department.

30. Immanuel Kant, *Kritik der Urteilskraft* [henceforth KU] § 45, Akademie edition: 5.306.

31. As Dieter Henrich, *Aesthetic Judgment and the Moral Image of the World* (Stanford: Stanford University Press, 1992), writes: "We must ... wonder how understanding, in its lawfulness, can enter a situation that cannot be elucidated by reference to the constitutive usage of the categories and that precludes general concepts." (47).

32. Kant, KU § 6 (5.211).

33. Kant, KU § 46 ff (5.307ff).

34. Kant, KU § 46 (5. 308) "He does not know himself how the ideas for [the beautiful work of art] come to him, and also does not have it in his power to think up such things at will or according to plan, and to communicate to others precepts that would put them in apposition to produce similar products."

35. Kant, *Anthropologie* (5.318n) "Genius ... glitters like a momentary phenomenon which appears and disappears at intervals, and vanishes again. It is not a light that can be kindled at will and kept burning for a period of one's choosing, but it is rather like a spark scattering flash which a happy seizure of the spirit entices from the productive imagination."

36. Kant, KU § 47 (5.309).

37. Kant, "*Die Einbildungskraft (als produktives Erkenntnisvermögen) ist nämlich sehr mächtig in Schaffung gleichsam einer andern Natur, aus dem Stoffe, den ihr die wirkliche gibt.*" *Ibid.*, § 49 (5.314).

38. Novalis, *Pollen*, in: Frederick Beiser, ed., *Writings of the Early German Romantics* (Cambridge: Cambridge University Press, 1996), 12.

39. See Peter Bürger, "Carl Schmitt oder die Fundierung der Politik auf Aesthetik," in: Christa Bürger, ed., *Zerstörung, Rettung des Mythos durch Licht* (Frankfurt, 1986). I owe this reference to Victoria Kahn, "Hamlet or Hecuba: Carl Schmitt's Decision," *Representations*, 83 (Summer 2003): 67-96. I came across this article after writing mine and am pleased that she starts hers with some of the same considerations I use.

40. I am indebted here to some conversations with Professor Jason Frank of Cornell University. On Freud see my "Psychoanalysis as a Vocation: Freud, "Politics and the Heroic," *Political Theory* , Vol. 12, Issue 1 (February, 1984): 51-79.

41. Aristide Zolberg, "Moments of Madness," *Theory and Society* (1972): 183-207, esp. 172. See also Sidney Tarrow, "Cycles of Collective Action: Between Moments of Madness and the Repertoire of Contention," *Social Science History*, Vol. 17, No. 2 (Summer, 1993): 81-307.

42. Pliny the Younger, *Epistles* 10.34.1: *Sed meminerimus provinciam istam et praecipue eas civitates eius modi factionibus esse vexatas. Quodcumque nomen ex quacumque causa dederimus iis, qui in idem contracti fuerint, hetaeriae eaeque brevi fient.*

43. Pliny, op cit, 10.9394: *non ad turbas et ad illicitos coetus, sed ad sustinendam tenuiorum inopiam utuntur. In ceteris civitatibus, quae nostro iure obstrictae sunt, res huius modi prohibenda est.*

44. Thus Paul founds the Christian Church. Cf Wittgenstein's remark in "Culture and Value," 35: "The spring that flows quietly & clearly in the Gospels seems to foam in Paul's Epistles."

45. The relation of love and law is a matter of considerable dispute in Christian theology. Some separate the two radically, others refer to a "law of love" which is the same as a "law of grace."

46. Slavoj Žižek, *The Ticklish Subject* (London: Verso, 2000), 115. My paragraph here is indebted to 113-116 of this book.

47. Of the seven epistles reliably attributed to Paul, he invokes his authority as *doulos* in three (Romans, Philippians and Philemon) and as *apostolos* (I and II Corinthians, Galatians, and I Thessalonians) in the others.

48.   Greek distinguished between a slave proper [*doulos*] and a slave taken in war [*andrapodon*].

49.   Taubes, *The Political Theology of Paul*, 41.

50.   See also I Corinthians 6. 15–17; I Corinthians 10. 15–17; I Corinthians 12.

51.   Tertullian, *Book of Apology Against the Heathen* (Oxford: Parker, 1842), §xxxix, 80.

52.   Romans 11.28: As concerning the gospel, indeed, they are enemies for your sake: but as regards the election, they are beloved of the Father.

53.   In Matthew 5.4445, Jesus orders that one love one's enemies: [44] *Ich aber sage euch: Liebt eure Feinde und bittet für die, die euch verfolgen,* [45] *damit ihr Kinder seid eures Vaters im Himmel. Denn er läßt seine Sonne aufgehen über Böse und Gute und läßt regnen über Gerechte und Ungerechte.*

54.   This raises another large question. For an initial entry to it, see Tristan Storme, *Carl Schmitt et le marcionisme* (Paris: Editions du Cerf, 2008).

TIME'S DELAYS: ANTICHRIST AND WORLD HISTORY

GARY SHAPIRO

> if there is one point where one realizes that Christianity has twisted humanity, it is to be found in all the connections that Christianity has entered into with politics, just as I do not doubt at all that here is the point at which it will one day succumb to a general contempt.
> — Franz Overbeck, letter to Heinrich Treitschke

> "we do not want the Kingdom of Heaven at all: we have become men — and so we want the Kingdom of Earth [*Erdenreich*]"
> — Nietzsche, *Thus Spoke Zarathustra*, IV.18

> Would you like a new name for me? The church language [*Kirchensprache*] has one— the Antichrist. Let's not forget to laugh!
> — Nietzsche, letter to Malwida von Meysenbug, 4 April 1883

> It is certain that the political philosophy of modernity will not be able to free itself of its contradictions if it does not become aware of its theological roots.
> — Giorgio Agamben, *Leviathan's Riddle*

The Birth of World-History From the Spirit of the Church

Christ and Antichrist are names having to do with time, more specifically with calculated time. If Christians begin their calendar with Jesus' birth (even if postdated four years) they have also frequently attempted calculations of the world's end, signaled by the Antichrist's coming. These calculations began in earnest with the church father Hippolytus around 210 CE, calculations Nietzsche would surely have discussed with his housemate, Overbeck, who wrote his doctoral thesis on Hippolytus' treatise *On Christ and Antichrist*. Overbeck's Latin dissertation concerns an important early patristic text in the tradition of eschatological speculation that grew up around the enigmatic references to the personification of evil. In the early third century, Hippolytus, living in Rome but coming from

New Nietzsche Studies, Vol. 11, Nos. 3 and 4 (Fall 2021 / Spring 2022), pp. 47–72.
© 2022 Nietzsche Society. ISSN 1091–0239.

a Greek cultural background, published a short treatise on Christ and Antichrist, defining several features of this figure taken up by many later writers.

Hippolytus' originality was in providing arguments that claimed to render intelligible the deferral and delay of the second coming and the end of time, an increasing worry in the second and third centuries. Very few non-theological philosophers have even heard of Hippolytus of Rome, but he has had an enormous if indirect influence on the course of philosophy, arguably enabling the movement of thought that eventually crystallizes as "world-history."[1] Hippolytus contributed to codifying church and European political theology for hundreds of years, consolidated and further defined the Christian picture of Antichrist and apocalypse, and, since the 1851 publication of his long lost *Refutation of All Heresies*, shaped the understanding of early Greek philosophy (perhaps it is fitting that this great thinker of deferral should have such a deferred effect).[2] His Biblical exegeses center around the names Christ and Antichrist.

The development of theology in the changing Christian community of the Roman Empire became Overbeck's lifelong theme, already foreshadowed in his dissertation on Hippolytus. Early theology began to ask questions like these: How and when would this world cease? How, in the meantime, can we live in a world of misery and pain? Eschatological beliefs, textual exegesis, and political theology contribute to various answers. Hippolytus expands the ideas of Irenaeus, his more original teacher. He shows a stronger interest in exegesis of sacred texts as a method of argument and exposition. Drawing especially on the Hebrew prophets, Daniel, and scattered Christian texts (there was not yet a codified New Testament), he claims that as Christ is the recapitulation [*anakephalaiosis*] of all good, so Antichrist is the recapitulation of evil. At the same time, Antichrist must mirror Christ by appearing in human form, being Jewish, sending out apostles, and building a temple in Jerusalem (corresponding with the temple of Christ's body). Hippolytus engages in ingenious interpretation of 666, the number of the Beast.

What are these names or titles—Christ and Antichrist—that occupied Hippolytus? In what sense are they names? As Agamben reminds us (and as many—even theologians—have forgotten!) "Christ" is simply the Greek translation of the Hebrew "messiah," as in the Septuagint. "Christ" is a Russellian definite description, not a name. That should direct us to look more carefully at Nietzsche's use of the title and "name" Antichrist. Nietzsche, the philologist, former student of theology, and Overbeck's friend, would have understood that *christos* is not a proper name, but a title or appellative. As Agamben points out, a general ignorance (or willful forgetting) of this fact has enabled a downplaying of messianic thought and an oblivion concerning messianic time in later Christianity.[3]

In addition to signaling an all-out assault on Christianity, the Antichrist title should be understood within a tradition we once again call political theology. Despite the obvious attempt to scandalize here, there is a theological history behind Nietzsche's declaration "I am in Greek, and not only in Greek, the *Antichrist*" (EH Books 2). The remark's context may seem to frame it as one more throw away witticism, but the "old philologist's" emphasis on language usually repays attention. The section in *Ecce Homo* that works up to this claim begins with the less outrageous assertion that Nietzsche has many sensitive readers, especially outside Germany. He says that he is well received by those sensitive to style and nuance — those able to listen, such as his *Doktorvater* Ritschl and the French critic Hyppolite Taine. Perhaps women listen more attentively than men. He is not like an ass or donkey, whose long ears betray his crudity. And only after such strong provocations to attentive listening does Nietzsche come to his philologically mediated identification as Antichrist: "I am the anti-ass [*Antiesel*] par excellence and so am a world-historical monster, — I am, in Greek, and not only in Greek, the *Antichrist*..."

This linkage of monstrosity, world-history, and the Antichrist can be understood in terms of a Christian tradition of political theology whose effect (and, doubtless, its occasional intention) is to obscure the consciousness of messianic time basic to the earliest Christian community. From the standpoint of world-history, Nietzsche acknowledges, he is a monster — but the careful listener might say, so much for "so-called world-history." Let us explore this conjunction of world-historical monstrosity and the linguistically inflected claim of the Antichrist name. Nietzsche's mention of Greek and unspecified other languages should lead to the question of the meaning and significance of the title Christ even before we consider the Antichrist figure. Nietzsche indicates that questions of time are at stake by calling himself a "world-historical monster" in the same sentence. As we know, world-history is itself something of a monstrosity for Nietzsche. What are the senses of time associated with the "idiot" Jesus, Christ as constructed by Christianity, the Antichrist and apocalypse, and the witches' brew of world-history that comes from the attempt to combine them? And what are the political implications of these forms of temporality? Can we demythologize the idea that the Antichrist is lord of the earth?

Nietzsche advises us to think of the name Antichrist in several registers, including at least its philological, philosophical, and theological contexts. Nietzsche calls for the Antichrist toward the conclusion of the *Genealogy*'s essay on "'Guilt,' 'Bad Conscience,' and Related Matters." In the long penultimate aphorism leading up to the writer's falling silent before the "younger" Zarathustra, he imagines "the redeeming human of the great love and contempt" who must come in a stronger time:

> This human of the future who will redeem us from the previous ideal as much as from that which *had to grow out of it*, from the great disgust, from the will to nothingness; this bell-stroke of noon and of the great decision, that makes the will free again, that gives back to the earth its goal and to humans their hope; this Antichrist and anti-nihilist; this conqueror of God and of nothingness—*he must one day come...*

The emphasis on the singularity of this anticipated figure certainly suggests a distinct individual, not simply one among others who are also opponents of Christianity. It is not merely the "previous ideal" —Christian ideals of compassion, selflessness or self-abnegation— which is to be destroyed but, emphatically "that *which had to grow out of it*," that is, I take it, Christian culture and institutions, in all their multiform transformations and disguises (the *Genealogy*'s third essay traces these types all the way down to the *Wissenschaftler* and the historian). The Antichrist "gives back to the earth its goal and to the human their hope." The Antichrist is not merely destructive, then, and in an important sense he is not completely original, for he gives back to earth and humans what had been lost or taken from them. "Giving back" suggests return, revolving back to an earlier condition, one of the core dimensions of "revolution." The implicit contrast then is between the Antichrist who restores these and Christ (or Christianity, which claimed his heritage) who is responsible for their loss or theft. Returning to *Zarathustra*'s crucial terms, *Erde* and *Mensch*, Nietzsche closes this essay in the *Genealogy* by reminding the reader (who has been advised to read the earlier book first) of the thematic relation binding earth and human. The idea of world-history, then, contrasts with that of the human earth [*Menschen-Erde*]: one forecloses the future and subsumes the earth within a closed system of meaning, while the other re-opens occluded horizons.

  The Antichrist's hyperbolic rhetoric alienates many readers, yet Nietzsche foregrounds his hyperbole in designating his alert readers as "the fewest," as Hyperboreans who dwell far beyond the north, and are like him in "seeing the wretched ephemeral chatter [*Zeitgschwätz*] of politics and national egoism beneath themselves" (AC, Foreword and §1). To see such chatter beneath one is not to ignore it altogether, but to see it in its appropriate position, from a higher perspective. This perspective brings together two important critiques. These are directed, first, at the foundations of *Zeitgschwätz*, the all too timely or *zeitmässig*, namely the philosophy and ideology of world-history on which it is parasitic (cf. UO III). The second critique focuses on Christian political theology, a set of doctrines and concepts embedded in institutional practice, which have the effect of obscuring the life and temporal experience of the earliest Christian community while lending support to the worldly powers of state and church. World-history and political theology mask the possibility of a politics of the earth by enabling and giving a framework to the distracting *Zeitgeschwätz* of the *Zeitungen*.

Antichrist and World-History

Who is the Antichrist in the discourse of the church [*Kirchensprache*]? The answer will help us understand how Nietzsche's project of a "philosophy of the Antichrist" could be a further twist in his thought concerning place and time: that is the earth and the world, *kairos* and *chronos*. The specter of the Antichrist helps to open up Nietzsche's perspective on political time (not mere *Zeitgschwätz*). Let's approach this question by considering the meaning of the figure in Christian political theology. This tradition claims its origins in letters attributed to Paul, was formulated explicitly as early as Tertullian in the second century, and has been explored by a number of more recent thinkers and scholars, notably Schmitt, Kantorowicz, and Agamben.[4]

In Christian political theology, as contrasted with the potpourri of passionate anathematizations and passing hysterias about supposed great events or cataclysms, it is not so much a question of naming the Antichrist as of understanding his, her, or their—for there can be many Antichrists, and perhaps by the logic of the simulacrum there must be—relation to political power. Briefly, in that long tradition, the Antichrist can be understood as the evil one(s), both enemies of Christ and figures capable of imitating his attributes, whose appearance is restrained or held off by the state. In the second letter to the Thessalonians, Paul (or whoever writes in his name) warns his addressees against expecting an imminent arrival of the last days, the end of the world. He says without much explanation that there is a restraining force or *katechon* [*Aufhalter*] that delays the appearance of Antichrist(s):

> Let no man deceive you by any means: for that day shall not come, except there come a falling away first, and that man of sin be revealed, the son of perdition; Who opposeth and exalteth himself above all that is called God, or that is worshipped; so that he as God sitteth in the temple of God, shewing himself that he is God. Remember ye not, that, when I was yet with you, I told you these things? And now ye know what withholdeth [*katechon*] that he might be revealed in his time [*kairo*]. For the mystery of iniquity doth already work: only he who now letteth will let, until he be taken out of the way (II Thessalonians 2: 3-7).

This is the rather enigmatic text that Tertullian applied to the Roman Empire around 200 CE, roughly a century before its official Christianization under Constantine. The theme of waiting, containing, warding off, and other apotropaic strategies has more general implications, and can be understood in such contexts as the Cold War doctrine of containment, slowing climate change, resistance to change by entrenched institutional interests, or the struggles of those with aging bodies to mitigate the processes of decay and degeneration.[5]

In his *Apology* Tertullian writes:

There is also another and a greater necessity for our offering prayer in behalf of the emperors, nay, for the complete stability of the empire, and for Roman interests in general. For we know that a mighty shock impending over the whole earth—in fact, the very end of all things threatening dreadful woes—is only retarded by the continued existence of the Roman empire. We have no desire, then, to be overtaken by these dire events; and in praying that their coming may be delayed, we are lending our aid to Rome's duration.[6]

When the Roman Empire becomes Christian and, later, Europe is ruled by Christian kings, such katechontic teachings become increasingly significant, providing ideological support for royal and imperial authority. It is not surprising then that Schmitt, Kantorowicz, and Agamben find the doctrine of the restraining force of the *katechon* essential in the claims to legitimacy put forward by medieval and early modern European states. For Schmitt, the state legitimated in terms of this teaching is the emblem and central institution of the temporal regime that began with the coming of Christ and will end in the world's last days as foretold in *Revelation*:

> The Christian empire was not eternal. It always had its own end in view. Nevertheless, it was capable of being a historical power. The decisive historical concept of this continuity was that of the restrainer: *katechon*. "Empire" in this sense meant the historical power to restrain the appearance of the Antichrist and the end of the present eon; it was a power that withholds [*qui tenet*], as the Apostle Paul said in his Second Letter to the Thessalonians.[7]

Katechontic political theology involves a very specific sense of *temporality*, one that helps to constitute the Christian core of *Weltgeschichte*, which Nietzsche saw as the dominant form of his age's temporal thought. Katechontic (and world-historical) political time contrast with the temporal consciousness of earliest Christianity, the community of Jesus' followers who believed that he had ushered in a new, messianic time. Paul writes

> But this I say, brethren, time contracted itself, the rest is that even those having wives may be as not [*hōs mē*] having, and those weeping as not weeping, and those rejoicing as not rejoicing, and those buying as not possessing, and those using the world as not using it up. For passing away is the figure of this world (I Cor. 7:29-32).[8]

We are to undertake all activities (work, marriage, civic relations) "as not" these activities. Time will be transformed. Yet as Agamben says "a messianic institution—or rather a messianic community that wants to present itself as an institution—faces a paradoxical task."[9] Institutions and communities are meant to endure. What then is an institution or community that expects an imminent end of all worldly institutions and communities? Agamben observes that both the Christian and Jewish traditions have entered an implicit agreement to see Paul as the founder of a new religion. In doing so "the aim is to cancel out or at least mute Paul's Judaism, that is to say, to expunge it from its original messianic context."[10] Agamben cites Jacob Taubes's 1986 final lectures (and draws on his own vast erudition) to support his stringent re-reading and re-evaluation of Paul. However, Nietzsche (cited extensively by Taubes) was already aware of the discrepancy between earlier and later responses to the Jesus event.

From Overbeck to Nietzsche

Martin Heidegger's student Karl Löwith wrote an ambitious and illuminating narrative titled *From Hegel to Nietzsche: The Revolution in Nineteenth Century Thought*. The book artfully combines aspects of a sequential history with a structure based on an array of philosophical topics. The last section is devoted to "The Problem of Christianity." Running his analysis again, more or less chronologically through a number of major figures, he concludes the section and so the entire book not with Nietzsche, but with "Overbeck's Analysis of Primitive and Passing Christianity." Of course Overbeck, who brought Nietzsche back to Basel after his collapse in Turin, had a productive life that continued for about fifteen years more. Löwith sums up his contribution as having achieved a clear understanding of why and how the Christianity of the bourgeois world came to an end. Yet since Overbeck's researches demonstrated "the abyss separating us from Christianity," Löwith ends his book with a qualification and a rhetorical question:

> This does not mean that a faith which once conquered the world perishes with its last secular manifestations. For how should the Christian pilgrimage *in hoc saeculo* ever become homeless in the land where it has never been at home?[11]

The expression *in hoc saeculo* is apparently a reference to Ephesians 1:21, where Paul writes (in the King James version), where he is describing the power given Christ by God:

> Far above all principality, and power, and might, and dominion, and every name that is named, not only in this world, but also in that which is to come.

The Greek term that the King James translates with "world" (and Luther with "*Welt*") is *aion*, also and more recently often translated as "age." The difference may not be very significant, since the world in Pauline perspective is always only that of an age or era that will give way to "that which is to come." Löwith, I assume, is playing on the relation between the *saeculum* and the secular or *weltlich*. He endorses Overbeck's view that primitive Christianity was rigorously unworldly. At the same time we can read something different in Paul's letter, from which Löwith draws this parting question. Yes, Christ's kingdom is not of this world or age, Ephesians implies, but it stands not so much or only outside them, but above them. It was openings like this that helped to make Christianity into the "secular" power that Löwith assumed (in 1939) it no longer was. Given the resurgence of religion and political theology, it should be worth exploring just how Nietzsche and Overbeck engaged with the problematic of Christianity and worldly power.

Nietzsche's *Bildung* prepared him to understand the striking archaeological gap between the early community and the church that eventually emerged. We will follow that understanding by placing him alongside his scholarly shadow Overbeck, whose work showed the way to that understanding in a voice that was as cautiously reserved and balanced as Nietzsche's was deliberately flamboyant and excessive. As we know, Nietzsche was brought up in a Lutheran pastoral family with ministers on both father's and mother's sides. He began university studies in theology before switching to classical philology. By 1865 he was having vigorous arguments with his sister Elizabeth, fueled by his reading of Strauss's *Life of Jesus*. It was the same year that he began to wrestle with Hegel's *Weltgeschichte*. In any case he certainly discussed early Christianity personally and in correspondence with Overbeck, for whom this contrast of earlier and later formed the basis of his lifelong investigations of church history.[12]

Overbeck was a penetrating student of the early theology and practice of the church, which he saw as attempting to make sense of the time opened up by Jesus' failure to reappear by constructing a narrative of historical time, building on such scanty and enigmatic Biblical passages as those on Antichrist.[13] The 1870's and 80's were marked by a flurry of critical and philological discoveries about early Christianity, its relations with Roman power, and the formation of the Biblical canon. Overbeck was a major player in this research activity. By 1886 Overbeck had informed Nietzsche that recent scholarship had identified Revelation as the rewriting of a Jewish apocalyptic text.[14]

In lectures on Gnosticism, Overbeck points out that in 150 a canon was unknown to those now considered mainstream Christian writers and church fathers, but by 200 it was more or less in place, although the process of its establishment was murky. Overbeck argues that it was the contest with Marcion's Gnosticism and its canon — which excluded the Hebrew scriptures—that led to the formation of what has since been recognized as the canon.[15]

In the struggle with Gnosticism the church developed a theory of time (as real and continuous rather than punctuated by absolutely abrupt revelations), a political structure (to combat heresy and order lives in the world), and an accommodation with the state (rather than dismissing it as merely an illusion of the fallen world).[16] The logic of theology as well as the strategy for suppressing Gnosticism pointed the Church in the direction of organization, doctrine, and practice that acknowledged history as it made its peace with the state.

As Nietzsche the philologist points out, presuming to name the Antichrist is a risky undertaking. Historically, the list of candidates has been extensive; a quick look at the internet shows that almost any significant political figure has been held to deserve the title, beginning with Nero, infamous persecutor of Christians (and philosophers). More recently, some pointed out that Ronald Wilson Reagan, each of whose names has 6 letters, displayed 666, the number of the Beast of the Apocalypse. During the thirteenth century struggle between Emperor Frederick II (one of Nietzsche's heroes) and the Pope, both sides argued that the opponent was Antichrist.

Jacob Taubes says that "Overbeck's voice was heard much more clearly from the grave than it was by his contemporaries."[17] The scope and depth of his research and his re-evaluation of Christianity and its theology has only begun to become evident in recent decades. Before a critical edition of Overbeck's works began to appear in the 1990's he was known mainly through a few very detailed philological and historical studies of early Christian texts and authors, and as "Nietzsche's friend." A few thinkers, notably Karl Barth, were deeply affected by the posthumous (and editorially problematic) compilation of some of his notes published in the 1920's. Despite Karl Löwith devoting the final, summary chapter of his magisterial *From Hegel to Nietzsche* to Overbeck, little has been done to clarify his intellectual relationship with his more famous friend. Yet surely it was Nietzsche, if anyone, who would have been familiar with Overbeck's program before the latter's posthumous work began to appear. In 1873 Overbeck published his iconoclastic *How Christian is Our Contemporary Theology?*[18] He argued that Christian theology, in accommodating state and history—notably from Paul to Constantine —was radically incompatible with the original Christian community's temporal consciousness. The latter involved rigorous rejection of the life and values of the "world," coupled with firm faith that its members were living in the last days before Christ's second coming, to be ushered in by catastrophes and tribulations forecast in apocalyptic texts. For a community living in expectation of the imminent end, accepting Jesus' counsel to take no thought for the morrow, to engage with the world "as not" in the world, theology would have been meaningless or superfluous. Nietzsche's portrait of Jesus is even more radical; Jesus lives in a pure present without any expectation of the last days, which was an addition by Paul and the early Church. John's first letter counsels "Do not love the world [*kosmon*] or anything in the world," (1 *John* 2:15) yet Christianity invents world-history as part of the complex process of its accommodation to the world. Overbeck thought that this must eventually lead to a rejection of Christianity; as he wrote to Heinrich Treitschke: "if there is one point where one realizes that Christianity has twisted humanity, it is to be found in all the connections that Christianity has entered into with politics, just as I do not doubt at all that here is the point at which it will one day succumb to a general contempt."[19]

For Overbeck, the most notable survival of the spirit of primitive Christianity's rejection of the world and its time was the monastic tradition in its most ascetic and unworldly varieties. Surveying the modern epoch, he (like Nietzsche) singles out Pascal as a unique Christian who managed to recreate something like the anti-worldly spirit of the first generations. For both, Pascal is the exception who demonstrates the degradation that has all but obliterated the earlier movement. Parallel to Nietzsche's attack on Strauss's "cultural philistinism" and Hartmann's *Weltprozess*, Overbeck saw contemporary liberal German theologians as shameless apologists for Bismarck's *Reich*. Later, thinking of his arch-foe Adolf Harnack who supported the *Reich*, Overbeck wickedly suggested a parallel with Eusebius, probably Christianity's first political theologian and certainly its most effective one, who provided the chief formulations for Constantine's "donation" of the Roman Empire to the Church. Both, he said, were "*friseurs* of the Emperor's theological periwig."[20]

In Overbeck's narrative, when apocalypse was delayed past the generation who would see the coming of the kingdom in their lifetime, as Jesus preached, explanations seemed in order. Followers of Jesus, as Overbeck insistently repeats, were at first deeply convinced of the misery of earthly life and they aspired, as in the *Acts of the Apostles*, to live in loving communion, their compassion for others rooted in freedom from "the world." But as time passed, the church increasingly made worldly concessions, eventually appropriating concepts of Greek and Roman philosophy to rationalize its position in the continuing fallen world. This struck Overbeck as an existentially bizarre transformation of early Christianity's sense that they were living in messianic time, that the *kairos* had arrived, that they were living in the time of the end, that the end times were near. In his commentary on Paul, Agamben explains that this was conceived as the time of the end, as distinguished from the end of time. Now, in Paul's terms, time had been contracted; *kairos* on this understanding is a contraction of *chronos*. Yet after the initial generation or so of the Christian community had died out, and at least through most of the second century, the meaning of Christianity "itself" was radically up for grabs, as multiple versions and "heresies" (as they were called retrospectively), including Gnosticism and various Judaizing, and anti-Judaizing sects, claimed legitimacy and authority. Overbeck's research concerned the formation of the Biblical canon which went hand in hand with the consolidation of the church, reaching a point of crystallization in the theology of Eusebius and Constantine's "donation" of the Roman Empire. Overbeck said that the upshot of this ferment, given form through fixing the canon and making Christianity the imperial Roman religion, was a Christianity that was nothing more than "the last phosphorescent glow of the decomposing ancients."[21]

There is an intriguing parallel between two texts on the Antichrist. Overbeck began his career with a dissertation on Hippolytus' treatise on the *Antichrist*, as Nietzsche completed his with a declaration of war and a curse on Christianity which he titled and signed with that name.[22] Overbeck, already distanced from traditional Christianity and feeling incapable of preaching and pastoral work, opted for the scholarly refuge of theology and teaching. As he wrote Treitschke, he chose Hippolytus as a subject because he feared that dealing directly with canonical New Testament writings could have involved an aspiring professor in conflicts for which he was not yet ready. At the opposite pole Nietzsche burned his academic bridges early with his *Birth of Tragedy*, and finally tempted the censors, flaunting the title *Antichrist* to signal that he was breaking history into two.

Even if young Overbeck was in part motivated by prudential concerns about his scholarly career, his choice of topic turned out to be significant for his later work, which focused on the contrast between early Christianity's awareness of messianic and eschatological time on the one hand and the later Christian accommodation to the world on the other. From Overbeck's perspective, early Christianity was fixated above all on the misery, evil, and corruption of the world; it anticipated a rapid transformation through Jesus' second coming. When this event was delayed, well past any living memory of Jesus' times, accommodation with the world became necessary. Part of this accommodation was theology itself. The very attempt to pose and answer questions about religious matters inevitably involved admitting some of the world's language and traditions of reasoning. Overbeck never stopped pointing out the ways in which Christianity was forced to use pagan learning and so, he sardonically observed, it became the vehicle through which that culture survived. In Nietzsche's more succinct words, Christianity became "Platonism for the people."[23]

From the beginning of his work Overbeck was inspired by a view which Nietzsche articulated much more dramatically in his later writing. He saw Christianity as necessarily containing the seeds of its own destruction. The title of Overbeck's posthumously edited "book" *Christianty and Culture* (a selection of his writings) could be taken as posing the exclusive alternative, Christianity or culture? His research focused on church history, seen as the process by which Christianity accommodated itself to the world. Yet terms must be clarified, for in the early centuries there was not one Christianity but a multiplicity of sects and groupings with competing social, sexual, and political practices, beliefs, and texts. The "world" was, by and large, the Roman Empire. Only with the Council of Nicaea and the donation of Constantine did the church achieve a tenuous stability in doctrine and structure. This complex history is the context for Overbeck's typical questions: How was the authority of the Church established? How were the canonical texts canonized?

Perhaps Hippolytus' greatest innovation was his redating of the final events to about five hundred years in the future. This opens up a time of waiting, expectation, and the possibility of accommodation to the world in the time that remains. From his reading of Daniel he deduced, for example, that there were still ten democracies and ten kingdoms yet to come, before the end of the world.[24] As I have been claiming, it is something like this time of waiting [*chronos*], which for Overbeck is both symptom and enabler of accommodation to worldly culture, and for Nietzsche a time that threatens to extinguish a vigilant watch for the opportunities [*kairoi*] offered by chance (BGE §274). Part IV of Zarathustra can be read as enacting a parody of the waiting which became basic to the Christian tradition. At the beginning of this section, Zarathustra explains his receptivity to the humans who may come to him in his mountain home:

> I still await the sign that it is time for my descent…not impatient, nor patient, but rather as one who has unlearned even patience— because he no longer "endureth" [*duldet*] …for my fate is leaving me time…I am grateful to it, my eternal fate, for not rushing and

pressing me, but leaving me time for jesting and wicked tricks...(Z IV.1).[25]

The rest of Part IV is given over to Zarathustra's "jesting and wicked tricks" with the higher men who come seeking him. This is not the resigned Christian endurance of life in a vale of tears, but a time that has opened and dilated for the pleasures of play. Waiting has been transformed into playfulness that enjoys rather than merely enduring.

Even after their common residency in Basel, and after Nietzsche had taken leave from the university there, he continued his reading of Overbeck's work and related research. Some of the signs are evident in Dawn, which contains an extended discussion of Paul entitled "The first Christian" (D §68), as well as many observations on Christianity inspired both by Overbeck and other contemporary scholars. Nietzsche worked on *Dawn* in 1880. The work's composition was accompanied by a flurry of correspondence with Overbeck concerning the latter's research and other recent work on Paul and early Christianity. In June 1880 Nietzsche writes to Overbeck that he has reread *How Christian is our Contemporary Theology?* and has understood much more than on his earlier reading, a reading that had already led them in 1873 to call their two-pronged assault on D.F. Strauss and liberal Protestant theology a *Waffengenossenheit*, or comradeship in arms. In July, Overbeck sends Nietzsche his relatively brief new book *On the History of the Canon*, along with others' books on Paul's anthropology and Justin Martyr. He writes that the studies in this book have the value for him of "preliminary works on the emergence [*Entstehung*] of the earliest Christian literature, and are important for that of the canon and its clear understanding."[26]

Already before *On the History of the Canon* Overbeck had been engaged in an acutely political reading of early Christian literature. In 1870 he published an introduction to *The Acts of the Apostles*, arguing that the text was written considerably later than the activities recounted there, and that the narrative had been shaped to suggest the compatibility of Christianity and the Roman Empire. I quote at some length to give the flavor of the analysis. Overbeck points to the political side of the Acts—its obvious striving to procure for the Christian cause the favor of the state authorities of Rome by the consistent representation of the good terms on which the personages of the Apostolic period, particularly Paul, stood with the Roman state and its officers…

Especially does the trial of Paul give the Roman officials the opportunity of showing the favorable opinion they have of him; and, shielded by the Roman laws, he is enabled, though still a prisoner, joyfully for a considerable time to fulfill in Rome his duties as an Apostle… Nay, the long detention of the Apostle is in part explained simply by forgetfulness of duty on the part of certain officials …In this account, to which the experience of Paul can hardly have corresponded, we cannot fail to recognize the design to avert political suspicions from Christianity, and such an account, in the form presented in the Acts, cannot have been intended for any other address than the Gentiles outside the Church.[27]

If such early texts are suspect, their canonization is even more so. Although the explicit subject of the longer of the two essays constituting *On the History of the Canon* is the question of establishing what can and cannot be known about the date and authorship of the Letter to the Hebrews attributed to Paul, it begins with a rather far-reaching declaration that might equally well have been written by Nietzsche: "It is part of the essence of all canonization to render its objects unknowable, and so it can be said of all of the writings in our New Testament, that in the moment of their canonization they have ceased to be understood."   Nietzsche was given to stronger formulations: "Paul understood the need for the lie, for 'faith'; the Church subsequently understood Paul" (AC §47).

Overbeck's book on the canon continues in the spirit of his analysis of Acts, demonstrating the philological acuity that Nietzsche so respected and admired. The motto of philology in Nietzsche and Overbeck's tradition might be "always more than one language" (paraphrasing one of Jacques Derrida's remarks on deconstruction). Philology is critical and diacritical, always marking differences in and within authors, texts, traditions, and interpretations. Overbeck's critical hermeneutical sensibility was aroused by discrepancies between Hebrews and Paul's other letters.[28]   Especially obvious (Overbeck is not the first to note this) is that the letter is composed in much more fluent Greek than the other letters, whose Greek is rather awkward (as Nietzsche wrote "It was subtle of God to learn Greek when he wished to become an author—and not to learn it better" [BGE §121]).[29] To be canonical it was required that a text's author be one of Jesus' apostles. Overbeck concludes that the text was attributed to Paul so that it could be pronounced canonical. The desire to canonize came, he argues, because the church found its content important and useful in securing its doctrines in opposition to Gnostic tendencies like Marcion's. It could also appeal to Jews who might "come to Jesus" if they felt that, far from surrendering their tradition, they could see this as its fulfillment. Nietzsche had read Overbeck's critical analyses. He recapitulates such inquiries from his own "physiological" perspective when he writes that

> One is not philologist and physician without also being at the same time anti-Christ(ian) [*Antichrist*]. For as philologist one sees behind the "sacred books", as physician behind the physiological depravity of the typical Christian. The physician says "incurable," the philologist "fraud"…(AC §47).[30]

Times and Temporalities of Christ and Antichrist

Overbeck's research and Nietzsche's judgments of Christianity coincide in emphasizing a radical break between the temporal experience and expectations of the early community and the church that slowly took form in the next few centuries. Katechontic time, the time of waiting and deferral has obvious political implications. With church and state established and coordinated, Christianity finds the basic lines of temporal life defined: the state, with the church's endorsement, resists the coming of Antichrist. History can now be plotted in terms of a story of deferred redemption with regular payments on the debt in the form of confession and penance. Yet the time of the *katechon* is only one mode of medieval Christian thought about time and history. At least since Bergson and Heidegger, philosophy has been aware of distinctions like those between chronological time and the lived experience of dureé, or between an authentic grasping of future possibilities and self-deceiving acceptance of the "objective" time of *das Man*. Nietzsche's writings abound in accounts of various phenomenological modes of temporal experience. He frequently reminds us that his many styles of writing are intended to convey varying tempos of experience. What needs emphasis is that this sense of temporal plurality is not restricted to purely individual experience. There are social, collective ways of marking and structuring time, not only by measurement and punctuations (for example, by holidays and intercalary days) but in terms of speeding up or delaying, contracting or dilating.

Historians of philosophical and religious thought, like Löwith and Taubes, see the tendency toward condensing the many varieties of temporality as stemming from the apocalyptic and eschatological commentaries and speculations of Joachim of Fiore, who elaborated a three stage conception of human history consisting of the epochs of God the Father, the Son, and the Holy Spirit. For Joachim the age of the Holy Spirit was to begin in 1200. Such critical studies lead Agamben to sharply distinguish messianic time (the time of the end) from eschatological time (the end of time).[31] Messianic time is experience free of obsessive hope, regret, and nostalgia; it lives in an expanded present, not in waiting or expectation of a future state. Eschatological thought expects, awaits, and frequently attempts to predict the ultimate end. Messianic time is apolitical. Eschatological time requires an interim politics adapted to the specific character of the destined end. For Nietzsche, it was Paul, the evangelist and community organizer, who laid the foundations for eschatological time and its politics.

Nietzsche hyperbolically restates Overbeck's thesis about the later oblivion of messianic time in Christianity when he writes "The word 'Christianity' is already a misunderstanding—in reality there was only one Christian and he died on the cross." In explicating this famous *bon mot* Nietzsche distinguishes between living "practice" and mere "belief," just as Overbeck distinguishes the first community around Jesus from the church and its doctrines:

> The "Evangel" died on the cross. What was called "Evangel" from this moment onwards was already the opposite of what he had lived: "bad tidings," a dysangel. It is false to the point of absurdity to see in a "belief," perchance the belief in redemption through Christ, the distinguishing characteristic of the Christian: only Christian practice, a life such as he who died on the cross lived, is Christian…(AC §39).

The "belief" in question here is a belief about what is to come, at the end of one's life or the end of time. The Stoics criticized time experienced as mere waiting and deferral, a critique that can be applied to the church's conception of katechontic time as that during which governments ward off the coming of the Antichrist. Stoics aimed at eradicating hope and fear, both of which blind us to the lived experience of the moment and the readiness for real opportunity or *kairos* when it arises.[32] As Seneca writes

> Two things must be cut short: the fear of the future and the memory of past discomfort; the one does not concern me any more, and the other does not concern me yet.[33]

Jesus, as Nietzsche understands him, was free from time-as-deferral but lacking a sense of *kairos*; this reading supposes that the idea of the imminent arrival of the kingdom, understood as total transformation or end of the world, is already an invention of Paul and the early church. Nietzsche engages in an abductive inference, leading him to his idea of Jesus as a Dostoyevskyan "idiot," living blissfully in the moment, announcing the kingdom of God and time's accomplished fulfillment, totally indifferent to institutional structures as he declares that we should "take no thought for the morrow." This blank canvas allows the inscription of history's palimpsest and is very close to Overbeck's picture of early Christian community psychology.[34] In Nietzsche's counter-narrative, Christianity was Paul's invention, positing Jesus' resurrection as history's turning point and the basis for a new, potentially universal faith community of both Jew and gentile. Nietzsche's parody of Paul (*The Antichrist*) offers another way of splitting history in two.

Nietzsche's deliberate caricature of church and theology coincides with the critique that Overbeck pronounces in more restrained but no less cutting fashion. The typical Christian theologian (in the spirit of Hippolytus) constructs a story about Jesus and the church which accommodates the persistence of mundane time when the *eschaton* fails to arrive. The theologian makes his peace with the "world" which the earliest Christian community prided itself on dismissing. The theologian *must* be concerned to *sublimate* the various forms of what Walter Benjamin called *Jetztzeit* that characterized primitive

Christianity, that amalgam of Gnostic salvation, Stoic *kairos*, and Jewish Messianic time. Eventually theology leads to the invention of world-history. Some of Nietzsche's most vicious remarks about the theologian as a type emphasize the theological core of German idealism. Kant was so well received by the Germans, Nietzsche says, because with his thought "a secret path to the old ideal stood revealed" (AC §10; cf. 8-11). That idealism culminates in Hegelian world-history which Nietzsche had been in the business of bracketing, exposing, and undermining since at least the *Birth of Tragedy*.

At the heart of Nietzsche's *Antichrist*, then, is the rejection of the theological time of waiting, deferral, and gradual culmination. Christian time eventually became world-history whose core is the state, "God's march through the world" as Hegel said. From this perspective, the final page, the "Decree Against Christianity"—signed "the Antichrist"—symbolically announces a new calendar and new experience of time. If time was measured previously from Jesus' birth, a new beginning is possible after the demolition of Christian world-history.

The last paragraph of the main text of *The Antichrist* promises a writing on the walls and a revision of the calendar based on Nietzsche's declaration of war on Christianity.

> Wherever there are walls I shall inscribe this eternal accusation against Christianity upon them—I can write in letters which make even the blind see... And one calculates *time* from the *dies nefastus* on which this fatality arose—from the *first* day of Christianity! *Why not rather from its last?—From today?—* Revaluation of all values! (AC §62)

In *Difference and Repetition* Deleuze writes of the profound structure that underlies this phantasm of the splitting of time. He contrasts the Cartesian *cogito* and the Kantian "I think." The *cogito* determines the I as a thinking being whose identity is dependent upon God. Kant saw that only the bare form of temporality was implied by the "I think," and so consequently "time signifies a fault or a fracture in the *I* and a passivity in the self."[35] Rational psychology must go the way of rational theology. Hölderlin and Nietzsche are the true heirs of Kant, rather than Fichte and Hegel. The time is out of joint and necessarily marked by a caesura. This "caesura, of whatever kind, must be determined in the image of a unique and tremendous event, an act which is adequate to time as a whole."[36] So Nietzsche's interruption of time, whether in the thought of eternal recurrence or in the introduction of a new calendar, is to be understood as a "symbolic image" of time out of joint.

The Antichrist's time is war-time, the war against Christianity and its "false reckoning of time." It is the war that follows in the wake of God's death. War-time cannot be planned, plotted, or predicted—or rather, these actions can all be attempted in full knowledge of their impossibility. In the parable of the madman, time is out of joint because the true news of God's death, like the light from distant stars, is still on its way to the traders in the marketplace. What they do not see, in their all too easy, all too human atheism, is that their Wall Street Journal is always already out of date, and that the market is deeply complicit with the more radical risks of war. In war we become other, reduced to our position in the ranks or reidentified with a *nom de guerre*. Nietzsche's war-time is the time in which "I is another," in which the *Antichrist* repeats the tragic age of the Greeks in its post-Christian and post-Cartesian difference.

The declaration of war, the "Decree Against Christianity," removed by Nietzsche's sister and early editors, was finally restored by Colli and Montinari.[37] Its title and form no doubt owe much to his studies in comparative political theology, from the interests he shared with Overbeck to his fascination with Jacolliot's book *The Religious Lawgivers*, and its eccentric translation of the *Law of Manu* along with quasi-Darwinian commentary. The "Decree," meant to form the last page of *The Antichrist*, could be the text of a public poster, defining the law of an occupying power—or as the parody of such an act, emphasizing the political thrust of the text. It declares that priests should be imprisoned, that "every participation in a religious service is an attack on public morality," that Protestantism is worse than Catholicism and liberal Protestantism its worst variety, that all preaching of chastity or denigration of sexuality are to be condemned, that eating with a priest is forbidden, and that ostensibly laudatory Biblical words like "God" and "redeemer" should be understood as insults. It is impossible to determine what in this decree is parodic and what is meant in total seriousness. Nietzsche, who constantly tells his readers that he expects the most subtle, philologically attuned ear for his writings, offers something in comic book or graffito style, a set of directives as shockingly simplified, if not more so, than the instructions and videotapes of many recent terrorists.

The dateline immediately following the title of the "Decree" reads "Proclaimed on the first day of the year one (—on September 30, 1888 of the false time scheme"). Nietzsche's career could be said to culminate in his failed project to recalibrate earthly time. He cannot avoid citing what he calls the old, false system of reckoning time. It should be day one, year one, of a time that has been newly divided in two — a new common era. Nietzsche's day one is put forward as an affirmative date, yet to the extent that it recognizes a prior time with which it marks a contrast, the question arises whether it can indeed be completely affirmative. In declaring war against Christianity he must mark time with a new calendar that is not indebted to the very system of values he is combating. But like Christianity and Islam, Nietzsche's calendar splits the history of humanity into two, unlike the Jewish calendar which begins with the creation of the world and so has nothing anterior to its basic date. Nietzsche's new way of reckoning time is tied up with wars and battles.[38] But then Christianity, as Nietzsche describes it very explicitly in the concluding pages of *The Antichrist* has always been at war. It has always been political, at least since the Church transformed Jesus into Christ. Whether surreptitiously conducting its vampiric raids on Rome, its Crusades against Islam, or its cultural wars—from Luther's attack on the Renaissance to Bismarck's *Kulturkampf* on behalf of the *Reich*—it is indeed a war-machine masked by its professions of peace.

The Antichrist began by taking its (or his) distance from *Zeitgeschwätz*, or the chatter of the media. It ends with a rapid fire, scathing review of Christianity as an embodied historical and political force, announcing a new way of reckoning time. Media chatter takes place unreflectively within the world; at its most ambitious it aims at positioning itself within its ultimate context of world-history. The final condemnation of Christianity and the curse upon portray it as an infamy on the earth. The "Decree" goes so far as to declare that churches must be regarded as pollutions or miasmas of the earth. To shift the focus from church and state to the earth they pretend to subsume and rule involves at least a sketch of what a "great politics of the earth" might be, and what kinds of things might be termed "great events." Ever since Nietzsche introduced that term in his last *Unmodern Observation*, describing what he then took to be the tasks of Alexander and Wagner, it had a scope that surpassed the "world-history" on whose discovery the nineteenth century so prided itself. So far as *The Antichrist* constitutes all or part of the project of transvaluing values, it raises the question of the earth's future in a way that neither the op-eds of the journalists nor the world-historical speculations of the Hegelians could. At the very edge and distant horizon of the Christian and world-historical traditions, forgotten, ridiculed, or marginalized by their modern heirs, the paleonym (or older name) of Antichrist was a way of thinking, about earth's future on a larger scale, however confusedly. Perhaps it is not surprising then that apocalyptic thought tends to resurge in times that fearfully anticipate climate change, trans-national religious war, shortages of basic resources, new waves of migration and nomadism, as well as rapid and unpredictable technological transformations that penetrate deeply into all social relations. Unlike those who scour the Biblical texts for literal, all too literal, news of the last days, Nietzsche's donning of the Antichrist mask can be read most fruitfully as a way of asking now, at this date—is it early or late?— how we might begin to think earth's times in ways that do not foreclose being open to great events and great politics.

Acknowledgments

This is the latter part of a preprint version of Chapter Six found in totality in Gary Shapiro, *Nietzsche's Earth: Great Events, Great Politics* (Chicago: University of Chicago Press, 2016).

Endnotes

1. According to Gilles Quispel "the Church Fathers, in their polemics against heresy, expressed for the first time the idea that there exists a development in history, the idea that in the education of the human race certain forms were justified in their time only to be rejected by a later epoch"; "Time and History in Patristic Christianity" in Joseph Campbell ed., *Man and Time: Papers from the Eranos Yearbook* (Princeton: Princeton University Press, 1973), 88.

2. The *Refutation* is a crucial source of what we think of as the fragments of presocratic philosophy and contains considerable testimony about them. It seems worth asking whether and to what extent some typical post-1850's pictures of the entire

"development" from Thales to Socrates are structured in some ways by Hippolytus' program, but that is a question for another occasion.

3.   Agamben, *The Time That Remains*, trans. Patricia Dailey (Stanford: Stanford University Press, 2005), 15.

4.   Carl Schmitt, *The Nomos of the Earth*, 59-60; Ernst Kantorowicz, *The King's Two Bodies*, 292; Giorgio Agamben, *The Kingdom and the Glory* 7, 15-16.

5.   The early Cold War doctrine of "containment" of the Soviet Union was formulated by George F. Kennan, who wrote in an influential (but at first anonymous) 1947 article in Foreign Affairs that "the main element of any United States policy toward the Soviet Union must be a long-term, patient but firm and vigilant containment of Russian expansive tendencies…. Soviet pressure against the free institutions of the Western world is something that can be contained by the adroit and vigilant application of counterforce at a series of constantly shifting geographical and political points, corresponding to the shifts and manoeuvers of Soviet policy, but which cannot be charmed or talked out of existence." But what happens when "liberation," the policy of Eisenhower's Secretary of State John Foster Dulles and of Ronald Reagan replaces "containment," finally resulting in the symbolic fall of the Berlin Wall and the collapse of the Soviet Union? As Leonard Cohen expresses it in his song "The Future" it may mean the end of all divisions and principles of measure, something that leads him to beg "Give me back the Berlin Wall, give me Stalin and St. Paul. I've seen the future, brother, and it's murder." Cf. KSA 13, 368 where Nietzsche speaks of the mediocre as "the *Verzögerer* [delayers] *par excellence.*

6.   Tertullian, *The Apology of Tertullian*, section XXXII. Similar observations are made by Jerome in his commentary on Daniel 7:8 and more of the same are attributed to Tyconius (d. ca. 390) in his *Commentary on Apocalypse*, a lost text, but one much cited, e.g. by Augustine.

7.   Schmitt, *Nomos*, 59-60. Schmitt's post-World War II *The Nomos of the Earth in the International Law of the Jus Publicum Europaeum*, trans. G.L. Ulmen (New York: Telos Press, 2003), with its articulation of the possibility of a global world order in the age of air power and its making explicit the katechontic dimension of political theology can be understood as sharing a problematic with what Nietzsche calls "a philosophy of the Antichrist."

8.   English translation based on Giorgio Agamben's Italian translation. Agamben, *The Time That Remains*, 23.

9.   Agamben, *The Time That Remains*, 1.

10.   Agamben, *The Time That Remains*, 2.

11.   Löwith, *From Hegel to Nietzsche: The Revolution in Nineteenth Century Thought*, trans. David E. Green (New York: Anchor, 1967), 385.

12.   It is tempting to think of Nietzsche and Overbeck as a kind of complementary yin and yang pair. Nietzsche was a flamboyant thinker who courted public discussion and opposition. He was proud of "having entered society through a duel? with his polemic against D.F. Strauss. Overbeck was modest and reserved; while he undermined the canon of Christian scripture by revealing falsifications and distortions, revealing the political motivations of canon formation, he did so quietly and without fanfare. While he published relatively little in his lifetime as explicit as his 1873 polemic, he left an enormous *Nachlass* of notes, memoirs, and essays very little of which as available until recently. In the 1990's some of this work was published, including a fair sample of his *Kirchenlexicon*, a massive cross-referenced personal encyclopedia consisting of 20,00 octavo pages. Previously an edition of some of these writings appeared as *Christentum und Kultur. Gedanken und Aufzeichnungen zur modernen Theologie*, edited by Overbeck's student. Carl Bernoulli. Bernoulli also produced the two volume heavily documented *Franz Overbeck und Friedrich Nietzsche, eine Freundschaft* (1908). Since the 1990s some German scholars, especially Andreas Sommer, have begun to consider the Nietzsche-Overbeck relation in a philosophical rather than biographical way. In the conflict between Nietzsche's "Basel" and "Weimar" friends, relatives, and associates,

Overbeck was overshadowed and considerably outlived by Nietzsche's sister Elisabeth, another factor that contributed to downplaying the relationship and producing the conventional picture of Overbeck as simply a "friend" who helped Nietzsche with financial and other practical matters, finally fetching him from Turin after his collapse. See Andreas Urs Sommer, *Der Geist der Historie und der Ende des Christentums. Zur "Waffengenossenheit" Friedrich Nietzsche und Franz Overbeck. Mit einen Anhang unpublitzierter Texte aus Overbecks "Kirchenlexicon" and Friedrich Nietzsche's "Der Antichrist": Ein philosophisch-historischer Kommentar* (Berlin: Akademie Verlag, 1997). For important evaluations see Karl Löwith's conclusion to *From Hegel to Nietzsche*, 374-385 and Jacob Taubes, "The Demystification of Theology: Toward a Portrait of Overbeck," in *From Cult to Culture: Fragments Toward a Critique of Historical Reason* (Stanford: Stanford University Press, 2010), 147-161. For a good introduction to Overbeck in his relation to Nietzsche see Lionel Gossman, *Basel in the Age of Burckhardt: A Study in Unseasonable Ideas* (Chicago: University of Chicago Press, 2000), 413-438.

13. As Taubes explains Overbeck's position: "History is not to be restrained by means of Christianity. 'Every attempt must be made to take the Christian periodization of history seriously' must shatter on this fact. The Christian reckoning of time would only be substantiated if Christianity had brought about 'a new era.' But Overbeck denies precisely this, for 'Christianity itself originally spoke of a new time under the prerequisite—one that was not met—that the existing world should perish and make room for a new one. This was, for a brief moment a serious expectation and, as such an expectation, surfaced continually but fleetingly, never becoming a fact of historical permanence—which alone could have provided the real basis for an incontrovertible account of time, one corresponding to the facts of reality. The world, and not the Christian expectation of it, is what held its own.'" Taubes, *From Cult to Culture*, 157.

14. Overbeck wrote Nietzsche, reporting that Eberhard Vischer "has made and published a very beautiful scientific discovery: the Johannine Apocalypse is a Jewish text that has been given a Christian rewriting" (Dec 12, 86) *Nietzsches Briefwechsel mit Overbeck*, 352.

15. Overbeck, *Werke und Nachlass*, ed. Ekkehard Stegemann et. al. (Stuttgart: J.B. Metzler, 2006), 9.319-349. Hereafter OWN.

16. On the Gnostic understanding of time, see Henri-Charles Puech, "Gnosis and Time" in Campbell, ed., *Man and Time*, 38-84, especially 80-83.

17. Taubes, "The Demystification of Theology," 147.

18. Overbeck, *How Christian is our Contemporary Theology?* trans. Martin Henry (London: Continuum, 2005).

19. Quoted by Taubes, "The Demystification of Theology: Toward a Portrait of Overbeck," 154.

20. Overbeck, *Christentum und Kultur*, OWN 6/1, 246. For Overbeck's 1873 critique of German theologians supporting Bismarck by arguments drawn from political theology, see *How Christian is our Contemporary Theology?*, 63-67.

21. Overbeck, OWN 4, 157.

22. Overbeck, *Quaestionum Hippolytearum specimen. [De Hippolyti libello de Antichristo. Dissertation.]*.

23. A very strong version of the "Platonism for the people"—or more precisely Stoic universalism — thesis is found in Bruno Bauer's eccentric 1877 book *Christ and the Caesars*, reviewed by Overbeck in 1878. Nietzsche and Overbeck were corresponding frequently about theological matters around this time, and Nietzsche mentions Bauer in several contexts KSA 6, 317, KSB 6, 242; 7, 270, 275; 8, 106, 205, 247, 370.

24. The multiplicity of regimes yet to come is compatible with Hippolytus' relatively anti-Roman stance, which can be contrasted with Tertullian's contemporary idea of Rome as *katechon*.

25. As Graham Parkes points out in his note on this passage, *duldet* is Luther's translation of the passage in I Cor. 13:7, where Paul writes of love or charity that it "endureth all things"; *Thus Spoke Zarathustra*, trans. Graham Parkes, 315.

26. Nietzsche to Overbeck, June 22, 1880; Overbeck to Nietzsche, July 10, 1880 in *Friedrich Nietzsches Briefwechsel mit Franz Overbeck*, 133-36.

27. Overbeck, "Introduction to The Acts of the Apostles," 23-24.

28. *Hebrews* is framed differently than those letters; it is not addressed to a specific group in a geographical location, and there is something odd about the supposed author, Paul, as apostle to the gentiles, writing to the Jews. As its title suggests, the text firmly links messianic faith to the Jewish tradition, citing sacred history and prophecy. The letter was accepted quickly in the Eastern church, but was suspect for some time in the West; under dispute were such theological issues as the rejection of rebaptism in *Hebrews* 6:4-6 as well as philological questions.

29. See Jacob Taubes's anecdote concerning his conversation with the literary scholar Emil Staiger in Zürich during World War II. Staiger had been reading Paul's epistles, but exclaimed bitterly: "But that isn't Greek, it's Yiddish! Upon which [Taubes] said: Yes, Professor, and that's why I understand it!" Taubes, *The Political Theology of Paul*, 4.

30. Here Nietzsche's usage does seem to permit reading *Antichrist* as simply anti-Christian.

31. Karl Löwith, *Meaning in History*; Jacob Taubes, *Occidental Eschatology*; Agamben, *The Time that Remains*, 62-3.

32. Agamben, "Time and History: Critique of the Instant and the Continuum" in *Infancy and History: On the Destruction of Experience*, 97-116.

33. Seneca, *Letters to Lucilius*, 78, 14. Quoted by Pierre Hadot in *Philosophy as a Way of Life*, ed. Arnold Davidson, 228.

34. Shapiro, "The Text as Graffito: Historical Semiotics," *Nietzschean Narratives*, 124-141.

35. Deleuze, *Difference and Repetition*, trans. Paul Patton (New York: Columbia University Press, 1994), 86.

36. Deleuze, *Difference and Repetition*, 89.

37. It was found in Nietzsche's papers glued to the last pages of *The Antichrist*; Colli and Montinari argue convincingly that it was intended to be the last page of that work (KSA 14, 448-54).

38. In the Jewish and Christian imaginary, which Nietzsche probably shared on this point, there is a tendency to think of early Islam as defined by its wars. But the Islamic calendar begins with the Hijra, understood as an act of complete submission: Muhammad saves the faith and its revelation by leaving Mecca for Medina. Since Nietzsche praises the Islamic war on Christianity he may have felt some kinship with what he took to be its associated way of dividing time into two parts. And like Jewish and Islamic dates, when presented in Christian or secular contexts, Nietzsche gives the other time scheme as a point of reference.

NIETZSCHE AS PROPHET: THE TIME OF ETERNAL RETURN

Marc de Launay

In the light of a fairly extended reception, it can seem that Nietzsche might be taken as having been a certain prophet; he would thus belong to a tradition instituted by the last of the three questions Kant asks to conclude *The Critique of Pure Reason*: "For what may I hope?" Was Nietzsche a prophet? In the vaguest sense of the term, we might consider that Nietzsche is at the very least engaged in prognoses concerning the proximate future: for example, predicting the coming of a "future age which will be that of great wars" (KSA 11, 413), claiming "to see coming a united Europe [*das Eine Europa*]" (KSA 11, 584), for the secret government of which he calls for the formation of a "new caste," whose will would be "capable of setting goals for millennia" (BGE §208) and the future of this Europe, to him, seems to depend on "both Jews and Russians who now are probably the two factors which will most certainly come into play in the great conflict of powers." (BGE §251) This "prophecy" stems at minimum from a representation of historical time which makes it possible to situate, in its unfolding, the moment when Nietzsche says he prognosticates: "We live *in the midst* of the time allotted to the human" (KSA 9, 541) and "the time is coming when the battle for the domination of the earth [*Erdherrschaft*] will be waged." (KSA 9, 546) What is more, Nietzsche himself is responsible for this self-image as he forged it directly in *Ecce homo,* presenting himself as "a bringer [*annonciateur*][1] of glad tidings like no one before me" (EH, *Why I am a destiny*, §1) to the point that "only beginning with me are there hopes again" (*ibid.*) which implies being just as much and "necessarily a man of calamity" who predicts once again that there will be "wars the like of which have never yet been seen on on earth." (*ibid.*) Moreover, in a letter written to Peter Gast, Nietzsche describes himself, in French, as « *poète-prophète* ».[2] However, and always in *Ecce homo*, when Nietzsche speaks of his Zarathustra, saying it is "the greatest gift ever given to humanity" (EH *Preface*, §4), it is immediately to emphasize that whoever speaks there "is no 'prophet,' one of those gruesome hybrids of sickness and will to power whom people call founders of religion." (Ibid.)   There is therefore at minimum ambiguity with regard to the meaning given to the term *prophet*. The word also appears in its rather banal usage, as in the Foreword to his lectures *On the Future of Our Educational Institutions*, or from the winter of 1872-1873, where Nietzsche takes up the old adage "no one is a prophet in his own land [*Kein Prophet gilt im Vaterland*]" (KSA 7, 548) or again in the spring of 1880, where the term designates one of the "inventions [*Erfindungen*] of the Jews." (KSA 9, 75)   These three examples dialogue with *Human, All-too Human* where Nietzsche mocks the gifts of prophecy recognized only when they work to comfort other interests (HH §574), and in November 1887-March 1888, where the old saying is considered an absurdity [*Unsinn*] inasmuch as the opposite is true "*das Gegentheil ist die Wahrheit*" (KSA 13, 11 [360], 159), and in the *Antichrist* where the prophet is an equivalent to the sectarian and man of the Church (AC §53). In the same work, however, Nietzsche recognized the merit in Isaiah of having been a "critic and a satirist of the hour [*Kritiker und Satyriker des Augenblicks, Jesaia*]." (AC §25)[3]

This equivocation does not dissipate but becomes intelligible on the condition of relating these different occurrences to the internal evolution of Nietzschean thought. During the summer of 1880, we see the theme of the "feeling of power" making an appearance for the first time and Nietzsche will not fail to put his analysis of this particular "feeling" with the forecast:

> [...] to be able to calculate, to know in advance! this means we deduce from the omniscience of God, his omnipotence—a common error of reasoning. The feeling of power in intellectual matters, which provides predictive knowledge, is illogically combined with that which is known in advance: as prophets, we imagine ourselves [*bilden wir uns ein*] to be magicians [*Wunderthäter*] (KSA 9, 193)

Yet not only is "willing a prejudice" but "all consciousness simply brushes the surface of things" so that the event "occurs despite everything outside of our freedom and often contradicts our superficial knowledge." Two years later, in a *Gay Science* aphorism (316) entitled

"*Prophetic Human Beings,*" Nietzsche elaborates a parable castigating the gifts of prophecy in order to substitute the real motives of anticipations, sufferings, and pain because "there is as much wisdom in pain as there is in pleasure" (GS §318), and knowing how to "scrutinize our lived experiences," he says in the following aphorism, is to demonstrate proof of an "honesty which has been alien to all founders of religion and their kind." (GS §319)

It is certain that prior to 1880, we find no text or fragment of the sort we encounter after this date, the kind that are both entitled "What will happen [*Das, was kommt*]" (the second of which bears the subtitle "a prophecy"), where Nietzsche evokes both the eternal return ("humanity must live in *cycles*; the only lasting form"[4]) and which indicate the "time" localized: "We are at noon." Henceforth, when it concerns what Nietzsche himself announces, the prophecy is of a different order: "This book [*Ecce homo*—dL] gives, I hope, a completely different image than that [(1861)] of a prophet [...] for hitherto all prophets have been liars [*denn alle Propheten waren bisher Lügner*]. ..." (KSA 13, 640) On the other hand, it is symptomatic that the term *Prophet* never appears in "Zarathustra," even if translations have difficulty in accounting for this, as Nietzsche uses the term *Wahrsager* which is very difficult to render otherwise. The *Wahrsager* is literally supposed to "say what is true [*Wahr*]," in the sense that the fragment quoted above affirms that what one "took until then to be the truth was a lie [*denn man hieß bisher die Lüge Wahrheit*]...," so that Nietzsche, prophet in an utterly new sense, can affirm neither more nor less than "the truth speaks through his mouth." It will be noted that, in *Zarathustra* there is also no occurrence of the terms "philosopher" and "philosophy" as systematically rendered by "*Weise*" and "*Weisheit*."

The place granted "Zarathustra" in *Ecce homo* is so obviously privileged that one will scarcely surprised to see Nietzsche doubt that there were even readers "worthy of hearing it" inasmuch as he affirms himself to have been the first to discover "the art of great rhythm" in the form of the dithyramb (i.e. a poem in honor of Dionysus) such as that which concludes the third part of *Zarathustra*, entitled "The Seven Seals," and of which Nietzsche says that it "flies [thus] a thousand leagues above what until then was called poetry." (EH, *Why I write such good books*, §4) The title of this concluding chapter of *Zarathustra* as it had been intended for the public is borrowed from the Apocalypse of John. To the breaking of the seven seals is supposed to follow a revelation, and this is indeed what Nietzsche says of his *Zarathustra*:

> Till then one does not know what is height, what depth; one knows even less what truth is. There is no moment in this revelation of truth that has been anticipated or guessed by even *one* of the greatest. (EH, Z §6)

The religious connotation is reinforced by the subtitle of the chapter: "The Song of Yes and Amen." (Z III, *The Seven Seals*) It is indeed indeed a kind of counter-revelation, counter-apocalypse, which comes at the end of a "counter-gospel," a counter-promise made to put an end to the "old tables" of Christianity.

The Seven Seals are each punctuated by a refrain:

> Oh how should I not lust for eternity and for the wedding ring of rings
> —the Ring of Recurrence! Never yet did I find the woman by whom I wanted children, unless it be this woman, whom I love: for I love you, O Eternity! For I love you, O Eternity!

The refrain is consequently the culmination of this revelation, for which each of the seals is a precondition. This revelation affirms the desire for the eternal return without however revealing what this ring of rings is; it is, however, a nuptial ring, which implies, as the chorus sings, not only that one must desire this feminine figure of the eternity of return, but also that the alliance thus concluded had not yet taken place —Nietzsche publishes in a way the banns of this union with her—and that she will have a future: "children." What is more, this nuptial "yes" is an acquiescence to something that already exists: eternity and the ring of rings which are not what is thus revealed, since what the veil is lifted over is only on the conditions that make it possible to say "amen" to what is. In other words, if there is, as Nietzsche writes, with regard to his bringing Christianity to light, in *Ecce homo* a "before and an after" (EH, *Why I am a Destiny*, §8), it is in no way because he would claim to be responsible for having introduced what is an essential or decisive modification; he is simply the one who realizes the apocalypse of what is.[5] This is exactly what a *prophatas* or prophet [*prophatas* ou *prophètès*] was in ancient Greece: as the Pythia installed on her bronze tripod above a volcanic fault inhaled the scents of the earth to give the god's answer to the questions of the faithful who came to question him [Apollo], the *prophet* became his spokesperson (this is the literal translation of the Greek term) by giving relatively intelligible form to what she [the Pythia] mumbled; thus the prophet formulated an answer interpreting, more or less, the barely coherent speech of the god transmitted by the Pythia in a trance. The prophet is neither diviner nor seer: he predicts nothing, saying what has already been announced, what comes out of the bowels of the earth.

"If I be a prophet and full of that prophetic spirit that wanders on high ridges between two seas, / wanders between past and future like a heavy cloud ...", this is how this concluding chapter of the *Seven Seals* begins.[6] The first condition required for this nuptial alliance with "eternity," that of return, is to be oneself endowed with a health which allows laughter acquiescing in what is, while being swollen with lightning and capable of enduring for a long time the mountain barriers which prevent the storm from bursting. The second condition is to have destroyed with mocking but not hateful joy (hence without resentment), the old tables, and to have blessed the world in the face of its detractors; the third is to be animated by the divine creative breath which tames chance and admits its creative effects; the fourth is to be the new "salt of the earth" thanks to which the redemption of good and evil takes place in their admixture finally recognized for the first time; the fifth is to be animated by the audacious spirit that animated Columbus when all known points of reference disappeared from his eyes: one must open up new seas, a future freed from the reassuring traditional tables but which is nonetheless subject to new tables; the sixth is the Alpha and Omega of this new alliance with what is: dance and laughter, that is to say: a state of mind where the healthy body devotes itself to the rhythmic dynamic drive finally admitted as the driving force of life; where laughter, annihilating at the same time as it is sanctifying as it admits what it has ruined in what it has liberated; the seventh is the refusal of the "high and low" of traditional values, of the hinterland; this refusal goes hand in hand with the resolution of an antinomy burdening language: "are not all words made for the heavy? Do not all words lie to the light? Sing! speak no more!" (Z *Seven Seals*, §7) Concepts betray what they designate just as signs are equivocal for weak minds who cannot decipher them, and just as we must now dance, we must sing, change style. Here Nietzsche rediscovers what he has already said in the form of a song, of his own discovery of the will to power, of his wisdom (Z II, *The Dancing Song*), henceforth superior to that of those who are "the wisest," and anticipates the accents of another chapter of the fourth part of the book, "The Drunken Song" (whose title is in fact "*The Sleepwalker Song*"):

> Joy [*Lust*], however, does not want heirs or children—joy wants itself, wants eternity, wants recurrence, [...]
>
> [10] ...Am I a prophet? A dreamer? A drunkard? An interpreter of dreams? A midnight bell?
>
> A drop of dew? An odour and scent of eternity? Do you not hear it? Do you not smell it? My world has just become perfect, midnight is also noonday. (Z IV, *The Drunken Song*, 9-10, 'This is my morning, my day begins: rise up now, rise up, great noontide!')

We will note, before coming back to this, that there is a singular temporality proper to the time of the announcement of the return, a temporality that is not confused nor can logically be confused with that of the eternal return. The eternal return is the reality of temporality; now the time of its announcement which does not predict but reveals it, is "Midday" or "Midnight" or even the "Middle", "because, to tell the truth, for such things there is no longer time on earth," writes Nietzsche at the conclusion of the IVth part of *Zarathustra*: "This is *my* morning, *my* day begins: *now arise, arise, great noontide*!" (Z IV, *The Sign*) And Zarathustra can finally leave his cave. (CW, *Preface*)

Writing several forewords to his published works in 1886, Nietzsche writes in his retrospective presentation of *Human, All Too Human, II*:

> My writings speak *only* of my overcomings: 'I' am in them, together with everything that was inimical to me, *ego ipsissimus* [...] To this extent, all my writings, with a single though admittedly substantial exception, {Zarathustra} are to be dated back—they always speak to something 'behind me'—

In the draft preface to the whole of the materials gathered under the heading entitled *Will to Power*, which Nietzsche wrote in the spring of 1888, one can read the same idea:

> What I tell is the history of the next two centuries. I describe what comes, what cannot come any other way [...] This history can be already be told: for it is necessity [*Nothwendigkeit*] itself that is here at work. [...]
>
> —The one who speaks here, on the other hand, has done nothing else but to *think himself as such* [*als sich zu besinninen*] [...] as a soothsayer-spirit-bird [*Wahrsagervogel-geist*] who *looks back* when he tells who will come. [...] (KSA 13, 189)

The method presupposed by this type of claim is, as we know, genealogy. It is a reflection on the opposition between the meaning of the university discipline of history and historical meaning:

> What I had to say against the "historical sickness," I said as one who had slowly and toilsomely learned to recover from it and was in no way prepared to give up "history" thereafter becausde he had once suffered from it. (HH II, *Preface*)

Foucault, in his beautiful study, "Nietzsche, Genealogy, History,"[7] clearly showed that genealogy is not opposed to history in Nietzsche but to the idea that the latter would be oriented according to a goal, as in the temptation to make it depend on ideal significations which would, as such, escape it. The genealogical method is directed against the idea of origin, for at least three reasons: firstly, because we imagine we are touching upon the essence of things when we manage grasping their origin; now, behind things, there is no essential secret except that they are without essence or that what one believes to be their essence also has a provenance; what we encounter, at the origin of things, is not their intact identity [*essence*], but their discord; nextly, because we imagine that originally, things would be in a perfect state, whereas Nietzsche insists on the fact that all beginnings are inglorious, sometimes derisory; finally, inasmuch as we associate origin and truth, and the latter, of course, also has a history in which myriad errors commingle to play an active role. Thus Nietzsche opposes origin to provenance and the emergent.

The notion of origination or provenance [*Herkunft*] makes it possible to undermine any reconstruction of identity and supposed coherences (that of the self, for example), and under the asserted synthesis, to demonstrate the accidents, deviations, dispersions, errors transformed into successes, etc. The search for provenance is not foundational; it fragments, on the contrary, what was held to be united, it destabilizes supposedly perennial legacies. Above all, however, provenance is associated with the body, which is the "guiding thread" adopted by Nietzsche for interpreting history:

> The human being of an era of dissolution which mixes the races together and who therefore contains within him the inheritance of a diversified descent in his body [*vielfältigen Herkunft im Leibe*], that is to say contrary and often not merely contrary drives and values [...], such a human being [...] will on average, be a rather weak human being [...]. If, however, the contrariety and war in such a nature should act as one *more* stimulus [...] if, on the other hand, in addition to powerful and irreconcilable drives, there has also been inherited and cultivated a proper mastery and subtlety in conducting a war against oneself, that is to say, self-control, self-outwitting: then there arise those marvelously incomprehensible and unfathomable human beings [...] They appear in precisely the same ages as those in which that rather weak type with his desire for rest comes to the fore: the two types belong together and originate in the same causes. (BGE §200)

The body—which also includes what it integrates in terms of climate, food, terrain—is the place of origin: it is in it that are born the different impulses and it supports their multiple conflicts of which it is itself the resultant. Genealogy, as an analysis of provenance, is situated, as Foucault says, "at the articulation of body and history."[8]

Just as origination does not imply uninterrupted continuity, generative emergence [*Entstehung*] cannot be explained by a final term. The metaphysics of history makes us believe in a finality which, at the end of an obscure undertaking, would be the realization and consummation of a process whose outlines would be present from the start. Genealogy, on the contrary, re-establishes the hazardous game of dominion. What is generated, always emerges from a struggle whose outcome was not given in advance, even if the variety of possible solutions to the conflict is limited. The eye was not intended for contemplation when it served mainly for hunting and warfare.

Emergence therefore always designates a field of conflict without one ever being able to imagine a reconciled humanity—it only goes from one transitory state of dominion to another, and there can be progress as well as regression in advancing from one state to another: "'Guilt,' 'conscience,' 'duty', 'sacredness of duty,' had its origin, its beginnings, like the beginnings of everything great on earth, soaked in blood thoroughly and for a long time." (GM II: 6) The different emergences are not the varied manifestations of the same meaning; they are only substitutions, conquests, reversals.

The future of humanity is only the series of interpretations, of evaluations whose engine is the configuration of the drives. To interpret is not to reveal a meaning hidden in an origin, but it is, at a given moment in the general conflict of drives, to take advantage of a favorable situation to impose a particular direction on a system of rules by bending it to a new will. The most striking example is given by Saint Paul installing a new reading of the Old Covenant, interpreting sin differently by making it original sin, and thus giving the body a reactive interpretation compensated by the promise of the glorious, risen body.

The historical meaning denounced in the second *Untimely Meditation* is that which always presupposes a supra-historical point of view, a philosophy of history which would synthesize in a totality (what was called at the time, *Weltgeschichte*) the finally reduced diversity of time; a history which would thus give to all the conflicts of the past the final form of reconciliation. The historical meaning then acquires support outside of time, for example in an absolute origin that goes hand in hand with the presupposition of an end of history; but the historical meaning will become historical meaning as soon as it abandons any absolute point of reference of this type, and history thus understood will reconvert into becoming everything that had seemed guaranteed to last by being. Unlike the Christian world and its Providence, unlike the Greek world divided between the reign of the will and that of the cosmos, real history knows, says Nietzsche, only "the iron hands of necessity which shake the dice-box of chance" (D § 130); chance as Nietzsche understands it is not a hazard of fate, but always a risk revived by the will to power which opposes it to any outcome of chance in order to master the risk of a still greater chance. Effective history is thus, for Nietzsche, as it is reestablished by genealogy, an instrument for the critical reading of values, comparable to physiology as it clings to the common thread of the body, and is unaffected by metaphysical illusions that want to believe in the immutability of being for fear of anything that bears the mark of becoming.[9] The historical sense, writes Foucault, "gives knowledge the possibility of making, in the very movement of its knowledge, its genealogy"[10] and, unlike the historical sense, it does not succumb to the illusion of objectivity, it knows that it is perspective. "There is no 'objective history' [*Historie*]" says Nietzsche in a fragment contemporary with the writing of Zarathustra, from Spring-Summer 1883, because "*history*" [*Geschichte*] has been the subject of "appropriation under the guidance of stimuli and drives." (KSA 10, 323) Now, if we apply his own method to what Nietzsche has just said, it is quite legitimate to wonder about the condition of the possibility of what he has just said: to speak of historical meaning from the point of view of historical sense and to affirm that there is no objective historical science while the reality of effective history would be that of appropriation by the body signifies that there exists at least a perspective from which such a statement is possible and simultaneously true; this perspective itself must have a provenance and must recognize its debt with regard to its emergence, this perspective is itself an event in history but also of history: "The doctrine of return marks the *turning point* of history" (KSA 10, 515) as Nietzsche writes in the fall of 1883.

The eternal return is not a common expression in Nietzsche and the least that can be said is that—in his published work—occurrences are very few apart from aphorism 341 of *The Gay Science* which evokes the notion without naming it at all explicitly, as well as aphorisms 43 and 56 of *Beyond Good and Evil*, which transpire in the same way, the expression is essentially to be found in two chapters of the IIIrd part of *Zarathustra* ("The convalescent," "The Seven Seals"), in a chapter of the IVth part ("The Song of Sleepwalker"); mention of the expression is subsequently found in *Twilight of the Idols* ("What I Owe the Ancients," §5) and, of course, in *Ecce homo* ("Why I am so Wise," §3; "Why I Write Such Good Books": "*The Birth of Tragedy*", §3, "*Thus Spoke Zarathustra*", §§1 and 6). This is where Nietzsche recounts when and under what external circumstances this idea came to him, and he copies fragment 11 {141} from the notebook dated "Spring-Autumn 1881" which is the first occurrence of the expression (KSA 9, 494f). Yet in none of the occurrences in his published work does Nietzsche explain what the eternal return is, any more than one might suspect, from just these occurrences, that the idea of eternal return appears a little less than a year after that of "will to power" as its inevitable consequence.

Only posthumous fragments, and in much smaller numbers than those that deal with the will to power, permit us to reconstruct what Nietzsche thus represented to himself. He represents the world as a quantum of forces which know neither interruption of their course nor diminution nor harmonious balance any more than there is globally a diminution of their intensity (KSA 9, 498); the circular course of these forces is not the result of an exit from a chaos gradually stabilized in orbital movement and Nietzsche denounces the analogy with the circular course of the stars. (KSA 9, 502) Moreover, it must be emphasized, the eternal return of the same is not the return of the identical [*Wiederkehr des Gleichen* isn't a *Wiederkehr des Selben*][11]:

> It is completely senseless to comment on the question of whether there has ever been an identical one [*Ob je...irgend etwas Gleiches dagewesen ist, ist ganz unerweislich*]. It seems that the general course of things creates something new even in the infinitely small parts of their properties (KSA 9, 523)

Otherwise "we should accept that the identical has existed from all eternity [*bis in all Ewigkeit zurück etwas Gleiches bestanden habe*], despite all the metamorphoses of facts and emergence of new properties—an impossible hypothesis!" (Ibid.) Since the quantum of the forces remains equal and the forces are "eternally active," these forces cannot "produce an unlimited number of cases," they must repeat themselves but not identically and without ever coming to a state of completion. There are therefore chances but within the limits of the framework thus fixed. The presuppositions of such a conception are borrowed by Nietzsche from what he understands of the thermodynamics of his time and which admits as a principle that of the conservation of energy. But he had already adopted these presuppositions, during the summer of 1880, by placing them at the foundation of his conception of the will to power: it was then not just a question of the world as a whole, but of the particular case that are individuals. which only represent a difference of degree and not of kind with respect to what Nietzsche designates by "will to power." The forces in question in the conception of the eternal return are already present in us and through us in the form of drive vectors which are never isolated and which all obey a single law, that of maximum effusion—always thwarted and deferred by the conflicts with the other vectors—, to a single dynamic which Nietzsche puts at the foundation of what we call value judgment, which consists in constantly deciding what is useful or harmful to this outpouring, constantly selecting the best way to promote this outpouring. The combination, as complicated as one would wish to imagine, of these drive vectors, bears for him the name of "life." The more the drive configuration increases in intensity, the more we are dealing with an ascending phase, the less intense it is and the more we are confronted by decadence. These two movements are never totally disjoint, one simply temporarily prevails over the other (this is why Nietzsche is not afraid to admit that he himself is a nihilist, even if he managed to overcome this nihilism), and this is how one rises or descends on the spiral that is the eternal return —it is definitely not a circle any more than it allows the evocation of a strictly cyclical history for nothing prevents continued decadence from leading to catastrophes whose magnitude would at the same time entail the disappearance of human life. The preservation of life has never been a goal of "will to power."

The fact remains that will to power and eternal return comprise what Nietzsche thinks of the motor and the dynamics of history:

> To imprint on becoming the character of being — this is the highest will to power [*Dem Werden den Charakter des Seins aufzuprägen — das ist der höchste Wille zur Macht*] [...] That everything recurs is the most extreme *rapprochement* of a world of becoming with that of being: the summit of contemplation. (KSA 12, 312)

In this sense, history is always in some way predictable, since all Nietzsche's effort concerning the past makes it possible to identify its laws without opening onto the promise of a future eschatological order. What Nietzsche limits himself to promising is the inevitable alternation of ascending and decadent phases: the conversion of values which reigned after that of Judaism and after the Greeks, the one which persisted, in spite of various reassignments, up to us in the present day, of what is named Christianity; and because Nietzsche is the 'first' to have the intuition of will to power and eternal return, he claims that with him begins the epoch of another history resulting from a another conversion of values, which he articulates.

This calls for two remarks: first, this new conversion has a goal which goes hand in hand with the end of Christianity; it is for Nietzsche, indeed, to realize the "redemption of all the past". He says so at least twice, in the third part of *Zarathustra*[12] and in *Ecce homo*.[13] Nietzschean prophetism therefore has as its essential *raison d'être* this emancipation from the past converted into *fatum* to which one can only say yes. The other remark touches upon temporality itself: "There is always a time when the most powerful of thoughts, that of the eternal return of all things, arises first in an individual, then in many, finally in all—it is, for humanity, every time, the noon hour [*die Stunde des Mittags*]" (9, 498) Nietzsche's insistence on "noon" may not be patent but a strange fragment from the same period sheds light on his conception: "There is a part of the night of which I say: 'Listen now, time stops !' [...] we experience a strange feeling of astonishment at this moment of the night [...], it was always 'much too short!' or 'much too long!', our sense of time feels an anomaly" (ibid., 539) which the Ancients expressed by *intempestiva nocte*. "Midday"—stopped time and at the same time "full time," conquered time, thus seems to be the untimely temporality that Nietzsche implicitly presupposed in order to be able to objectify the law of temporality itself. Now, this dominated time implies that historical temporality in its totality is also to be mastered.

We must therefore seek to confirm both the evolution followed by Nietzsche from his first critique of historical science to his project of the revaluation of values and the transformation undergone by the content of effective history with respect to the new conception establishing "will to power" and its two consequences, the eternal return and the revaluation of values. Since Nietzsche's main adversary is Christianity and since Nietzsche also owed much of his education to the Protestant presbytery, it is legitimate to choose an eminent figure of the reformation, Luther, and to examine the treatment Nietzsche reserved for Luther.

In the second of his lectures *On the Future of Our Educational Institutions*, Nietzsche says of the Marquis of Posa, the prominent figure in Schiller's *Don Carlos*, that he is "the noblest and most German of his figures." (KSA 1, 678) In Act III, Scene 10, Posa is summoned by Philip II who seeks to circumvent him and here is how Posa responds to him:

> *The Marquis*: The policy of the crown has created a new happiness which it is still rich enough to spread; in the hearts of men it has aroused new desires which this happiness can satisfy. She strikes a truth in her effigy. The truth she can bear. [...] But is what satisfies the crown enough for me? Can my love for my brothers lend itself to the belittlement of my brothers? [...] Do not choose me, sire, to expand this happiness struck in your corner. [...] I cannot be a servant of any prince.
>
> *The King*: You are a Protestant.
>
> *The Marquis*: [...] My hand, before you, has removed the veil that hides the secrets of royalty. Nothing assures you that I will still hold holy what no longer frightens me. I am dangerous because I meditated on myself. [...] The century is not ripe for my ideal. I am a citizen of the centuries to come.

Independently of the immediate echoes Posa's disposition does not fail to evoke[14] in Nietzsche's perception of his own approach, it corresponds to a profound component of German culture where the figure of Luther lends him a status that may not be reduced to a particular confessional choice, transmuting the Teutonic into the recipient of the divine word by way of the new translation of the Bible, thereby establishing the German language as such. We should not be surprised to find that at the time of these lectures, Nietzsche will rank Luther among those he calls the great German minds, i.e., Goethe and Schiller. (KSA 7, 645) When Nietzsche composes the second *Untimely Meditation*, Luther is present in spirit, via a bias revealing, at minimum, connivance: ""Luther himself once thought that the world could only have arisen from an oversight of God," because, and here Nietzsche reprises a quote from Luther recorded several times in his notebooks during this same period, "if God had thought of 'heavy artillery' ['*schwere Geschütz*'], he would not have created the world." (KSA 7, 626, cf. 706) Germanic gifts manifested themselves first in Luther and later in

German music and both phenomena are believed to have prepared the Germans for the Dionysian (275). The Lutheran spirit in which Nietzsche at that time recognized a genuine health, "would rise up against the repugnant state of mind of the propertied classes, against their stupidity and lack of thought [*Dummheit und Gedankenlosigkeit*]." (718) Again, in 1875, Nietzsche noted a quote from Luther he appeared to make his own:

> I have no better instrument than anger and zeal, because when I want to compose, to write, to pray and to preach, I must be angry [*so muss ich zornig sein*], it refreshes all my blood, gives sharpness to my spirit... (KSA 8, 111)

For Nietzsche, in sum, Luther is first and foremost part of the pantheon of Germany as he conceives it as his own, and if one aspect of his attitude towards the great reformer never changes, it is his admiration for Luther as stylist and writer, translator of the Bible. In a letter to Rohde dated 22 February 1884, Nietzsche, putting the finishing touches to Parts II and III of his *Zarathustra*, tells his friend of a "confession which I cannot keep to myself—I imagine myself, with this Zarathustra, having completed the German language. After Luther and Goethe, there remained a third step to be taken." Even more, the justification of the originality of "Zarathustra" is drawn from a personal innovation of Nietzsche: "Luther's language and the poetic form of the Bible as the basis of a new German poetry—that is my invention!" (KSA 11, 60) And until the final year of his intellectual activity, Nietzsche acknowledged, even negatively, his debt to Luther:

> It would not be possible without an antithetical kind of race [*eine Gegensatz-Art von Rasse*], without Germans, without those Germans, without Bismarck, without 1848, without the "wars of independence", without Kant, without Luther himself [...] There is nothing that I want otherwise [...] *amor fati* [...] even Christianity becomes necessary: the highest form, the most dangerous, the most seductive in its negation of life, which provokes its highest acquiescence—me. (KSA 13, 641)

Previously, Nietzsche limited himself to noting, in 1876, a destiny that concerned him in the same way: "According to their place of birth, human beings become Protestant, Catholic, Turkish, quite as one, born in a land of vineyards, becomes a wine drinker." (KSA 8, 334) And he went so far as to embellish his family genealogy by claiming to descend from Polish nobles driven out by the Counter-Reformation since they were Protestants (KSA 9, 681).

It should also be emphasized that it is the words of Luther before the Diet of Worms that are taken up by Nietzsche to express, in the fourth part of *Zarathustra* ("Among the Daughters of the Desert"), the *amor fati* at work in the acceptance of being a European—"Here I stand. I cannot do no other [*ich kann nicht anders*]." These same words are commented on in 1880 in a fragment characterizing the German spirit: "The German does not admire in Luther, for example, the man who submits ... to a law, but, on the contrary, he who despite all the orders and all the prohibitions, remains faithful to himself ..." (KSA 9, 116) This is nothing less than the problem of authenticity Nietzsche outlines here, which characterizes the Lutheran question of faith posed in the perspective of an immediate relationship with God, what was called, throughout the nineteenth century, *Gottunmittelbarkeit*: "North German culture did not come from a nobility [*Adel*] like French culture, but of teachers (teachers, organists, etc.) and preachers. It is quite a different subjection; always with the ulterior motive that there is something higher than princes [*Fursten*] (Luther)" (382)—a direct echo of the statements of the Marquis of Posa.

The Lutheran imprint [*l'imprégnation*] of Nietzsche—son, grandson, great-grandson of a pastor—is evidently not a superficial one and all the criticism he undertakes of Luther as of Christianity in general, retains Protestant elements, even if, for the most part, no longer solely at a structural level. His attitude towards Luther began to change around 1876-1877 at the same time as he began to write *Human, All Too Human*; with this work begins, to last four years, a resumption of the criticism addressed by the Enlightenment to Christianity. Luther, once recognized with Goethe, Schiller and Beethoven as a pillar of the German spirit, finds himself reduced to being no more than an instrument in the hands of the pope and the emperor:

> It was an extraordinary chance political constellation that preserved Luther [...], for the Emperor protected him so as to employ his innovation as an instrument of pressure against the Pope, while the

Pope likewise secretly befriended him so as to employ the Protestant princes of the Holy Roman Empire as a counterweight to the Emperor. (HH I, §237)

And Nietzsche then accuses Luther and the German Reformation, described as an energetic "protest by retarded spirits," of having inhibited the evolution of the Italian Renaissance, thwarted the deployment of "all the positive forces to which we owe modern culture"; but, above all, Luther and the Reformation delayed "the full development and uncontested domination of the sciences." Nietzsche goes further: he contests with Luther the originality of his conception of justification by grace, of which he attributes the paternity to the Italians:

> But Luther's bony head [...] bristled up: because justification through grace seemed to him his great discovery and motto, he did not credit this proposition when it was uttered by Italians: whereas, as is well known, the latter had discovered it much earlier and, in profound quietness, had propagated it throughout all Italy. (*Assorted Opinions and Maxims*, §226)

The real turning point in Nietzsche's critique of Luther and of Christianity, more generally, took place rather precisely during the summer and autumn of 1880, when Nietzsche sketched out his concept of the "will to power" for the first time in the notebooks of posthumous fragments which would also serve as palimpsest for the *Dawn*. In aphorism 262 of this work, Nietzsche, who has just written that "Not necessity, not desire—no, the love of power is the demon of men," pretends to only take up an idea of Luther, that is to say to interpret from the perspective of "will to power" some verses of the reformer: "Luther has said it already, and better than I, in the verses: 'Let them take from us our body, goods, honour, children, wife: let it all go—the kingdom [*Reich*] must yet remain to us!' Yes! Yes! The 'Reich'!" (D §262) It is the same process that he used, in aphorism 88, when he denounced in Luther a spirit too rustic to admit the effective reality of the *vita contemplativa*, and when he credited him with having, for this reason, wanted to put an end to the cult of the saints. The motive that Nietzsche imputes to him then is none other than *ressentiment*, rancour.

It is therefore no longer simply a question of a critique of Lutheran conceptions devised from the "historio-critical" perspective adopted by Nietzsche between 1876 and 1877, beginning with the first aphorisms of *Human, All Too Human*, in *Assorted Opinions and Maxims*, as well as in *The Wanderer and his Shadow*, it is no longer a question of a criticism modeled on that of the Enlightenment—in the name of science—, but of a denunciation that proceeds *ad hominem* on the basis of "will to power." Luther, like all of Christianity, now represents a kind of instinctual configuration whose general dynamic tends to deny all that is earthly, immanent, contradictory, conflicting, changing, exuberant, in favor of a single experience privileged among all, that of faith, that is to say an illusion based on the interpretation of a promise ascribing hope to another world.

By undermining the belief in conscience, which is nothing more than a kind of fiction,[15] Nietzsche deprives the Protestant so to speak of his favorite vice: constantly appearing before this tribunal which he naively grants to be of exemplary stability and permanent rigor. The ego is in reality only a "plurality of personalized forces" and the "subject is unstable." (KSA 9, 211) The theory of instincts that Nietzsche was developing at that time ruined any attempt to take seriously the purposes of humanity inscribed on the pediment of history, any meaning given to existence in general (cf. KSA 9, 290f). It is not a question of "living to live [*leben, um zu leben*]" (KSA 9, 270) but of "living in such a way that our energy knows its maximum intensity[16] and joy—and [of] sacrificing everything for that." (KSA 9, 271) The "will to power" manifestly does not have the goal of preserving life and genuine "nature" (the instincts and their combinations) does not have life as its goal but "expenditure."

From the outset, a theory like this reduces any Christian conception to a kind of ideology that endeavors to master time and history by making all of us equally prisoners of a past from which we cannot escape and over which we have no control—original sin:

> As all of our actions are absolute necessities [*absolute Nothwendigkeiten*] and equally absolute unknowns to us, all "you must unconditionally [*du sollst unbedingt*]" are just empty words. (KSA 9, 225)

The critique of "ideals" founded on "will to power" does not primarily or essentially target Christianity but any moral doctrine and, more generally, any theory that seeks to subsume the reality of "nature" understood as instinctual economy, beneath principles dictated by the intellect which is, for Nietzsche, no more than an "instrument" in the service of the expenditure proper to the instinctual dynamic. However, the critique of Christianity which continues to develop throughout the *Daybreak*, *The Gay Science*, *Zarathustra*, *Beyond Good and Evil*, and *On the Genealogy of Morals*, sometimes takes a 'Protestant' turn,[17] thus Nietzsche mobilizes what must be called a reformed *topos*—the critique of ecclesiastical and scholastic tradition carried out in the name of a fidelity to the letter of the biblical text:

> What should we expect from the later effects of a religion which, in the centuries when it was founded, indulged in unheard-of philological buffoonery on the Old Testament: I am talking about the attempt to hide the Old Testament from the Jews under their noses, claiming that it contains only Christian teachings and that it belongs to Christians who are the true people of Israel [...] Let us remember that the Church did not hesitate to lengthen the text of the Septuagint (eg, at Psalm 96, verse 10) and then exploit the fraudulently interpolated passage in the sense of Christian prophecy. (D §8)

Likewise, it is a mixture of philologist and Protestant who speaks provocatively in *Beyond Good and Evil*:

> In the Jewish 'Old Testament', the book of divine justice, there are men, things and speeches of so grand a style that Greek and Indian literature have nothing to set beside it. [...] the taste for the Old Testament is a touchstone in regard to 'great' and 'small' [...] To have glued this New Testament, a species of rococo taste in every respect, on to the Old Testament to form a *single* book, as 'bible', as 'the book of books': that is perhaps the greatest piece of temerity and 'sin against the spirit' that literary Europe has on its conscience. (BGE §52)

The same perspective is expressed in aphorism 26 of the third part of *On the Genealogy of Morality*, which accuses Christians of idolatry, just as the reformers denounced the pagan auras encumbering idolatry with which—often for reasons of proselytizing politics—the apostolic and Roman Church encumbered itself.

The form of this criticism which opposes the biblical text to the institution basing its justification and its legitimacy on the monopoly of its interpretation, which opposes the person of Jesus and his practice to the priests and their doctrine, the founding Old Testament to the "New," which wants to be the fulfillment of the promises decreed by it to be the sole legitimacy of the first, this form is essentially due to a Protestant atmosphere, much more than to the spirit of the Enlightenment which still animated the frontal rejection of Christianity as an illusion of symbolic "representation," in a meaning that remained close to Schopenhauer's lexicon.

One year after Nietzsche had the intuition of the "will to power," he accesses his "abyssal thought," the idea of eternal return, during the summer of 1881. The eternal return is a "logical" consequence of "will to power" but it entails a very different conception of history. Even if Nietzsche seemed to defend, in the second *Untimely Meditation*, an idea of history that he tried to make reconcilable with the requirements of "life," and even if the idea of "eternal return" appears there (KSA 1, 261), neither life nor the eternal return still refer to the "will to power," except to give an illusion in retrospect. Nor does the Eternal Return remove its validity from the parallel undertaking and constantly sharpening critique of Christianity, but it nevertheless considerably inflects the very perspective of the attack on the Christian religion or on one or another of its remarkable figures, Paul, Luther and, above all, Jesus.

In fact, the idea of eternal return has as corollary a conception of history in which "tables of values" constantly succeed one another, that is to say, inversions of values eclipsing and reversing "former tables." The eternal return does not mean the return to the identical *stricto sensu*, for example, of the person of Jesus but the inevitable struggle between ascending drive configurations and decadent configurations, the outcome of which is always the triumph—itself likewise transitory—of new ascending values always more crude in style than the refinement attained by the ultimate decadent values at the twilight of their "validity." What the eternal return designates is no definite content but the dynamics of the whole of history which becomes a kind of spiral, without assignable or discernible origin or terminus, on the turns of which, incessantly, "cultures" rise or fall. The fact of considering that the idea of eternal return "splits history in two" entail, henceforth, that is to say if we adopt this Nietzschean conception, that we can only evaluate the totality of history from the inevitably ironic and at the same time passionate viewpoint of the philosopher-artist or "overhuman": from a point of view where the mixture is achieved between instinctual adhesion to ascending values and the consciousness of their inevitable decadence—therefore from a point of view which, logically, is at the same time contradictory since it is, in fact, extra-historical, the one that Nietzsche designates by the expression *amor fati*. This is the only position one can adopt if one wants to "save" the whole of the past (cf., accordingly ZII, *The Tomb Song*) and snatch it from the *fatum* of original sin.[18]

Two consequences with regard to the critique of Christianity: on the one hand, it then finds itself totally justified, in the name of *amor fati*, as an irruption of formerly ascending values, and Protestantism is no longer anything more than an avatar in the history of this axiological configuration seeking to increase the intensity of its expenditure; on the other hand, and since Nietzsche wants to announce new values which are more 'true' than the previous ones in the sense that they are less contradictory to the "terrifying text of nature," since they are a better interpretation of this fundamental text with which they seek to reconcile humanity (cf. GS §109), decadent Christianity once again becomes the main enemy, and Christ is the only serious competitor who therefore deserves the promulgation of new theses posted at the door, no longer of one church, but of all: this is the very purpose of the value conversion project. Thus *Twilight of the Idols* is the "first book of the revaluation of values," inaugurating Year I of the new era, while *The Antichrist* is the second, and ends, as we know, with all the revolutionary ceremonial borrowed from the French, with the promulgation of the "Law against Christianity" explicitly dated "September 30, 1888 of the false calendar."[19]

As for Luther, if he remains the enemy, it is now for other reasons: the Renaissance is, in effect, perceived by Nietzsche as an attempt to convert Christian values, "an attempt with all available means, all instincts and all the resources of genius to bring about a triumph of the opposite values, the more noble values" (AC § 61) The exemplary figure of this war against Christianity waged at the very heart of institutional Christianity, the papacy, is that of Caesar Borgia:

> *Cæsar Borgia as pope!* . . . Am I understood? . . . Well then, *that* would have been the sort of triumph that I alone am longing for today—: by it Christianity would have been *swept away*!—What happened? A German monk, Luther, came to Rome. This monk, with all the vengeful instincts of an unsuccessful priest in him, raised a rebellion against the Renaissance in Rome . . . . Instead of grasping, with profound thanksgiving, the miracle that had taken place: the conquest of Christianity at its capital—instead of this, his hatred was stimulated by the spectacle. A religious man thinks only of himself.—Luther saw only the *depravity* of the papacy at the very moment when the opposite was becoming apparent: the old corruption, the *peccatum originale*, Christianity itself, no longer occupied the papal chair! Instead there was life! Instead there was the triumph of life! (Ibid.)

Henceforth, in other words, it is Luther who delayed the coming of what Nietzsche prides himself on being at the same time the herald henceforth, promulgator and craftsman: the liberation... of time, the emancipation from all past history, the restoration, *ad integrum*, of the past.

The condition of possibility of this promulgation of the new era nevertheless remains... the existence of Nietzsche himself:

> If I wage war on Christianity, I am permitted to do so only because I have never experienced anything troubled or sad from that side—on the contrary, the most estimable people I know have been Christians without guile [...]. Myself, I am descended from Protestant ecclesiastics: had I not inherited from them a high and pure meaning, I would hardly know where the right would originate to go to war against Christianity. My formula for this, the very Antichrist,[20] is itself the necessary logic in the evolution of a genuine Christian; in me, Christianity overcomes itself. (KSA 13, 622)[21]

Nietzsche once again turns Protestant critique against Protestantism[22]: first, attacking the Christian spirit in the name of the text relating the deeds and gestures of Jesus, and, secondly, in the name of this practice against any doctrinaire sedimentation which would deprive "life' (henceforth understood as synonym of "will to power") of this action in becoming and dispense anyone from making an authentic attempt at it, from risking the experience of it. Henceforth, that is, from the viewpoint of eternal return or *amor fati*, "Christ is a 'free spirit', he does not care about anything that is fixed (word, formula, Church, law, dogmas)," because "everything that is fixed kills [*alles, was fest ist, tödtet…*]"; he believes only in life and in the living—and what"is" not but becomes, "he speaks only of what is most intimate", of lived experiences: everything else has the meaning of "a sign, an instrument of language." (KSA 13, 164)

"Faith" understood in this way is a thousand leagues from any dogmatic repetition or codification, any demonstration, "it is in itself, at all times, its own miracle" (AC §32)—said otherwise, in his ascending phase, Jesus is a … Dionysiac figure. The "message" of Jesus is no longer the content of what the Gospels relate from the point of view of inchoate doctrine "but to demonstrate how one should live." (AC §35) Thus the true legacy of Christ to humanity is that part of his *res gesta* which refutes the distinction between faith and works and goes so far as to "abolish the idea of 'fault'" (AC § 41) by going so far as to deny "any gap between the human and God," living this unity "not as a privilege, but as his Good News!" (Ibid.) It is the culmination of a critique of Christianity carried out in the name of a typically Protestant *Gottunmittelbarkeit* which ends up bordering on Gnosticism since, following Jesus, the other Good News is that which Nietzsche announces with the revaluation of values, even arrogating to himself the Christian symbol *par excellence*—*Ecce homo*. New age, new "time," new calendar, new "prophet", in a particular sense as Nietzsche is both the one who announces and the one who is the content of the promise, in the double sense of *epangelia/épangélia*. Christianity had distorted "life," betrayed "nature"; Nietzsche undertakes to redeem it by installing himself in the pose of the Gnostic magician who alone holds the true light—*amor fati* resulting from the double intuition of the "will to power" and eternal return—and who, thus, undertakes to save the world, doomed, without it, to endlessly pursue a "history" unconsciously undergone through alternations of ascendancy and decadence which would seem to be due only to chance.

Translated by Babette Babich-Strong and Tracy Burr Strong

Acknowledgments
This text appears as "Nietzsche et le prophétisme," *Les Études philosophiques*, n° 73 (2005/2): 183-192. Thanks are due to the author for his gracious permission to include this essay in the current volume. This translation was begun with the late Tracy Burr Strong (1943-2022), interrupted by his untimely death on 11 May 2022.

Endnotes
1. *Botschafter*, which means both ambassador and evangelist, that is to say announcer of a promise [*annonciateur d'une promesse*]—*épangélia*.
2. Letter of 21 March 1885, the period during which Nietzsche wrote the fourth part of his "Zarathustra" (which, it may be remembered, would only be printed at the author's expense, in fifty copies sent uniquely to "friends" and of which Nietzsche would seek to recover the vast majority).
3. This he had already noted in fragment 11 {377}, November 1887-March 1888, where the prophets of Israel are described as anarchist-rebels against the established authorities. (KSA 13, 182) [Nietzsche cites Renan here, in French.— trans.]
4.   KSA 10, 44; [*Das, was kommt. / Eine Prophetie*]. KSA 10, 45.
5.   Cf. "He that is enlightened about that, is a *force majeure*, a destiny." EH, *Why I am a Destiny*, §8?
6.   "Prophet" is there articulated by the term *Wahrsager*, and "prophetic" by the adjective *wahrsagerisch* which consonates with *ja sagen*: "to say yes," which, immediately afterwards, Nietzsche makes use of.
7.   This appears in the volume *Hommage à Jean Hyppolite* (Paris, PUF, 1971) [Foucault, "Nietzsche, la généalogie, l'histoire" in: François Dagognet, Suzanne Bachelard, Georges Canguilhem, Jean Hyppolite, *Hommage à Jean Hyppolite* (Paris: PUF, 1971), 145-172.}
8.   Ibid., 154.
9.   Cf. TI *Reason in philosophy*, §§ 1 et 4.
10. Foucault, *Hommage à Jean Hyppolite*, 163.
11. Nietzsche goes as far as to coin the substantive *"das Selbige"* to introduce a sort of dissonance into his allegorical presentation of the eternal return in the chapter "The Convalescent" of the third part of "Zarathustra."
12. Cf. "Old and New Tablets" §12 *in fine*.
13. *Ecce homo*, "Why I write such good books," "Thus Spoke Zarathustra," §8; it is in in fact a reprise of a passage of the IInd part of *Zarathustra*, "Night Song."

14. Very early on, Nietzsche perceived himself as a dangerous thinker (cf. his letter of 13 May 1878 to R. von Seydlitz, as well as the one testifying to his jubilation after the review by a Swiss newspaper of *Beyond Good and Evil*, cf. the letter of 31 October 1886 to P. Gast).

15. Cf. D §119: "all our so called consciousness is a more or less fantastic commentary on an unknown, perhaps unknowable, but felt text?" Cf., *The Gay Science*, §109 (*in fine*), §335, as well as *Beyond Good and Evil*, §§22, 230.

16. On intensity as criterion for evaluation, cf. "Will? What properly takes place in all feeling and knowing everything is an explosion of forces (extreme intensity…), we call this concurrence [*Geschehen*] 'wanting [*Wollen*]'." (KSA 11, 64)

17. D §88 also recognizes, in a typically Protestant way, that we owe to Luther the "benefit" of having "aroused distrust of the saints and of the whole Christian *vita contemplativa*."

18. We must not forget that "original sin" means, in German, "hereditary sin [*Erbsünde*]."

19. It is both the date chosen by Nietzsche to be that of "the day when the first book of the Conversion of all values was completed," as he writes at the end of the foreword to *Twilight of the Idols*, and that which corresponds to the "day of redemption," the "first day of Year I," a dating placed in the subtitle of the "Law against Christianity" on which *The Antichrist* ends.

20. Remember that the German *Antichrist* means both "Antichrist" and "anti-Christian."

21. The Hegelian formulation should not mislead: there is no teleology of the Spirit in the background of the eternal return, Nietzsche repeatedly fought this representation of universal history. Cf., for example, GS §1.

22. Cf., here the penetrating analysis offered by Eric Blondel, *Nietzsche. Le «5ᵉ Évangile»?* (Paris, Les Bergers et les Mages, 1980), 172ff.

Jacopo Tintoretto, *Bacchus, Venus and Ariadne* (1576-1577).

19th C. Reproduction. Photo Credit: Worcester College, University of Oxford.

DIONYSIAN REDEMPTION, ARIADNE'S DEATH, ASSES' EARS—AND NIETZSCHE'S DEBTS

BABETTE BABICH

ὡυτὸς ʽΑίδης καὶ Διόνυσος / *Hades and Dionysus are the same.*
— Heraclitus

Dionysos:
Sei klug, Ariadne ! ...
Du hast kleine Ohren, du hast meine Ohren :
steck ein kluges Wort hinein ! —
Muß man sich nicht erst hassen, wenn man sich lieben soll?...
Ich bin dein Labyrinth...
— Nietzsche, *Klage der Ariadne*

A Problem Like Ariadne...

There is a long-standing tradition of scholarship on Nietzsche's Ariadne and Jacques Derrida wrote about Nietzsche's ears,[1] and Nietzsche invokes Dionysus and his ears and Ariadne's ears in his *Klage der Ariadne* [Ariadne's Lament]. Scholars raise the question of Ariadne in Nietzsche's texts as the name seems to code for another name, assigning various candidates, including Nietzsche himself.[2]

As Adrian del Caro puts it, the labyrinth seems emblematic: no sooner does one "try one's hand" than one seems induced to abandon the project, joining the ranks of the "many respected voices in Nietzsche scholarship who have closed the book on Ariadne," but del Caro cautions that thereby one closes scholarly

> access to one of the more obscure, secretive locations within the Nietzschean philosophical topography. Ariadne is Cosima Wagner, Cosima Wagner was Nietzsche's secret and long-standing love, Wagner was Theseus (sometimes), Nietzsche was Dionysus ...[3]

Del Caro cites "respected" scholarship, and if, in the interim, one scholar has managed to connect Ariadne and Jordan Peterson, the Nietzsche specialist, Claudia Crawford, so far from any danger of 'closing the book' has dedicated an entire book, if little received (perhaps because stylistically challenging), on the complexities of the Ariadne question and language and style,[4] while other, if no less esoterically styled, authors focus on the labyrinth.[5]

New Nietzsche Studies, Vol. 11, Nos. 3 and 4 (Fall 2021 / Spring 2022), pp. 99–130.
© 2022 Nietzsche Society. ISSN 1091–0239.

Still other authors focus on Nietzsches's Ariadne dithyramb and of course 'Ariadne' features in feminist readings.[6] In music scholarship, Richard Kuhns connects von Hofmansthal and Nietzsche to illuminate Richard Strauss' opera of the same name,[7] and David Farrell Krell, very prolific on the theme of Ariadne, mines for his own purposes the insights of the most eminent of the respected names who have written on Ariadne, Karl Reinhardt,[8] in Krell's *Postponements*.[9]

Everyone seems to know, everyone tells us.

Beyond Nietzsche's Ariadne, there are inconsistent elements in the myth of Ariadne (this being the way of myths)[10] as the story evolves between Greece and Rome.[11]

Fig. 1. Sarcophagus with Dionysus and Ariadne, 190-200 CE. Walters Art Museum, Baltimore.

The mystery cult of Dionysus/Ariadne concerns life after death. Here, glossing Robert Turcan's earlier exposition, the Latinist expert on women in religious history, Britt-Mari Nässtrom, observes that

> Ariadne's temporary death illustrated the experience of physical death by the individual who had been initiated into the mysteries. For this reason, Dionysus's wedding on Naxos is represented on many sarcophagi, which represent him as the lord of nature and nature's reviving power.[12]

To discuss Nietzsche's Ariadne, at issue is Ariadne's relation to Dionysus, her divine husband, who comes upon her in death or else as she 'sleeps' and, through marriage, elevates her to divinity. This encounter is likewise complicated, and interpreters read this sleeping encounter as nuptial and erotic given morphological parallels with satyr encounters and maenadic vulnerability (though, the nuptials being beyond dispute, just for whom this might be 'erotic' as such is typically unreflected).[13]

Ovid tells us that Ariadne is not dead but beside herself in anger and grief, abandoned as she was by Theseus whose life she had saved. Her 'discovery' (and there are multiple and conflicting stories of this) by the god Dionysus thus becomes the basis for the Dionysus-Ariadne death cult, as he redeems her. Prior to Ariadne's apotheosis via Dionysus, there was a (consummated) relationship with Theseus who slew Ariadne's brother, the Minotaur, quite dependent as Theseus was on Ariadne's help to do so, by which act she betrayed not only her brother but her father and her mother and all of Crete in the process. On Claudia Crawford's account, Ariadne's father was Midas although most traditions tell us his name was Minos.[14] There is conjunction via metonymy: the names sound or begin by sounding the same—think the ancient philosophers whose names begin with *Anax*: Anaximander, Anaximenes, Anaxagoras[15]—and the ambiguity persists inasmuch as both Midas and Minos had asses's ears. (Parenthetically, for Nietzsche, it is worth noting that asses' ears may be distinguished from horse's ears in terms of length hence Paul Deussen takes pains to inform us that Nietzsche once undertook to measure the ears of the horse he was riding to be sure he was not riding an ass—or a mule.)[16]

Minos, father to both Ariadne and the Minotaur, was brother to Rhadamanthus and Aeacus/Aiakos, all three of whom were judges of the underworld. If Pindar emphasizes Rhadamanthus in the second Pythian ode, Minos has a more enduring name, as he is depicted standing at the wide gates of hell in Dante's *Inferno*, associated with a snake, that would be his own tail, which he wraps around the damned, relegating them to whatever correspondent level of hell—think the derivative contortions of the 'sorting hat' in J. K. Rowling's *Harry Potter and the Philosopher's Stone*.

In Dante, the 'sorting' is self-referred as Minos wraps his tail around himself, the vehicle of scandal for Michelangelo who used the same figure of Minos, ears and all (Figs. 2 and 3), judging himself, and the fact that the figure resembled the Papal Master of

Ceremonies, Biagio da Cesena,[17] set at eye level in the crowded tableau of the *Last Judgment.* Horst Bredekamp emphasizes the painting's figural orientation.[18] For Bredekamp, Michelangelo precisely "literally" marginalizes Minos, setting him "against the edge,"[19] thus counterbalancing Charon. There's a snake biting the penis of the tormented figure which had in the past been painted over for modesty, a detail now restored. Art historians/tour guides highlight the effects of calumny (nudity and snakes signify erotic intemperance, not unlike Ixion whose unhappy tale is told as part of the cautionary word in Pindar's 2nd Pythian Ode, so important for Nietzsche).

Fig. 2. Michelangelo, Minos. *Last Judgment.*   Fig. 3. Cherubino Alberti, *Minos and Demons.*
1536-1541. Sistine Chapel.   After Michelangelo. 1553–1615. Art Institute Chicago.

Nietzsche relates *Midas'* judgment concerning what is or *would be* best for the human being "not to hear" in *The Birth of Tragedy* (BT §3). Once again, both Midas/Minos have long, asses' ears, as evident in Michelangelo's painting of Minos and likewise emphasized in Cherubino Alberti's later sketch (Fig. 3 above).[20]

As Pasiphae's consort-king, Minos had demanded a bloodthirsty tribute of human sacrifice to feed their son, the Minotaur—seven youths and seven maidens.[21] Nor were Minos' ears the only physiological troubles of a husband married to Pasiphae, the Cretan queen who afflicted him with ejaculate of scorpions *and* spiders *and* millipedes, so to punish his human lovers.

Minos, Ariadne's father, encircled by his snakes, might be among the foregrounded figures in Titian's *Bacchus and Ariadne* (1522-1523), depicting a startled Ariadne after her fatal abandonment, surprised by Dionysus vaulting an awkward vault, as if theatrically lowered, *ex machina*, a strobe light moment: the visual almost center of the painting, illuminating the line of vision, Dionysus seeing Ariadne, note the crown of stars above her, seeing Dionysus. (Fig. 4)

Fig. 4. Titian (1488-1576), *Bacchus and Ariadne* (1522-1523). National Gallery, London. Public Domain.

Ecstatic, with layered grounds, including the background landscaped distance and in the foreground, carrying the fruits of the ritual σπαραγμός aloft, the slightly built, so hard to place as Silenus, but sylvan, Pan-figure to the viewer's right, wearing soft and flowery satyr chaps behind the slightly off-center presence—the *center* being a baby, boy satyr—of a naked, muscular figure that could be Minos: grappling with his snakes, swarthy, widow's peak, seemingly graced with horns suggested by two white lines on either side of his head or maybe these are long ears, hard to tell with his wild hair. Some scholars, thinking only of the snakes, identify the figure as Laocoön, if absent his two sons, others claim that the "'Laocoön'" quotation, reading between Giordano and Titian, and focusing on musculature *per se*,[22] must be Silenus—but why the Laocoön? Because, of course, mimesis. Other scholars track the figure to Catullus' account, ergo, and in either case, metonymically, noting his struggle with the serpents surrounding his body (and in his hands), as Michelangelo's Minos is girt about by snakes, signifying, true in da Cessna's case as in Laocoön's case as in Ixion's case, erotic excess.

In an earlier version of this essay, I highlighted the focus on Apelles,[23] the unfairly calumniated 'truth-telling' artist depicted by Botticelli and Dürer. Here, looking at Michelangelo and Titian to get to Poussin's *Bacchanale*, I am concerned to note the relation between philosophy and the Orphic tradition as this is also one of the reasons Albert Camus writes about Sisyphus[24] and Simone de Beauvoir writes about woman as *mare tenebrae*.[25] Philosophy in this lineage is the *art of living* beyond life and consequently a *school for dying*.

I highlight the importance of a *material* hermeneutic as Nietzsche learnt this not from the Friedrich Ritschl from whom he learnt the classical tradition of historical and *literary* hermeneutics but Otto Jahn's 'monumental' or archaeological hermeneutics as I argue that this may help us to 'read' Nietzsche's notion of 'monumental' history typically misread when one parses 'monumental' in today's honorific sense of the term as opposed to its physical or archaeological sense.[26] Object discoveries like those of the Orphic gold tablets, which Nietzsche knew, and, more recently, like the Derveni Krater (Figs. 6 and 7) along with the Derveni (and other) papyri, should *change* philosophy even if scholars have been slow to acknowledge this, shattering what we take philosophy to be. In addition to the Orphic tradition relevant for understanding the inception of philosophy whether one speaks of the beginnings of philosophy in terms of the Pre-Socratics *à la* Diels, or the Pre-Platonics *à la* Nietzsche,[27] this illuminates our reading of Dionysus. In his *Philosophy in the Tragic Age of the Greeks*, Nietzsche refers to Kant in the context of Anaxagoras' νοῦς in the mechanico-technological context of our age (as opposed to a theatrical) *deus ex machina*, instead once "Anaxagoras' circle is moved, once *Nous* has started it on its revolution, all order, all conformity to law and all beauty of the world are but the natural consequences of that first impulse to move" (PTAG §17, cf. GS §109). Thus Nietzsche explains:

Anaxagoras could have used words as proud as Kant (in his *General Natural History and Theory of the Heavens*) to take credit for the disposal of mythological and theistic miraculous interventions and anthropomorphic purposes and utilities. ...Instead of seeing in it the intentions and the intervening hands of a machine god [*eines Maschinengottes*], he derived from a type of oscillation which, once having begun, is necessary and predictable in its course and attains effects which are the equal of the wisest calculations of ratiocination, and of the utmost planning of purposiveness—but without being them. (PTAG §17)

Here Nietzsche's concern is *cosmological*, referencing the Kant-Laplace hypothesis before citing Kant's 1755, *Universal Natural History and Theory of the Heavens*,[28]

"I am enjoying the pleasure," said Kant, "of seeing a well-ordered totality, creating itself, without the aid of arbitrary fictions, only by the impulses of ordered laws of motion, which is so similar to that world system which is our own, that I cannot keep from taking it to be the same. [...] It seems to me that one might say at this point, without presumption, 'Give me materiality and I will build a world from it!'" (Ibid.)[29]

The *economics* of the universe, this is the *Timaeus* with its reference to the Platonic ouroboros, is crucial for Kant leading to a physics of world-generation— cosmogony—that goes of itself. This legacy is part of the reason Henri Poincaré would offer a stochastic proof for the theory of eternal recurrence,[30] quite as Nietzsche in this same locus cites Afrikan Spir *vis-à-vis* Kant (§15).

Reading Nietzsche's lectures on the tragic age would make every difference. But, given the obstacles (lack of translation, contested reception), scholars rarely read Nietzsche's university lecture courses on *The Pre-Platonic Philosophers*, much less *The Divine Service of the Greeks*, or *Greek Lyric*, and so on. Typically, scholars fail to reference these courses and some argue, on the basis of little evidence, that they were merely announced and 'never presented,' implausible for courses repeated over several years and irrelevant in the case of *Vorlesungen*: written texts composed for presentation and intended to be heard. Hence whether read outloud to students or not (Newton lectured to the walls, as we know, if he had no hearers), these are texts written to be read out loud, in the *acroamatic* context Nietzsche emphasizes in a series of then-contemporary public lectures *On The*

Future of our Educational Institutions.[31] To date, there are no plans for a comprehensive English edition of these lectures and critical commentary remains rare for specialists in Nietzsche's thought and rarer still for classical philology in general.[32]

'Surviving' the underworld after death is *the* challenge for the Greeks as the soul loses coherence and sanity after death: its passage into the world of shadows is confusing as the Orphic tradition along with Homer and Plato (*and* the satires of the 2ⁿᵈ Century CE Lucian) tell us. This is the key to the Dionysus-Ariadne death cult, as this endures in Greek and Roman antiquity, here to repeat Heraclitus: ὡυτὸς ʿΑίδης καὶ Διόνυσος / *Derselbe aber ist Hades und Dionysus* / *The same however are Hades and Dionysus* (DK 15), quite in the dithyrambic context of bacchantic procession, that is to say, explicitly phallic celebration. Scholars contrast morphological complexities, juxtaposing Dionysus in Greek ceramics with Roman frescoes or noting Dionysus' physical disposition *vis-à-vis* Ariadne, his naked leg over her draped leg, a formal characteristic of Ariadne who holds her own veil open with one raised hand, lifting it from her head, and the naked Dionysus, hand resting over his own head, on the Derveni Krater. (Fig. 6)

Fig. 6. Derveni Krater (330 – 320 BCE). Dionysus and Ariadne. Detail. Bronze. Thessaloniki, Archaeological Museum. Public Domain.

A 'Little Sleep'—A 'Little Death'

Ariadne's 'sleep' is a word for death. Thus Plutarch tells us that one myth has Ariadne hanging herself after being abandoned while Homer's *Odyssey* tells us that Artemis kills Ariadne. What is certain is that the Dionysus/Ariadne mystery cult is commonly depicted on sarcophagi (e.g., Fig. 1 above, Fig. 16 below). On the Derveni Krater, the transport/transition between life and death may be symbolized by the solitary booted sandal worn by the triumphant huntsman (Fig. 7), signifying movement (or travel) between the world of the living and the underworld where shoes and every other physical attribute, so Lucian points out, can be of no use.

Fig. 7. Derveni Krater. Hunter (shod/unshod) and ithyphallic satyr/maenad (unshod).

Theseus who manages to 'forget' Ariadne or else to have been swept away by the waves such that he could not help his boat sailing away from Naxos or else fleeing in deference to a dream in which Dionysus commanded him to leave, and so on and so on, 'abandons' Ariadne. A princess (more than a priestess *per se*), unmarried and pregnant with Theseus' child, lacking protection, would not have survived in any case, even assuming/accepting any of the excuses above (nor would Theseus be the first man to abandon a woman under similar circumstances).

Angelika Kauffmann's 1974 *Bacchus und Ariadne* (Fig. 8) can seem to draw on some of the ancient, Greco-Roman, iconography, including a veil being raised, hence the discovery, variously interpreted as a wedding veil but which may also be a burial shroud, lifted by Eros/Cupid who also takes Dionysus by the hand, to aid his 'discovery.' In Kaufmann's painting, Ariadne is awakening from sleep (or death?), resting on her left arm, closed hand against her cheek, raises her right, palm outward, in a stylizedly apotropaic, classically erotic, gesture.

Fig. 8. Angelika Kauffmann, *Bacchus und Ariadne*. 1794. National Trust. Wikimedia. Public Domain.

The Ariadne who cries, as Nietzsche writes in the *Dionysian Dithyrambs*, "Who still warms me, who still loves me?" refers us to the cold of death. In his *Nachlaß*, Nietzsche gives us the etymological intersection with Dionysus as 'Zeus-killer' or '-huntsman,' "Ζόννυξος ... *Zeusjäger*".[33] Later, in the *Dionysian Dithyrambs*, Nietzsche continues,

> Unutterable, veiled, terrible one!
> Huntsman behind the clouds ... you unknown—*god*.

Nietzsche's lament, intriguingly echoing one of his youthful poems to an 'unknown god,' is spoken in the interval before the appearance of the deity, when the clouds break, staccato drama, complete with stage instructions: "A flash of lightning. Dionysus becomes visible in emerald beauty."

Along with Jacques Taminiaux' *Le théâtre des philosophes*, Tracy B. Strong amplifies the political reference to theatre as this resonates with an essay he intended to update for presentation at the Texas meeting of the Nietzsche Society: "Where are We When We are Beyond Good and Evil?"[34]—here to recall that the ass appears, specifically on stage, 'beautiful and strong' (BGE §9).

Fig. 9. Melchior Meier, *Apollo and Marsyas and the Judgment of Midas,* 1581.
Metropolitan Museum of Art. Public Domain.

Ariadne's apotheosis is clearly divinely redemptive where her father Midas's asses' ears are a similarly divine punishment: Apollo, displeased with Midas's judgment of Marsyas as victor, graces him with the ears of an ass to show him up for his poor judgment, before the god proceeds to flay Marsyas for his skin[35] as we see in the gruesome 16th century engraving by Melchior Meier (Fig. 9), Apollo displaying the tortured satyr's skin to a very long-eared Midas.

Similarly, Bartolomeo Manfredi depicts *Apollo and Marsyas* (Fig. 10 below), at once beautiful and calmly horrific: Apollo skins the satyr alive to take his skin—still a practice with farm-reared and trophy animals to this day.[36] Thinking Apollo remains a challenge for us as he seems so very self-evident a god, at least by contrast with Dionysus, but this is an error as we recall from Marcel Detienne's (1935-2019) critical discussion of ancient polytheism, *Apollon le couteau à la main.*[37] The plagues wreaked on Troy to turn the tide in the Trojan war are, as Homer tells us, the 'work' of Apollo, and we remember that Apollo's lyre was made of animal body parts: from the sound box[38] wrought from the shells of the tortoises one can still see if one climbs the acropolis near Athens, covered taut with animal skin, to goat horns, strung with gut, fitted with findings of bone, ivory, and mother of pearl.[39]

Fig. 10. Bartolomeo Manfredi, *Apollo and Marsyas* (1615-1620). Saint Louis, Art Museum. Public Domain.

If philosophers of science, with exceptions including the current author, typically pay little attention to Nietzsche, students of ancient history, philology, or philosophy *likewise* exclude Nietzsche. Contemporary scholars leave Nietzsche out because to include him 'upsets,' as he writes about the Spanish, 'all their prejudices,' adding stylistic fluidity and complexity. In addition, it should be observed that it also permits one to borrow the bits one likes (hardly uncommon) whilst excluding those one does not. To this extent, Nietzsche remains a secret resource for classicists and Jonathan Barnes adverts to this as does Hugh Lloyd Jones along with André Laks,[40] co-editor of the recent, multivolume Loeb edition of *Early Greek Philosophy*. The advantage of a non-received resource is that one may read without exigence. Scholars are free to use *and* to condemn Nietzsche's scholarship in favor of their own.

"Adventavit asinus, / pulcher et fortissimus."

A depiction of what Nietzsche clarifies as the inevitable confession of what he calls the "philosopher's conviction," is the 'advent' of the ass: 'beautiful and (melodic) strong,' complete with a mystery cult with both a long history and an even longer future (think Shakespeare's *Midsummer Night's Dream*) in Lucian's *Onus* (or, as the tradition also likes to claim, some other author's) *Lucius and the Ass*,[41] a tale of scopic misadventure, complete with the same roses Midas will use to bind Silenus, qua deceived or plied with wine and thereby 'tortured' as Nietzsche tells us in his *Florentinische Tractat über Homer und Hesiod, ihr Geschlecht und ihren Wettkampf.* Nietzsche repeats the Greek "πᾶσαν μηχανὴν μηχανώμενοςτο," to explain that Midas uses every extreme device to extract an answer) explaining that what is at stake in *The Birth of Tragedy* is the desire to learn the answer to the question of what would be best for the human, the same question, Lucian has Menippus ask Teiresias in his Νεκυομαντεία.[42]

Fig. 11. Barberini Faun. Munich: Glyptothek. Author's photo.

Roses, used to bind the captured Midas, play a role as fetters in Lucian's *True History* when the narrator and his companions first encounter Rhadamanthus. Roses also have an erotic resonance for Nietzsche and I write about this in connection with Zarathustra and the sublime as this matches a certain statue's, the Barberini Faun's, disposition (Fig. 11), which happens in turn to be not unlike the convention used to indicate Ariadne and Dionysus, whereby, the sleeping hero, the satyr (the Faun being very much alive) sleeps sublime: "arm resting above his head" quite as Nietzsche writes.[43]

Fig. 12. Martin Luther, *Wider das Papstthum zu Rom vom Teuffel gestifft*, 1545. Wittenberg durch Hans Lufft. Cover after Lucas Cranach. Public Domain.

Significantly, as this concerns the questions of both judgment and of redemption,[44] Martin Luther uses the allegory of the ass in the polemical title-page wood-cut for his *Wider das Papstthum zu Rom vom Teuffel gestifft*, featuring the pope—in a fairly crowded figure (Fig. 12 below)[45]—depicted with long, asses's ears, legs outstretched, hands folded in prayer, carted off by demons as if seated in the church choir, as one also sees the apse including the arch of church windows behind the pope, likewise carried off, the whole poised for a fall into the leviathan- or eel-like maw of hell, surrounded by hordes of demons with horns *and* long ears, epitomized as "*Papstesel mit langen Eselsohren und verdammtem Lügenmaul.*"[46]

Although his theme is neither Nietzsche nor Ariadne, Robert Bernasconi recalls Pliny's discussion of the Greek painter, Apelles (of whose celebrated painterly work, like Menippus' celebrated writing, there are no surviving illustrations) reflecting on Heidegger's lecture courses on Nietzsche and art. Bernasconi's essay is titled with Pliny's proverb '*Ne sutor ultra crepidam*' reading Erasmus—that great Lucian enthusiast—together with Dürer.[47] As Lucian's *Slander* is based on Pliny's account,[48] it is worth noting, to add to Bernasconi, that Botticelli's depiction of Apelles in his *Calunnia* [The Calumny of Apelles] (ca. 1494) draws on Lucian's ekphrasis.[49]

Well-discussed in art history—the secondary source being *Vasari's Lives*—the hero of the story is Apelles, the blamelessly accused who exacts revenge (this is the creative power of *ressentiment*), think of Michelangelo painting Biago da Cesena as Midas, painting the king listening to slander. Sovereigns, thus the need for Lucian's satire, are less than 'sovereign,' all-too liable to having their ears turned.

Fig. 13. Botticelli, *Calunnia* [The Calumny of Apelles] (ca. 1494). Detail: Ignorance & Suspicion on either side of King Midas. Galleria degli Ufizzi, Florence. Public Domain.

Prior to Luther's attack on the pope (cf., again, Fig. 12) but after Botticelli (Fig. 13), we may note Albrecht Dürer's 1520-1521, *Die*

Verläumdung des Apelles where Dürer's characters are labeled after Lucian (Fig. 14).

In Dürer's fresco, the king's furry ears are fully unobscured (unlike the hands-on tactics of the whisperers, Ignorance and Suspicion, attending Botticelli's king, traditionally named Midas in Fig. 13).

Fig. 14. Albrecht Dürer, *Die Verläumdung des Apelles*, Ignorance/Suspicion, detail. Altes Rathaus, Nürnberg, Großer Saal: North wall. 1521-22. 1613 and 1904/1905. (Destr. Bomb strike, 1944/1945). Deutsche Digitale Bibliothek.

At issue when it comes to asses' ears is the matter of judgment. Calumny, especially calumny at the court, is the art of besmirching, pointed, again this is Lucian's clarification, contra the king's stupidity or gullibility—hence the long ears—pulled by the two ladies on either side, as the king is moved to extend his hand to Slander who is escorted by Envy in the company of Treachery and Deceit.

Nietzsche also uses the metaphor of long ears in his Zarathustra book, nowhere more conspicuously perhaps than in his parodic fourth book, *Conversation with the Kings*, observing that he had long ago unlearned how to take consideration for 'long ears,' to the interruption of the ass: 'I-A'

Poussin's magnificent *Midas and Bacchus*, shows us why Midas might have inspired the god's sympathy, quite beyond his restitution of the god's companion, Silenus, originally baited and 'detained' by the king in the first place (Fig. 15). Here a a drowsy Silenus, depicted as a bacchic figure inclined to excess, with wine jug still in his hand, is to the far left in the painting, along with a fairly Apolline Dionysus, indeed, looking so very Apolline that, in spite of the painting's title, scholars identify him as Apollo, here in a red cloak and a drained wine cup, complete with a bacchantic figure in the background, perhaps Pan, playing the double aulos (but not a syrinx). Kneeling, we see the supplicant, King Midas, ears tucked discretely beneath his diadem, with a sleeping Ariadne—or Maenad—arm over her head, and so on.

Fig. 15. Nicolas Poussin, *Midas and Bacchus*, 1629-1640. Munich, Alte Pinakothek. Wikimedia. Public Domain.

Poussin features almost all the signifiers of wine as we know—so it goes with associations with Dionysus—that Midas had captured Silenus using wine to ply the forest god, as noted above. And as Hyginus takes some care to explain, the 'torture' is largely a symbolic affair: this being what it is to be bound with roses (the same point holds for Lucian's satirical *True Story*), whilst queried on "nature's mysteries and the events of long ago." In this scene, after keeping Silenus for ten days, Midas restores him, drunken as he would have to be, to Dionysus who, as reward for the safe return of Silenus, grants Midas any wish.

Here, it is enough to get the sense of the argument where it concerns the matter of judgment as this bears both on Ariadne and

Theseus but also discernment just when it comes to the 'art,' as Nietzsche names it, of ending.[50]

Midas lacked judgment—quite as Apollo recognized. Thus, misguidedly, Midas asked Dionysus that everything he touched turn to gold. Later, realizing the deadly consequences of his wish, Midas prays to Dionysus to pity him—and Poussin twice paints this sequence—with the god taking Midas to bathe in the river Pactolus.

'You have small ears, you have my ears'

Ariadne inherits her father's poor judgment but not his long ears. In the voice of Dionysus, Nietzsche teases Ariadne, "Be clever [*Sei klug*], Ariadne, you have small ears, you have my ears…" a caution soon converted to the provocation of the aphorism, *On the Beautiful and the Ugly*, asking, why her ears are not longer? (GD, *Streifzüge eines Unzeitgemässen* §19; DD, KSA 6, 401; cf. KSA 13, 498)

Ariadne is also connected from the first of the *Untimely Meditations* with the labyrinth and she is explicitly invoked towards the end of *Beyond Good and Evil*, as Nietzsche quotes Dionysus:

> "Under certain circumstances I love what is human" and with this he alluded to Ariadne who was present—"the human is to my mind an agreeable, courageous, inventive animal that has no equal on earth; it finds its way in any labyrinth, I am well disposed towards him; I often reflect how I might yet advance him and make him stronger, more evil, and more profound than he is." (BGE §295)

The satiric element is patent in the allegory including the reference to long ears.

Nietzsche sets Dionysus as response to Ariadne's lament, a he-god's reply that takes little account of what she, as mortal, says and, yet, as deity, still answers her as he redeems her:

> *Ein Blitz. Dionysos wird in smaragdener Schönheit sichtbar.*
> *Dionysos:*
> *Sei klug, Ariadne ! …*
> *Du hast kleine Ohren, du hast meine Ohren :*
> *steck ein kluges Wort hinein ! —*
> *Muss man sich nicht erst hassen, wenn man sich lieben soll ? …*
> *Ich bin dein Labyrinth…* (*Dionysos-Dithyramben*, KSA 6, 401)

The theatrical appearance of Dionysus in 'emerald beauty' is key to the ecliptic, elliptical, ecstatic, labyrinthic element that remains.

We may cite instances, as many of the art historians already quoted do, of the significance of the approach of Dionysus to

Ariadne emblematic of translation—hence a common motif, as noted, to decorate sarcophagi, including the gesture of revelation/ discovery in the case of Ariadne (bottom right in Fig. 16 below), a matter of passing, crossing over to life beyond life, the awakening of psyche, the soul, from earthly death to a life eternal.

As sleep is akin to death so passage to the afterlife is akin to a wedding night.

Ariadne had more than a few reasons to lament. Here we recall Hyginus' fable, as after Ariadne helps Theseus murder her brother, necessary to halt the tribute Minos demanded, a tribute to have included Theseus, who brings Ariadne with him on his return to Athens yet abandons her, 'asleep' on Naxos. But what could Theseus have done with the daughter of the king who had demanded such a tribute for the hunger of her brother? Ariadne, even explaining the help she gave him in his escape/triumph, would not be welcome in Athens. Abandonment to a god's redemption is the only possible rescue for Ariadne: "Liber [Dionysos], falling in love with her, took her from there as his wife."

Fig. 16. Roman sarcophagus showing Dionysus approaching Ariadne. Ca. 230-240 AD. Louvre, Paris. Public Domain.

Note that the figure of Ariadne asleep has the same formal attributes as Ariadne in death and depictions include as her attribute a shroud (or veil) not only in funerary art but many paintings, most particularly perhaps the 1626 *Bacchanale*, featuring Dionysus' discovery of Ariadne by Poussin, and, in this case, her veil or shroud is black, perhaps with a winding sheet or wedding garment or, as it may appear, nudity, underneath. (See Fig. 17 below.)

This is what the coming of this particular tempter god signifies.

Certainly: Poussin's *Bacchanale* (and Poussin enthusiasts object to the attribution to Poussin) is somewhat more centered than Titian's. There is no 'vault' towards Ariadne and there is no shock as in Titian (above: Fig. 3), but, with tenderness, the god lifts her from her shroud into his chariot.

The gesture is one of rescue: redemption or salvation. In just this measure, this is a cult for all humankind. At the same time, there is the color (black) of Ariadne's covering shroud or veil as she is embraced and as she is lifted up to Dionysus by Eros as one of Poussin's winged putti.

Fig. 17. Nicolas Poussin, *Bacchanale*, 1626. Museo del Prado, Madrid.   Public Domain.

Do these reflections solve the 'problem' of Ariadne or the problem or fetish of/with her ears? Not too likely, but perhaps it helps for other questions.

Certainly we know a little more about Ariadne's lament as Nietzsche writes, again to cite: "Who still warms me," she asks, "who still loves me?" I've sought to make the case that we need the half-truth that it is to speak of being "half-dead." Ariadne is dead;

Dionysus, marrying her—this is death as birth and as rebirth—saves/redeems/transfigures her.

Having arrived at this point of all-too-human abandon (Theseus) and divine salvation/redemption (Dionysus), we are fairly distant from the contest between Homer and Hesiod of which Nietzsche writes. We are also seemingly at a distance from the folk elements of what Nietzsche named a 'witches brew' of sensuality and cruelty in *The Birth of Tragedy out of the Spirit of Music* although we will need both by the time Nietzsche comes back to Beethoven at the end of his first book.

If our concern is with the 'real' Cretan princess, as if this were history, as it is not, and as opposed to myth, as it is, we could note that Ariadne, fatally abandoned on Naxos, is cold quite as Nietzsche writes: "*Wer wärmt mich, wer liebt mich noch?*".

Talk of myth is talk of the gods, typically these are 'gods' we moderns neither believe nor, indeed, disbelieve. If we happen to be theists, our faith is monotheistic (Nietzsche speaks of ('monotono-theism') but if we call ourselves atheists, as Sartre likewise reminds us, it is that same one god we refuse. The myriad old gods are no deities for us today.

Fig. 18. Max Klinger, *Christus im Olymp*, 1897. Österreichische Galerie Belvedere. Public Domain.

Ariadne's lament is *Nietzsche's lament*—quite as Ariadne, qua *myth*, speaks through Nietzsche's mouth, just as she speaks to us through Ovid or Strauss, etc. For this reason, I conclude with a leveled out or 'flattened' Parnassus, *Christus im Olymp*, a destroyed and since 'reconstructed' painting by Max Klinger (1857-1920), as this painter also illuminates Nietzsche not on Ariadne but Eros. (Fig. 18)

Klinger was inspired by the theologico-political contrast that was Nietzsche's, echoing Hölderlin's elegiac account of the old gods in the persons of Saturn/Kronos and Jupiter/Zeus. Hölderlin, who also sings *To the Titans*, names Saturn the deposed, "the guiltless god of the golden age [*Schuldlos der Gott der goldenen Zeit…*} in his *Natur und Kunst/Nature and Art*. The cycling of gods parallels the decline of ages, gold to silver to bronze and iron, and in *Die Titanen*, Hölderlin inquires after these older gods, to remind us that "we lack / the song that liberates the spirit [*es fehlet / Gesang, der löset den Geist*}."

We remember Nietzsche's critical remonstration: "2000 years and not a single new god."[51] It is the succession of gods that inspires the artist's peripety depicted in Klinger's *Christ on Olympus*. Damaged, which is to say: destroyed in the second world war—and subsequently only badly restored—Klinger's painting shows the advent of the new order. Christianity contra the old gods.

Klinger dramatizes the ascendance of the new cult Nietzsche predicts in his first book, parallel to Socrates:

> the new Orpheus who rose up against Dionysus and …put the powerful god to flight. The god, as when he fled Lycurgus, king of the Edoni, escaped into the depths of the sea, the mystical floods of a secret cult that was gradually to cover the whole world (BT §12)

Klinger gives us a painterly ekphrasis via transference of Nietzsche's Eros aphorism, ecstatic, as Nietzsche writes in 1886: "Christianity gave Eros poison to drink—he did not die, to be sure, but degenerated into vice." (BGE §168)

One may hear echoes of Lucian's 'atmospheres' and I write about these in a theo-political context,[52] i.e., 'air,' as Nietzsche writes, as *Die Wüste wächst* [The Desert Grows]. In *Ariadne's Lament* this includes reflection on death as such, not Zarathustra's death as this is well-known—Lucian jokes about it in his dialogue of the dead, *Menippus or the Consultation of the Corpses*[53]—but Nietzsche's own presentiment of his own death as of our own: everyone's. 'Sniffing' paradise:

> I sit here sniffing the finest air,
> air of Paradise, truly,
> bright, buoyant air, gold-streaked,
> as good air as ever
> fell from the moon—
> came it by chance,
> or did it happen by wantonness,
> as the old poets tell.[54]

We can read Ariadne's last verse in Nietzsche's dithyramb before the gnomic reply comes with Dionysus in glowing greenness, 'emerald beauty,' a color to recall Lucian's colors—along with violet and gold—of the afterlife, the answer from the "unknown god," "veiled," Nietzsche says here, and he says it twice, "in lightning."

On Madness, Debt, and Ending—at the Right Time

If we read this by way of Lucian's *Slander*, related themes in Nietzsche of Oedipus' eyes and Odysseus' stopped-up ears[55] acquire a different sense. One may be deceived via one's own blinders *or* one's blindness, one's hearing *or* one's deafness. Thus 'oblivion' is ascribed since antiquity to the Theseus who 'abandons' Ariadne, the Cretan princess crucial in the context of the labyrinth—and the danger of the Minotaur—but a liability in the after-story. She could not have been, *she would never have been*, welcome in Athens as his bride.

There is a fatefulness here and to this extent, the Nietzsche who lost his father at a very young age (the traumatic memory is emblematic in Zarathustra) was concerned with the theme of endings and death, emphasizing, as a relatively young man, the importance of 'dying at the right time.' This was not a matter of a long life as he often wrote, and scholars inform us that he would have been thinking of his teacher Ritschl such that one can outlive one's victories—the same would not have been true of his father, thus the sentimental reminiscence at the start of *Ecce Homo*. The reference to ending well is physiological, geographic, and atmospheric. Thus Nietzsche refers here to the bay of Rapallo and to Portofino.

I go further than Crawford cited above to argue the likelihood, there is no way to be certain in any case, that Nietzsche began by feigning his madness, in a parallel with Hölderlin (I concur with Pierre Bertaux), as the poet's life and 'madness' may have inspired Nietzsche's own (arguably) planned 'retreat.' As plan, the strategy had its costs which had to be endured even had it proved successful, nor did it succeed in Nietzsche's case. If almost forty years of 'madness' was hardly ideal for Hölderlin, it did relieve the poet of the demands and strains of everyday life (and of engaging with his mother). But, Nietzsche, at the end of their shared 19th century, could not repeat the poet's achievement some 90 years earlier. As brutal as psycho-medical interventions were in Hölderlin's day, they were far worse in Nietzsche's day, continuing to worsen to the present day, as the late Thomas Szasz argued in book after book.[56]

If we know Nietzsche requested drugs from doctors and that he often self-prescribed for his ailments, with iatrogenic consequences affecting his eyes, his digestion, etc., it would be the (then novel) psycho-pharmaceuticals that came to be prescribed for those afflicted with psychological disturbances and collapse, given the scene as it had been set in Turin, that made all the difference. Catastrophic and effectively unpredictable—doctors did not under-stand their side-effects at the time nor, to be sure, do many doctors today, again to reference Szasz quite in addition to recent research on the empirical uselessness of many psycho-pharmaceuticals—the effects would be cumulative and life-long.[57] Thus even if the case may be made that Nietzsche initially *feigned* mental instability, it is certain that he would end his life in (iatrogenic) madness.

At issue for research are the months leading up to Nietzsche's collapse in Turin along with the circumstances of his collection from his lodgings in Turin, at the hands of Overbeck, who made decisions on his behalf, just where it may plausibly be supposed that doctors would have been involved, along with pharmacological intervention even before but certainly on the train to Basel, this last on Overbeck's assessment less of Nietzsche's needs (we are told that he screamed and that he was agitated) than a concern for propriety. Nietzsche's subsequent 'treatment,' various as this was (if largely unrecorded) followed at clinics in Switzerland and Germany in accord with his mother's decisions in Naumburg which included pharmacological intervention (here we do have apothecary records), interventions which would, after his mother's death, be continued in Weimar in accord with his sister's decisions on his behalf. This has been generally, if incompletely, documented. Here, the lack of a full record is consequent to the losses of two world wars, compounded by a divided Germany in addition to the novelty of the medicaments involved, themselves inadequately studied in terms of side-effects and factively uncommunicated between physicians who, in addition to being unaware of the cumulative effects of Nietzsche's personal drug habits throughout his life, had their own ideas for 'treatment.'

In our day, given the popularity of 'asymptomatic' illness and where the notion of malingering seems to have disappeared from the social alphabet, where we suspect communicable disease on all fronts, visible and invisible, that is, again, symptomatic and not, it can be difficult to imagine that Nietzsche might have feigned madness. But if he did, and there is very good evidence as Crawford and others argue he did, the consequences would not have been possible for him to predict nor would the option of ending the ruse have been available.[58]

Nietzsche would have been financially motivated to feign illness. Oddly, despite Nietzsche's well-known penury, usually mentioned abstractly, as if this were some romantic detail and otherwise irrelevant, scholars rarely advert to Nietzsche's economic resources when it comes to his *Ecce Homo* or his desire to re-issue his extant books in new editions, complete with new prefaces composed to this end. To date, scholars remain preoccupied by Nietzsche's *Nachlaß* notes along with their reconstructed plans for books he never wrote.

With respect to the "last things" Nietzsche spoke of beginning with the first section of *Human, All too Human*, it makes all the ontic difference that Nietzsche's Basel pension (1000 Swiss francs, as Curt Paul Janz tells us, with supplements to a total of 3000 per year, along with a small sum as supplement, officially scheduled to expire after six years) had, apparently by administrative inadvertence, been extended (to follow Janz's account), from the six years first awarded to ten years. Nietzsche had thus benefitted from four years of overpayment of funds to which he was not entitled, whereby the original pension limits would have been, to repeat Janz' lapidary articulation: "*weit überschritten*."[59]

Illness (and Nietzsche was always ill) and mortality, given his father's early death, along with what would in end-effect have been insuperable debt could not but have been on Nietzsche's mind. Nietzsche was not *likely* to run out of money: he had done that. 'Underwater,' in past-due debt, he would have owed repayment for pension funds overpaid, the same money he still needed to live. Thus Nietzsche's need to support himself as author—*Why I Write Such Excellent Books*—meant that *new* editions of extant books would have been of more immediate or practical urgency beyond any search for popularity as we understand this today,[60] even beyond a planned masterwork, no matter whether 'The Will to Power' or 'Revaluation of Values,' etc. Such could come, but only after Nietzsche had resolved the economic challenges of everyday life. Thus Dave Allison, agreeing with Crawford, suggested Nietzsche's last postcards be read as testifying to a deliberate collapse.

There is additional discussion needed to raise the question of the different psycho-pharmaceuticals Nietzsche was prescribed in addition to the more popular studies that have focused on the drugs Nietzsche self-prescribed throughout his life.[61] The side-effects of these would complicate the psycho-pharmaceutic treatments prescribed beginning with his collection in Turin before his transport to Switzerland and continuing in Germany, all involving drugs to contain/control symptoms that whether feigned to begin with or not could not but become, that is just how psycho-pharmaceuticals work, all-too-real in the end.

If there was an Ariadne-Dionysus death cult, and if, in death, Ariadne would be redeemed or transfigured by Dionysus, in his lifetime, Nietzsche would have no salvation, no 'safety': his 'madness' and his silence assured until the day he died by his mother, his sister, and, above all, by pharmaceutical ministrations.

Acknowledgment

A preliminary draft of this essay was written at the invitation of Carlos Segovia for his collective project on the complex (and contested) topic of "conceptual *personnae*." The current version draws on a lecture presented for Tracy Strong, *in memoriam*, at the Nietzsche Society meeting, October 2022 at Texas A&M.

Endnotes

1.   Jacques Derrida, "Otobiographies: The teaching of Nietzsche and the Politics of the Proper Name," trans. Avital Ronell in: *The Ear of the Other: Otobiography, Transference, Translation: Texts and Discussions with Jacques Derrida* (New York: Schocken Books, 1985), 1-38.

2. Erich F. Podach, *Ein Blick in Notizbucher Nietzsches: Ewige Wiederkunft, Wille zur Macht, Ariadne* (Heidelberg: Verlag Rothe Drucke, 1963). And see, for brevity, Gilles Deleuze, "Ariadne's Mystery," *ANY: Architecture New York*, No. 5, Lightness (March/April 1994): 8-9 and Derrida, *The Ear of the Other: Otobiography, Transference, and Translation ... Discussions with Jacques Derrida*, Peggy Kamuf, trans. See for example, and indebted to the literary scholar, Wolfram Groddeck, Claus Zittel's "'Gespräche mit Dionysos'. Nietzsches Rätselspiele," *Nietzsche-Studien*, 47 (2018): 70-99. And see too, importantly, Andreas Urs Sommer, *Kommentar zu Nietzsches "Jenseits von Gut und Böse"* (Berlin: de Gruyter, 2016).

3. See Adrian Del Caro, "Symbolizing Philosophy. Ariadne and the Labyrinth," *Nietzsche-Studien*, 17 (1988): 125-157, here 125.

4. Claudia Crawford, *To Nietzsche: Dionysus, I Love You! Ariadne* (Albany: State University of New York Press, 1995) and see Karsten Harries, "Nietzsche's Labyrinths: Variations on the Ancient Theme" in: Alexandre Kostka and Irving Wohlfarth, eds., *Nietzsche and "An Architecture of Our Minds"* (Los Angeles: Getty, 1999), 35-52.

5. Holger Schmid, "Zur Epistemologie des Labyrinths," *Revue Internationale de Philosophie, Nietzsche*, Vol. 54, No. 211 (March 2000): 135-147. For Schmid, Ariadne's lament may be regarded as "Nietzsche's 'most mysterious poem'"(144), observing that it is Dionysus in his to and fro, his coming and going, that "'is' the labyrinth" (quite as Nietzsche also suggests) and which Schmid connects with Nietzsche's: "Es giebt kein Außen." 146. See further on Dionysus' appearance/disappearance in this respect, Marcel Detienne, *Dionysos at Large* (Cambridge: Harvard University Press, 1989).

6. Kelly Oliver, *Womanizing Nietzsche: Philosophy's Relation to the "Feminine"* (New York: Routledge, 1995).

7. Richard Kuhns, "The Rebirth of Satyr Tragedy in *Ariadne auf Naxos*: Hofmannsthal and Nietzsche," *The Opera Quarterly* (January 1, 1999): 435-448.

8. Krell cites the 1977 English translation but see Karl Reinhardt, "Nietzsches Klage der Ariadne" in Reinhardt's important: *Vermächtnis der Antike. Gesammelte Essays zur Philosophie und Geschichtsschreibung* (Göttingen 1960), 310-333, quite in addition to Hellmut Flashar, "Die Klage der Ariadne," *Hyperboreus* 16/17 (2010/2011): 501-512.

9. Krell, *Postponements: Woman, Sensuality and Death in Nietzsche* (Bloomington, 1986).

10. See, for an object compilation of sources, Richmond Yancey Hathorn, *Greek Mythology* (Beirut: University of Beiruth Press, 1977).

11. See on Dionysus and Sabazius in Ancient Rome, Robert Turcan, *The Cults of the Roman Empire* (Oxford: Blackwell, 1996), 291f.

12. Britt-Mari Näsström, "The Rites in the Mysteries of Dionysus: The Birth of the Drama, *Scripta Instituti Donneriani Aboensis*, 18 (January 2003): 139-148, here: 142, citing Turcan, *The Cults of the Roman Empire*, 312-314. Cf. with respect to the fifth century CE poet, Nonnus, David Hernández de la Fuente, "The Awakening of Ariadne in Nonnus: A Deliberate Metaphor" in: Filip Doroszewski and Katarzyna Jażdżewska, eds., *Nonnus of Panopolis in Context III: Old Questions and New Perspectives* (Amsterdam: Brill, 2020), 226-247. Oddly even those who write directly on Nonnus do not discuss Nietzsche save peripherally, perhaps (oddly) assuming that Nietzsche did not know Nonnus, thus Robert Shorrock, author of *The Myth of Paganism: Nonnus, Dionysus and the World of Late Antiquity* (London: Duckworth, 2011) manages to make no mention of Nietzsche apart from the opposition between Apollo and Dionysus, which Shorrock does note. But Nietzsche (one really has to emphasize that this should go without saying) discusses Nonnus and his Dionysiaca in his Basel lecture courses on Greek Literature. See, for example, KGW II5, 70f. Cf. Carlos A. Segovia, "Rethinking Dionysus and Apollo: Redrawing Today's Philosophical Chessboard," *Open Philosophy* 5 (2022): 360-380.

13.   See for one discussion of the motif, including the conflation of sleeping maenads 'discovered' by marauding satyrs depicted " with arm arched over her head, the stock gesture indicating sleep and perhaps sexual vulnerability" with reference to a 5th C. BCE kylix by Makron held at the Boston Museum of Fine Arts as see Lillian Joyce, "Ariadne Transformed in Pompeii's House of Fabius Rufus" in Maura K. Heyn and Ann Irvine Steinsapir, eds., *Icon, Cult, and Context Sacred Spaces and Objects in the Classical World* (Los Angeles: The Cotsen Institute of Archaeology Press, 2016), 47-64, here p. 49, although it is somewhat dissonant to describe the scene as illustrated (Joyce's Fig. 5.2, p. 50) in tems of possible, i.e., of 'perhaps sexual vulnerability' just given that the scene depicted is an edge scene of an unpleasant ('unpleasant' once again for whom?) awakening for the sleeping maenad.

14.   See Hathorne cited above for collected loci and cf. John Forsdyke, "Minos of Crete," *Journal of the Warburg and Courtauld Institutes*, Vol. 15, No. 1/2 (1952): 13-19.

15.   See the first chapter, "Entstehungsgeschichte. Die Vorplatoniker" of my *Nietzsches Antike: Beiträge zur Altphilologie und Musik* (Berlin: Nomos/Academia Verlag, 2020), especially in connection with Nietzsche on the ancient notion of teacher-student succession: 36f.

16.   See Paul Deussen, *Erinnerungen an Friedrich Nietzsche* (Leipzig: F. A. Brockhaus, 1901). This is also available in an old translation into English by Paul Carus. And see too Udo Friedrich, "Die Paradigmatik des Esels im enzyklopädischen Schrifttum des Mittelalters und der frühen Neuzeit," *Zeitschrift für Germanistik*, Neue Folge, Vol. 25, No. 1 (2015): 93-109.

17.   Norman E. Land, "A Concise History of the Tale of Michelangelo Biagio da Cesena," *Source: Notes in the History of Art*, Vol. 32, No. 4 (2013): 15-19.

18.   Horst Bredekamp, *Michelangelo* (Berlin: Wagenbuch, 2021).

19.   Ibid., 527.

20.   Although my attention to discomfit is not his theme, see Paul Barolksy, "The Meanings of Michelangelo's Minos," *Source: Notes in the History of Art*, Vol. 25, Nr. 4 (Summer 2006): 30-31.

21.   Europa was the mother of three sons with Zeus, hence genealogies matter. See for discussion, P. B. S. Andrews, "The Myth of Europa and Minos," *Greece & Rome*, Vol. 16, No. 1 (Apr., 1969): 60-66.

22.   See for discussion Maria H. Loh, "New and Improved: Repetition as Originality in Italian Baroque Practice and Theory," *The Art Bulletin*, Vol. 86, No. 3 (2004): 477-504.

23.   See Babich, "Nietzsche's Ariadne: On Asses's Ears in Botticelli/Dürer – and Poussin's *Bacchanale.*" *Open Philosophy*, Vol. 5 (4 Aug 2022): 570-60. https://www.academia.edu/84112636/Nietzsches_Ariadne_On_Assess_Ears_in_Botticelli_D%C3%BCrer_and_Poussins_Bacchanale.

24.   There is a published version, "Retrieving Agamben's Questions," *FORhUM Forum za Humanistiko Forum für Humanwissenschaften/Forum pour les sciences humaines/Forum per gli studi umanistici Forum for the Humanities*, 28 May 2020 http://www.for-hum.com/ , online, but see, likewise, online my blogpost of this essay, for illustrations: https://babettebabich.uk/tag/the-myth-of-sisyphus/.

25.   See Babich, "Between Nietzsche and de Beauvoir: Becoming Woman," *Estudios Nietzsche: Nietzsche und die Frau*, 23 (2023). 15-45.

26.   Babich, "Nietzsches hermeneutische phänomenologische Wissenschaftsphilosophie. Unzeitgemäße Betrachtungen zu Altphilologie und Physiologie" in: Helmut Heit, Günther Abel, Marco Brusotti, eds., *Nietzsches Wissenschaftsphilosophie/Nietzsches Philosophie of Science* (Berlin: de Gruyter, 2012), 291-311.

27.   In my own life time as a scholar, what had been the Kirk/Raven edition of *The Presocratic Philosophers* would be augmented in Kirk/Raven/Schofield by their chapter "The Forerunners of Philosophical Cosmogony" — a bit of a misnomer as Carlo

Rovelli and others like Paul Feyerabend and Thomas Kahn and F. M. Cornford told us for years that *Philosophical* Cosmogony is, morning star/evening star, *Scientific* Cosmogony. See for one helpfully historical reflection, Jan Bremer's "Rationalization and Disenchantment in Ancient Greece: Max Weber among the Pythagoreans and Orphics?" in: R. Buxton, ed., *From Myth to Reason? Studies in the Development of Greek Thought* (Oxford: Oxford University Press, 1999), 71-83.

28. Not here that this is a locus that would inspire Hans Vaihinger's 'fictionalism' but not less further reflections on axiomatic systems in astronomy and cosmology continuing to this day. I talk about some of this in an essay on Kant and Nietzsche's philosophy of science that appeared last year, Babich, "On the Very Idea of a Philosophy of Science: On Chemistry and Cosmology in Nietzsche and Kant," *Axiomathes. Special Issue Epistemologia*, 31/6 (December, 2021): 703-726.

29. Thus Nietzsche cites Kant. Cf. "Now, I confidently apply this concept to my present enterprise. I summon up the material stuff of all worlds in a universal confusion and create out of this a perfect chaos. According to the established laws of attraction, I see matter developing and modifying its motion through repulsion. Without the assistance of arbitrary fictions, I enjoy the pleasure of seeing a well-ordered totality emerge under the influence of the established laws of motion, something which looks so similar to the same planetary system which we see in front of us, that I cannot prevent myself from believing that it is the same. ... 'Give me only the material, and I will create a world out of it for you.'" *Preface* to Immanuel Kant, *Universal Natural History And Theory Of The Heavens Or An Essay On The Constitution And The Mechanical Origin Of The Entire Structure Of The Universe Based On Newtonian Principles* (1755). Georg Reimer's edition of the complete works of Immanuel Kant (1905). Taken from Ian Johnston's online translation: https://johnstoi.web.viu.ca/kant/kant2e.htm.

30. See on this, Milič Čapek's several essays on cosmological proofs for eternal recurrence, for example, "The Theory of Eternal Recurrence in Modern Philosophy of Science, with Special Reference to S. C. Peirce," *Journal of Philosophy*, 57 (1960): 289-96. I cite this along with the relevant constellation in Nietzsche's writing in my *Nietzsche's Philosophy of Science* and elsewhere including my edited volumes on *Nietzsche and the Sciences*. And see for a useful discussion especially re Nietzsche's sources, Paolo D, Iorio, "Nietzsche et l'éternel retour. Genèse et interprétation" in: *Nietzsche. Cahiers de l'Herne* (Paris: l'Herne, 2000), 361-389 in addition to Juliano C. S. Neves, "Nietzsche for Physicists," *Open Edition Journals* (2016). Online: https://arxiv.org/pdf/1611.08193.pdf.

31. See for discussion of Nietzsche on the acroamatic as such in a broader context, along with further references, my "On Distinguishing the Acroamatic from the Dogmatic," *Journal for the Philosophical Study of Education*, Vol. 4 (2023): xii-xix.

32. I argue that this has much to do with the fact that Nietzsche's posthumous works were published– in full–only late in the last century, although his notebooks were fully available to the editors of early editions of his completed works. See, again, the first chapter to my *Nietzsche's Antike*, cited above.

33. Tracing as this is key to the etymological method, i.e., philological hermeneutics, Nietzsche highlights in a Nachlass note dating from the time of his Basel lecture courses, "Ζόννυξος im Lesbisch-aeolischen Dialekt. /Ursprünglich wohl Διόνῡξος). Dies führt auf einen Stamm νεκ also νεκρός usw – *neco*. //... Kuretenkult des Zeus ursprünglich. / Ζόννυξος ist der todte Zeus: oder der 'tödtende Zeus' – Zeusjäger = Ζαγρεύς und ὑώμηρτής." (KSA 7, 82)

34. See Jacques Taminiaux, *Le théâtre des philosophes. La tragédie, l'être, l'action* (Grenoble: Jérôme Millon, 1995) in addition to Tracy B. Strong, "Where Are We When We Are Beyond Good and Evil: Nietzsche and the Law," *Cardozo Law Review*, Vol. 24, No. 2 (2003): 101-127.

35.   Martin Vogel, "Der Schlauch des Marsyas," *Rheinisches Museum für Philologie, Neue Folge*, 107. Bd., 1. H. (1964): 34-56.

36.   Babich, *Nietzsches Antike*, iv. And for further references, 312ff. Cf. Titian's painting of the same flaying of Marsyas for greater verisimilitude and, oddly, thus less jarring. See for discussion, Anthony Apesos, "Titian's 'Flaying of Marsyas': 'Colorito' Triumphant," *Artibus et Historiae*, Vol. 39, No. 77 (2018): 111-143, here 111.

37.   Marcel Detienne, *Apollon le couteau à la main. Une approche expérimentale du polythéisme grec* (Paris: Gallimard, 1998).

38.   See David Creese, *The Origin of the Greek Tortoise Shell Lyre*, PhD Diss., Dalhousie, 1997.

39.   See further Babich, "Nietzsche und die reine Musikalität des Dionysischen: Rhythmus und Dithyrambus" my last chapter, in *Nietzsches Antike*, 299ff, especially my reference to the work of the archaeo-musicologist, Richard Dumbrill on the challenges of reconstructing the silver lyre of Ur (312-314) by contrast with Martha Mass and Jane Snyder's research on the relative lack of physical evidence permitting the reconstruction of Greek lyres and other stringed instruments (328-330). Thus Nietzsche is hardly the only one to make this observation, as Mass and Snyder observe (albeit after making it explicit that they are not/would not be reading Nietzsche), "Whereas Egyptologists can study a number of harps, lutes, and lyres, as well as instruments of other kinds, often preserved in excellent condition, Hellenists have almost nothing except some ivory ornaments and facings, a few plektra, and fragments of tortoise shells." Martha Mass and Jane Snyder, *Stringed Instruments of Ancient Greece* (New Haven: Yale University Press, 1989), xvi-xvii. See too a recent discussion, which repeats on the very first page "the shadow of Nietzsche's Apollonian/Nietzschean dichotomy," in an (uncited) echo of Mass and Snyder, Theodor E. Ulieriu-Rostás, "Dionysiac Strings? Towards An Iconographic Reassessment of Late 5th and Early 4th Century Athenian Perceptions of Mousike?" in: Luigi Bravi, et al. ed., *Ultra Lyra e Aulos. Traduzioni Musicali e Genera Poetici* (Pisa: Fabrizio Serra Editore, 2016), 327-354.

40.   In André Laks, *The Concept of Presocratic Philosophy* (Princeton University Press, 2018) Laks assesses Zeller and Diels as "just as much 'inventors of the Presocratics' as is Nietzsche, to whom this title has been attributed because of the decisive role he played in the extraordinary philosophical and intellectual prominence they enjoyed in the twentieth century." 21. Cf., here, as despite his own philological emphases, Laks does not discuss as Jaap Mansfeld and David Runia do, the initial plan that set Nietzsche and Diels together on the project Diels would finish alone, or indeed the relevance of Nietzsche's extensive source scholarship on Diogenes Laertius, the first chapter, "Entstehungsgeschichte" in Babich, *Nietzsches Antike*.

41.   I recommend the title page of Joel Relihan's recent translation of "Lucian (?)," if only, and there are abundant other reasons, for its clarification/exemplification of questions attending scholarly attributions which Relihan precises at the level of the title: "The Tale of Lucius Or, The Ass (*Onos*) An anonymous Greek reworking (doubtfully attributed to Lucian) of the lost, anonymous Greek *Metamorphoseis* (falsely attributed to Lucius of Patras)" (Indianapolis: Hackett, 2023).

42.   "the best way of life, the kind that one would choose if one's right mind." See Lucian, *Three Menippean Fantasies*, trans. Relihan (Indianapolis: Hackett, 2021), 14.

43.   I take this up, including related citations, in a chapter on the eroticism of Nietzsche's description of statues–and the sublime in an erotic context, "Zarathustras Statuen" in Babich, *Nietzsches Plastik. Ästhetische Phänomenologie im Spiegel des Lebens* (Oxford/Berlin: Peter Lang, 2021), 217f. and earlier (in several essays) discussing Nietzsche and Archilochus–and lyric poetry.

44. John Elbert Wilson, *Schelling und Nietzsche zur Auslegung der frühen Werke Friedrich Nietzsches* (Berlin: de Gruyter, 1996), 334.

45. Martin Luther, *Wider das Papstthum zu Rom, vom Teufel gestiftet* (Wittemberg: Durch Hans Lufft, 1545). There is, if anything might go without saying, a correspondingly large literature on this.

46. Luther, *Wider das Papstthum zu Rom*, 228.

47. Robert Bernasconi, "*Ne sutor ultra crepidam*: Erasmus and Dürer at the Hands of Panofksy and Heidegger" in: *Heidegger in Question: The Art of Existing* (Atlantic Highlands: Humanities Press, 1996), 117-134. Cf., too, the art historian, E.H. Gombrich, likewise concerned, as Bernasconi is concerned, with verisimilitude, although perhaps closer to Patrick Aidan Heelan's studies of Cezanne and Van Gogh in his *Space-Perception and the Philosophy of Science* (Berkeley: University of California Press, 1983) in a medieval *and* renaissance perceptual context, not unrelated to Merleau-Ponty's own analyses of color, Gombrich's signal essay in his *The Heritage of Apelles* (London: Phaidon, 1994 [1976]), 1-19.

48. See again my earlier discussion where, among others, I cite David Cast's *The Calumny of Apelles: A Study in the Humanist Tradition* (New Haven: Yale, 1981).

49. See for an overview, very much as an articulation of ekphrasis as such, and with a range of references, including a lovely representation/discussion of Lysippos' *Kairos* (39f), Barbara Borg: "Bilder zum Hören–Bilder zum Sehen: Lukians *Ekphraseis* und die Rekonstruktion antiker Kunst Werke," *Millennium*, Vol. 1 (2004): 25-57.

50. See too Babich, "Ageing, Aura, and Vanitas in Art: Greek Laughter and Death," *Slovak Journal of Aesthetics*, Vol. 12, No. 1 (2023): 56-86.

51. See further, my "Nietzsche's *Antichrist*: The Birth of Modern Science out of the Spirit of Religion" in: Markus Enders and Holger Zaborowski, eds., *Jahrbuch für Religionsphilosophie* (Freiburg i. Briesgau: Alber, 2014), 134-154.

52. Babich, "L'atmosphère, le parfum et la politique de l'utopie : Lucien, Nietzsche, et Illich," *Diogène. Revue internationale des sciences humaines*, n° 273-274 (janvier-juin 2021 [2022]): 124-46.

53. Lucian, "Menippus or the Consultation of the Corpses" in *Three Menippean Fantasies*, here referring to "the disciples and successors of Zoroaster," 14.

54. I cite here Reg Hollingdale's translation of Nietzsche, in *Dionysus Dithyrambs* (London: Anvil Press Poetry, 1984), 33. Cf., in the same Dithyramb, of 'round, maiden gullets,' Babich, *Nietzsches Antike*, 332.

55. In what is either a misprint or an oversight, *both* blinded eyes and stopped up ears are (inaccurately) attributed to "Oedipus" in the Stanford edition of *Beyond Good and Evil*.

56. Thomas Szasz famously made this case in *The Myth of Mental Illness: Foundations of a Theory of Personal Conduct* (New York: Harper and Row, 1961) an argument that would be understood as Szasz pointed out that there was no physiological way to differentiate between a patient suffering mental illness, a patient pretending to suffer mental illness, and a healthy patient. As Szasz himself reprised his claim, retrospectively, in 2011: this amounted to "the systematic misinterpretation of unwanted behaviours as the diagnoses of mental illnesses pointing to underlying neurological diseases susceptible to pharmacological treatments." Szasz, "The Myth of Mental Illness: 50 Years Later," *The Psychiatrist*, 35/5 (2011): 179-182. In an overview of the ongoing lack of fundamental research–most drugs are repurposed and mood benefits claimed anecdotally, Ross J. Baldessarini, confirming (without mentioning his name) Szasz's intitial claim, updated to reflect present diagnostic techniques: "As increasingly technically sophisticated and detailed information is developed in such fields as neuroimaging and neurogenetics, we are repeatedly reminded that almost all major mental disorders remain fundamentally idiopathic."

Most lack not only known etiologies but also even a coherent pathophysiology" and emphasizing, as he repeats, "that the disorders considered to lie within the province of psychiatry remain idiopathic." Baldessarini, "The Impact of Psychopharmacology on Contemporary Psychiatry," *Can J Psychiatry*, 59(8) (2014 Aug): 401-405, here 402. Baldessarini is the author of *Chemotherapy in Psychiatry: The Pharmacologic Basis of Treatments for Major Mental Illness* (New York: Springer Press, 2013). See too from an insider's perspective that does not disagree with these fundamental claims and featuring a a fairly unambiguous title, Edward Shorter's *The Rise and Fall of the Age of Psychopharmacology* (Oxford: Oxford University Press, 2021).

57. Several years ago Michael P. Hengartner, argued with respect to anti-depressants across the board, i..e, not specific to one drug or another, that "Due to several flaws such as publication and reporting bias, unblinding of outcome assessors, concealment and recoding of serious adverse events, the efficacy of antidepressants is systematically overestimated, and harm is systematically underestimated." Among the listed side-effects are "Insomnia, fatigue, loss of appetite, psychomotor agitation, and suicidal acts are recognized depression symptoms, but newer-generation antidepressants may cause precisely these symptoms. This is not what we would expect from drugs that effectively treat depression. Moreover, emerging evidence from well-controlled long-term pharmacoepidemiologic studies suggests that antidepressants may increase this risk of serious medical conditions, including dementia, stroke, obesity, and all-cause mortality." Hengartner and Plöderl, "Statistically Significant Antidepressant-Placebo Differences on Subjective Symptom-Rating Scales Do Not Prove That the Drugs Work: Effect Size and Method Bias Matter!" *Frontiers in Psychiatry*, 17 October 2018. More recently the argued serontonin causal mechanism has been debunked. Joanna Moncrieff, Ruth E. Cooper, Tom Stockmann, Simone Amendola, Michael P. Hengartner and Mark A. Horowitz, "The Serotonin Theory of Depression: A Systematic Umbrella Review of the Evidence," *Molecular Psychiatry*, 21 June 2021.

58. Things are no different today, as demonstrated more than fifty years ago (without being contravened in the interim, despite circular defenses from the side of psychiatry) by the experiment that led to the publication of David Rosenhan's famous "On Being Sane in Insane Places," *Science*, 179, 4070 (19 January 1973): 250-258. Rosenhan argued, with respect to the power dynamics involved (follow up experiments added race and gender) that the only way to get out after being classified as insane is by agreeing with the diagnosis, humoring the psychiatrist, and persuading them that their treatment is improving one's mental state. See too, in addition to the late editor of this journal, David Allison's work on Munchhausen-by-Proxy syndrome, Rob Wipond, *Your Consent Is Not Required: The Rise in Psychiatric Detentions, Forced Treatment, and Abusive Guardianships* (Dallas: Ben Bella, 2023)

59. Thus see for one discussion, Curt Paul Janz's account of Nietzsche's departure from Basel, including a brief account of his pension, *Friedrich Nietzsche. Biographie. Kindheit, Jugend, Die Basler Jahre* (Frankfurt am Main: Zweitausendeins 1993 [1978]), 848.

60. Cf., for example, Claus-Artur Scheier's edited compilation of Nietzsche's late prefaces, *Ecce auctor : die Vorreden von 1886* (Hamburg: Felix Meiner, 1990) as well distinguishing the sense in which Nietzsche's *Ecce homo* might or might not be read as autobiography, Sarah Kofman, *Explosion I. De l'"Ecce Homo" de Nietzsche* (Paris: Galilée, 1992).

61. See the work, among others, of Peter Sjöstedt-Hughes, "Antichrist Psychonaut: Nietzsche and Psychedelics" in: *Noumenautics: Metaphysics – Meta-Ethics – Psychedelics* (Falmouth: Psychedelic Press, 2015), 59-74, the issue of side effects of therapeutic psycho-pharmaceuticals is something else again although, perforce, compounding these effects.

Eros, Dionysus holding a chelys, and Ariadne. Red figure Kylix, ca. 390 BCE.
British Museum. Public Domain.

Eugène Delacroix, *Automne: Bacchus et Ariane*, 1862.
Museu de Arte de São Paulo - São Paulo, Brazil. Public Domain.

BOOK REVIEWS

CAMBRIDGE INTRODUCTIONS TO
KEY PHILOSOPHICAL TEXTS

Nietzsche's
On the Genealogy of Morality
An Introduction

Lawrence J. Hatab

Nietzsche's
Genealogy of Morality

DAVID OWEN

Nietzsche and
Eternal Recurrence

Bevis E. McNeil

palgrave
macmillan

Nietzsche
on
Love

FRIEDRICH NIETZSCHE
EDITED AND TRANSLATED BY ULRICH BAER

EDINBURGH CRITICAL GUIDES TO NIETZSCHE

Jeffrey Church

Nietzsche's

*Unfashionable
Observations*

David Owen, *Nietzsche's Genealogy of Morality*. London: Routledge, 2007. 192 pp., bibl.; index.

Lawrence Hatab, *Nietzsche's Genealogy of Morality: An Introduction*. Cambridge: Cambridge University Press, 2012. 292 pp., bibl.; index.

The following review essay examines two commentaries on Nietzsche's *On the Genealogy of Morals*. With most review essays, the primary task of the review is to explain the thesis of the book under consideration, to examine whatever merits the book has to offer and to offer criticisms, where appropriate. This essay, however, will deviate. Before reviewing each work, I begin by analyzing the philosophical methods Nietzsche employs in *The Genealogy*. This analysis is important as it will serve as a lens through which I will examine the virtues/problems of each work reviewed. After providing this analysis, I demonstrate that Nietzsche's perspectivism is a key feature to any genealogical inquiry. Finally, I examine the merits of each work, outlining each book's distinctive features, qualities, and problematic aspects.

Philosophical Genealogy

Philosophical genealogy refers to the method of historical and philosophical investigation developed by Friedrich Nietzsche upon his reading of Paul Ree's *The Origin of Moral Sensations*. As the name itself implies, genealogy is a distinct method of practicing philosophy that entails examining the historical origins of present-day philosophical concepts, ideas, practices, emotions, and discourses. The purpose of this examination is to take ideas long thought to be innate, immutable and absolute and instead demonstrate that such entities are constructs of sorts: they are elaborate assemblages constituted from previous concepts, behaviors and, even feelings.

Nietzsche's analysis focuses primarily on tracing the latter of these, for "feelings not thoughts are inherited," he writes in *Daybreak* §30. However, feelings are often beyond one's conscious understanding. They are, as Jon Elster shows all too often perverted and subverted by reason. One cannot understand the purpose, biological or otherwise, of one's feelings by winding one's way through the labyrinth of the mind. Thus, according to Nietzsche, then, the body must serve as the main device a genealogist uses to uncover primal affects to see how such feelings evolved into more complex emotions. In this vein, Nietzsche utilizes the body in two ways: first, he likens the body to a document that is overwritten by history, culture, and religion and yet a document that may be recovered.

Nietzsche's conception of the body as a historical document is evident in section 13 of the second essay of *On the Genealogy of Morals*. Nietzsche there shows that most moralists do not go far enough when it comes to tracing the necessary condition for morality because they are too terrified to undertake the study. For the actual precondition of morality is the creation of memory and to ensure that particular values, precepts, or codes found themselves 'stuck' within the mind of early humans it was necessary that the body be "conditioned" to accept it. Such conditioning, Nietzsche maintains, required torture: the first moral code, consisting of "five or six 'I shall nots'" were only remembered because of this long historical conditioning of the body that preceded it. Thus, it is the genealogist who must unpack the mnemonics that created values. What's more, the only manner in determining how these mnemonics were created is to study the variety of gruesome forms of punishment inflicted on early humans.

The lesson to be learned, Nietzsche evinces, is that one can discover the underpinnings of a concept by examining the sequence of bodily procedures that produced it. In other words, and in a counter-intuitive way, one gets a better understanding of what some idea entails by understanding the how behind the notion. 'How was the idea first ingrained in human beings?' 'How are bodies managed by the idea?' 'How does the idea reconfigure the body?' Indeed, if one were only to understand an idea regarding its content or the what of the notion, for example, e.g., What is justice? Within a defined historical narrative, then one would not be able to go beyond the narrative. Genealogy can go beyond and delve deeper into the roots of some concept, value or practice by showing that the historical self-understanding of the particular object under investigation is but one perspective a historian of morality may use to understand some idea's perceived value.

Nietzsche extrapolates from his analysis of section 13 to create one of the most important distinctions and key methodological procedures of genealogy: one must keep meaning and interpretation separate from the technologies of the body. Nietzsche remarks that, in the case of punishment, for example, the procedural is the enduring part of the punishment, "the custom, the act, the "drama," a certain strict sequence of procedures." The other aspect is the fluid element – the meaning, the purpose, the expectation of punishment, etc. These two aspects are distinct from one another, and we make a grave mistake if we think, as some naïve historians of morality, that the meaning of punishment can be projected back onto the procedures of punishment. That is, the second aspect, the meaning aspect, always comes later; it is a rationalization that is reinterpreted according to the group who is being 'punished.'

This tracing of values to their mnemonic roots causes us to see our values in a different light, so Nietzsche argues. Values such as self-sacrifice, upholding a duty and remembering a promise cannot be decoupled from the very tangible physical forces that shaped, contoured and indeed ingrained themselves within our early ancestors. More pointedly, Nietzsche reveals that such values are informed and driven because they are infused with a particular feeling. For example, failing to uphold a promise may cause us to experience mental anguish and even profound physical suffering, but the reason behind our pain has nothing to do with the promise itself rather Nietzsche declares it has to do with the tortuous breeding our ancestors went through and that we rather miraculously inherited. Anguish and promise keeping were fused not because they are conceptually linked because, say, to break a promise is to break my word and my word is a reflection of my character (this conceptual tethering is a superficial relationship that comes later). Rather, promise-breaking and anguish were fastened to one another through torture. Moreover, we, Nietzsche claims, inherited this emotional fastening from our ancestors. Understanding this dual process of inheritance and tethering, Nietzsche thinks, allows us to see the value (as in the case of promise making) in a different light. It allows the genealogist to take up a new and unique perspective on our historical reality.

Nietzsche, as a genealogist, is at his best when he reveals the genealogical origin of guilt in the second essay of *On the Genealogy of Morals*. According to Nietzsche, guilt is neither something *sui generis* (it is not a gift from God) nor is it a natural development of an instinctual feeling. Guilt is a discrete yet contingent interpretation and evolution of "the bad conscience": a more basic, quasi-physiological response to physical trauma. Guilt, Nietzsche reveals, is a complex physiological, psychological, and social phenomenon. It is a tapestry woven by many weavers using different threads and one that begins with the very looping of the thread of subjectivity itself: the internationalization of our animal-like ancestors via civilization.

The idea that guilt is an original formatting of sorts creating the human being from some "half-animal, half-man creature" because of actions taken by partisan groups with their own values demonstrates that ideas, discourses, and values are born from a struggle for power (GM: II, 16-17) According to Nietzsche, it was the warrior-artists who initiated the process of the creation of the modern subject by first erecting walls in early human communities and secondly inventing painful techniques of torture to deter early humans from climbing them. The result of blocking natural and instinctual desires for adventure, roaming, hunting and the like was the creation of a new type of creature who expressed his will to power inwardly. Our early ancestors' once animal-like drives turned inward carving out the faculties of subjectivity itself in first creating the bad conscience and then more complex attributes such as introspection, conscience, guilt, strategizing and planning, internal monologue, etc.

These warriors, though, were soon displaced by the forerunners of the priestly type: shamans, witch doctors, and soothsayers. In a masterstroke of genius, these proto-religious types re-constellated the bad conscience by giving it meaning: they explained that this negative affect was the result of early humans' unworthiness in the eyes of some god, spirit or other. They used the bad conscience as a tool in their war against the warrior caste for control: they wanted power over the huddled masses of early human communities. The priestly caste re-worked and further advanced the drive toward internalization creating the soul – a substance which could be used for further self-torture. Finally, Nietzsche declares, the invention of an all-powerful God who gave his only Son such that all of humanity would be saved is the coup de grace of this long history in the formation and imprinting of guilt.

The above is a much-simplified story of how the soul as the internalization and redirection of primal appetites came to be formed. Nietzsche fills in these details in the second essay of the genealogy. The point in elaborating on this was to show the history of so-called 'civilization', begins through an act of will to power: the creation of walls is an effort to enslave one group for the sake of increasing another group's power. Genealogy demonstrates that history is not working towards some hidden *telos* as the Whig Historian would have it, but is rather best understood as a struggle between contending forces. Ideas, discourses, practices and even feelings, are the sign-language of evaluation and all evaluation presupposes evaluators. History is a struggle between groups for power.

By unmasking the origin and subsequent lines of descent of a feeling, such as guilt, the philosophical genealogist effectively demonstrates the great sign-chain of interpretations that produced the current emotion. A genealogist's task then, is, ultimately, to unravel the tapestry: to determine the threads used and the tools utilized to weave the threads and the pattern, if any, the threads now make.

The above analysis as to the 'true' origin of guilt is referred to as the diagnostic component to the genealogical inquiry and for a good reason: Nietzsche often called himself a physician of culture. Moreover, like any good doctor, Nietzsche develops a curative component, too. To this end, Nietzsche called genealogy the path to (*gay scienza*) or gay science. Genealogy is a curative science: it exposes the flaws in the tacit beliefs we currently hold to be true. By demonstrating that specific life-denying ideas or feelings long thought to be true, innate, immutable and unchanging, are in fact mutable, contingent and arbitrary, Nietzsche's genealogical investigations allow us to cast doubt on such modes of life thereby enabling us to establish new beliefs and attitudes in order to live more creatively, joyfully and indeed, experimentally than our prior beliefs allowed. Uncovering the sources of our contemporary feelings reveals that our previous understanding and perspective of said values was through a dark and unjustified prism.

Problems with Genealogy

With this short description of genealogy as a method out of the way, I now wish to examine some of the potential problems with the method itself. One problem has to do with the significant difficulties regarding the epistemic justification of genealogy. One rather strong and philosophically interesting reading of the *Genealogy* suggests that the central thesis of the work is to persuade its readers that tools for rational thinking, for judgment, for reasoning are themselves constructions of power. But if this is true, namely, if rationality is itself merely a product of a peculiar confluence of power, then standards of reason, warrant and justification are themselves nothing more than an emergence of a regime of power which takes such rational procedures to be the metric by which some statement is accepted to be true. Statements that purport to be true cannot be decoupled from evaluative claims. Moreover, evaluative claims, so suggests this reading, are shot through with agenda, or perspective. Alastair MacIntyre expresses the shocking and disconcerting consequences of this position well when he writes:

> The ruptures in that history (of science), as identified by Bachelard and Kuhn, moments in which a transition is made from one standardized understanding of what is to be rational to some other, sometimes incommensurable standardized understanding of rationality, are also secondary phenomena. For they, like the standardized orders which they divide and join, are the outcome of assemblages and confluences in the making of which distributions of power have been at work, in such a way that what appear at the surface level as forms of rationality both are and the result from the implementation of a variety of aggressive and defensive strategies, albeit strategies without subjects. Truth and power are thus inseparable. And what appears as projects aimed at the possession of truth are always willful in their exercise of power.

MacIntyre's insightful upshot of genealogy, namely, that truth claims are never value-neutral – they are perspectival – has surprising ethical implications but very troubling epistemic consequences. Turning to the ethical merits of the position first, adopting a perspectivist view allows one to realize that some truth claims such that 'the good shall be saved and the wicked punished' are thought to be true at least to some only because they express a discrete group's system of values. They are not facts that have been discovered. In fact, Nietzsche claims, there is no such thing as a fact: even facts are valuations; they are perspectival. A fact is infused with power, perspective, and agenda.

This realization, however, as to the perspectival nature of facts themselves is freeing so suggests Nietzsche's commentators because it emancipates us from feeling troubling and painful emotions like guilt should we fail to live up to strict codes of Christian conduct for example (if we feel so inclined by our social upbringing). Even though guilt causes us pain, it is not a feeling that denotes a punishment from God. It is a feeling that we inherited in a rather contingent way. Now that we acknowledge that guilt is not metaphysically necessary, it is not a punishment ordained by God, the pain once experienced by this feeling is blunted significantly. With this realization, we may not feel the sting of guilt as we otherwise would.

Turning now to the epistemic issues with perspectivism it may be difficult to interpret, coherently, the claim itself. One question that immediately arises when discussing perspectivism is the following: 'How is perspectivism underwritten?' For notice that if truth statements are themselves merely expressions of value, then what can be said for Nietzsche's own position on perspectivism? Is perspectivism itself merely an evaluation? If so then why believe it? On the other hand, if it is not an evaluation, i.e., it is objectively true, then how does it avoid self-referential contradiction?

A partial solution to assist us in making sense of perspectivism and resolving some of the questions noted above can be gleaned by noting the problems with pure objectivity. In essay three, section 12 of Nietzsche's *On the Genealogy of Moral* we find the most incisive critique of objectivity to be found in Nietzsche's published writings. According to Nietzsche, pure objectivity is incoherent because it postulates a non-relational relationship between the subject of knowledge and the object desired to be known. In more meta-phorical language, Nietzsche claims that pure objectivity entails seeing an object with an "eye turned in no particular direction" and thus paints, in the language of Wittgenstein, an impossible mental 'picture.' Further reflection on this paradoxical 'picture' of know-ledge leads Nietzsche to extol "that there can only be a perspective seeing and a perspective knowing..." and Nietzsche's celebrated doctrine of perspectivism is born.

At this point, things get rather murky: though pure objectivity is clearly impossible, it is unclear exactly what Nietzsche means by "a perspective seeing and a perspective knowing" or indeed what perspectivism entails as a philosophical position proper. For if we may only have perspectives on the world, then how could we ever claim that another perspective is false? It is clear that Nietzsche does believe that some claims are both more epistemically worthy than others and that some claims are simply untrue. In the *Genealogy*, there are several passages where he not only suggests that the English genealogists, such as Herbert Spencer, take the wrong path when it comes to examining the true history of morality, but that Nietzsche's genealogical approach is better justified, epistemically speaking.

These questions must be answered, or so I argue because genealogy as a method stands or falls on the doctrine of perspectivism. Perspectivism is important to genealogy as a method for two reasons. Firstly, perspectivism justifies Nietzsche's most profound claims that facts are infused with value; that such values evolve as the evaluators themselves change and vice versa and that genealogy can provide an accurate tracking of such values. Also, Nietzsche claims that genealogy is superior to other methods of historical inquiry, such as the English method of moral investigation, because it is more in keeping with naturalistic assumptions and therefore inherently more justifiable. The search for objective truth is a fool's errand or so argues Nietzsche; all investigations are conducted with an aim or agenda in mind. Only a genealogical approach for the search for origins is thereby warranted because only genealogy accepts the 'truth' of perspectivism.

Secondly, perspectivism underwrites the great emancipatory power of genealogy: Nietzsche believed himself to be a cultural physician – we are poisoned or so argued Nietzsche by our values. Genealogy allows us to cure us of the poison that we so desperately and inexplicably love. Perspectivism is the essential ingredient to this antidote because it shows that no account has a monopoly on truth; there are different truths and many ways of speaking the truth. It is of paramount importance that the problems raised above are addressed, or otherwise perspectivism becomes just another interesting idea but without epistemic justification.

Lawrence Hatab on Perspectivism
Lawrence Hatab in his book, *Nietzsche's On the Genealogy of Morality: An Introduction* attempts to addresses these related problems of perspectivism by performing an end-run. For Hatab, the epistemic problems noted above are the result of a category mistake. We see a problem with both the epistemic, ontic and ethical problems of perspectivism insofar as we are captured by a false picture: some statements are true and believed to be true while other statements are false but believed to be true. Perspectivism as an epistemic doctrine, we mistakenly believe, or so argues Hatab, must belong to either one or the other category. If this logic holds then perspectivism is either objectively true and therefore false (because it is self-contradictory,) or is merely a perspective and therefore mere subjective opinion. Perspectivism must then be incoherent.

This analysis of perspectivism as an incoherent doctrine, however, presupposes the very categories of subjective and objective that perspectivism seeks to explode. As I understand his position, Hatab argues that the doctrine of perspectivism is a practical "guideline" that emerges from the inexorable truth that life is simply a collection of forces held in tragic, agonic tension. "Accordingly, Nietzsche's texts cannot be reduced to doctrines or positions that call for assessment or philosophical positions such as will to power, perspectivism, and especially eternal recurrence." (17) Nietzsche's position, according to Hatab, is that life cannot be constrained or reduced to some category such as being, for example. "In restoring legitimacy to conditions of becoming, Nietzsche advances what I call an existential naturalism. The finite unstable dynamic of earthly existence – and its meaningfulness – becomes the measure of thought." (9) Furthermore, life cannot be restricted to a process or higher synthesis a la Hegel. Life cannot be construed as the synthesis of being and becoming and nor can such a synthesis represent a stepping stone to some higher, syncretic fusion. "Life," according to Hatab's reading of Nietzsche is essentially anti-binary: it is a flow of tensions, a continuum of inconsistencies, a co-mingling of contrary feelings. Perspectivism is the only epistemic doctrine we can fathom as humans that best represents this 'essential' anti-binary 'feature' of life (137). Perspectivism allows us to recognize multiple meanings in the world while keeping the tragic forces of life at bay. Perspectivism affords Nietzsche to recognize the truths contained in conflicting positions, which, according to binary thinking, are logically contrary and, therefore, irreconcilable. This recognition so argues Hatab, provides us with a deeper comprehension of life because we are attempting to understand life according to its full, immanent logic. Hatab's interpretation of the *Genealogy* suggests that we can better glean the perspectival nature of life itself by viewing it from within the context of Greek tragedy.

According to Hatab, Nietzsche seeks to reinvigorate the spirit of Greek tragedy and claims that in accepting such a spirit we lead more joyful and, presumably, authentic lives. The essential plank in the Greek narrative was the recognition that mortals were not the central players on the stage of history. Mortals were at the mercy of the gods; essentially they were the gods' playthings. But the idea that mortals were the mere toys of the gods, strangely, did not prevent the Greeks from participating in their Dionysian festivals nor from producing the great works of Greek tragedy. The Greeks recognized that ecstatic joy and profound despair were two sides of the same coin: on which side the coin would land was something determined by fate.

The Greeks embodied the spirit of *amor fati* – the love of fate. *Amor fati* is one of the most important and well – known virtues extolled by Nietzsche, but unfortunately, the conceptual characteristics of the idea are not always well-explained in the secondary literature. For example, is *amor fati* necessarily grounded on eternal recurrence or can it be naturalized? If the former, can it be equated "with love of destiny?" If the latter, then can we equate *amor fati* with love of physiology? Implicit in Hatab's reverence for the Greek affirmation of life, I would suggest that he holds a third interpretation. For Hatab, *amor fati* means "love of agon."

To love of *agon*, as the Greeks did, is to embrace two notions: 1) that one is at the mercy of the gods; the gods perpetually and without warning interfere in the lives of mortals. 2) One is free to acquiesce to this in this overarching schema or to resist it. Hatab illustrates this point in a rather lengthy excursus on the subject of Agamemnon's theft of Briseis – a maiden of Troy who was initially claimed by Achilles as a prize of war. Agamemnon never regretted his 'decision' to steal Briseis away from Achilles. Although Agamemnon's action is considered ignoble, at least to Achilles's lights, and to some extent by Agamemnon, it becomes clear that Agamemnon had no control over his actions; a god possessed him. Agamemnon's behavior leads to Achilles' refusal to return to the battlefield which in turn leads to the deaths of many Achaeans as the tide of war begins to turn in favor of the Trojans.

Given the Greeks' misfortunes of this singular event, one would think that Agamemnon would curse the god or gods who used him as a puppet. But he does not do this. Instead Agamemnon offers an "acceptance speech" as it were. Quoting Hatab, Agamemnon says:

> "I am not responsible, he says, because Zeus and the fates cast upon my heart a fierce delusion that day, when in my arrogance I took from Achilles his prize. But, what could I do? It is god that brings all things to completion." (59)

The notion that the gods could interfere with our very psychological make-up at any time to the extent that we feel what they want us to feel is deeply disturbing. Bizarrely, Agamemnon seems indifferent to this actuality. Hatab writes: "Yet the heroes do not seem to rebel against such intercessions as diminishments of their worth or to bemoan ruinous consequences as unfair or wretched enslavement to cruel deities. Once again, the Homeric self is a confluence of fate and freedom, of noble achievement in the midst of forces larger than its own efforts." (59) Though the ancient Greek did not have control over his life, he was able to affirm his own existence. Hatab uses the above intuition, drawn as it is from the well-spring of ancient Greek thought, fruitfully, as he then presents his own interpretation of *amor fati*, grounded as it is on the above insight.

Hatab employs this interpretation to extricate Nietzsche from of the moral entanglements produced by an acceptance of eternal recurrence. In a section entitled "Eternal Recurrence and Moral Tragedy," Hatab argues that the most incisive critical response to the idea of eternal recurrence is the moral repugnance objection. From an uncritical interpretation of eternal recurrence, Nietzsche is asking us to affirm all historical events: good, bad or morally indifferent. However, this interpretation is problematic for several reasons. Firstly, it is too much to ask for humans to affirm this notion because it is clearly impossible; if we are honest with ourselves we cannot affirm all events in our lives unedited – we cannot help contem-plating "what ifs" and wishing for "do-overs." (201) Secondly, to avow all historical events is to avow heinous actions undertaken by others. This affirmation would effectively mean that I must affirm such events as the Holocaust while being unable to prevent them from happening. And as Magnus, whom Hatab quotes, suggests, only a detached god (or perhaps psychopath) could affirm such atrocities. (199)

Hatab suggests that we may resolve this problem by reassigning what we are affirming. According to Hatab, what Nietzsche is asking us to affirm is not the event itself, but the perturbation provoked by the event in question. Thus, the eternal recurrence requires that we accept (but not to affirm) the cyclical pattern of history vis a vis as cycle of events but asks us to affirm the reactions we have to said events. As Hatab writes: "Eternal recurrence, therefore, cannot entail the approval of everything that returns. If I will the return of something I find heinous, I also will the return of my opposition to it." (201) To love fate is to accept the external events of history, without qualification, exactly as they happened but also to affirm our opposition to these events again and again and again. Concluding his view on *amor fati*, Hatab writes: "Amor fati cannot mean the indiscriminate love of all things but rather the love of the agonistic necessity that intertwines everything." (201) This agonistic necessity is the tragic Greek love described above: it is a love of one's station in life, a love of godly intercession, a love of glory. But above all, it is a love of competition – it is a love of struggling against enemies both mortal and immortal alike.

Hatab's thesis, namely, that Nietzsche seeks to re-inject a tragic sensibility into modern living is insightful, fecund and deeply profound. As well, Hatab provides a brilliant new interpretation of *amor fati* that resolves some of the issues regarding eternal recurrence discussed in the secondary literature. I do not wish to critique Hatab on these points. What I take issue with is Hatab's construal of perspectivism itself. In a sense, I think there is a way to eat one's perspectival cake and have it too, without creating a two-world distinction to which Hatab eventually succumbs. One may adopt a perspectival position while also acknowledging that some positions are less justified than others.

Here I turn to examine Hatab's definition of perspectivism: "There are many possible takes on the world, and none could count as exclusively correct." (15) I call this position naïve perspectivism because it would seem to assume a whole host of theses both epistemic and ontological that go unrecognized. As I see it, there are several problems with this position as stated here. First, it is important to recognize that the above sentence makes two epistemic claims. The first is that there are in fact different "takes" or "perspectives" but, and this is crucial, that all such "takes" refer to the same world. Thus, just as one might acknowledge that there can be different interpretations of the same text, it is agreed that all interpretations refer to the same object, namely, the text itself. To concretize this insight we might say that it is possible for two scholars to have very different views on say Descartes' *Meditations*, but both interpreters recognize that they are referring to the same text; one is not confusing the text with a blender. However, this analogy does not work in the context of naïve perspectivism. For the perspectivist cannot know whether all perspectives refer to the same object, namely the world, without undermining her very position. To make such a claim would be to hold either an aperspectival view on the world itself (but what is the world independently of a perspective?) or perhaps to claim that all perspectives ultimately refer to some non-object such as a plenum of absolute agonic becoming. The first position is self-contradictory. The second leads to self-contradiction or to a position that is by its nature non-cognitive and therefore incomprehensible.

Hatab opts for the second of these choices and in my view, attributes a two-world view to Nietzsche and thus turns Nietzsche into an idealist of some stripe. For according to his interpretation, Nietzsche is still committed to the existence of a 'world,' tragic and incomprehensible though it may be, which exists independently of a perspective. Although the world is perhaps best described as a "plenum of agonic becoming", notice that it can still be described independently of a perspective. Notice, also, that if one were unable to describe even this "baseline" notion of the world, namely, the intuition that the world, at the heart of its core is tragic, then Hatab's position would be breathtakingly incoherent. This interpretation is confirmed in several places. I quote two representative passages: "Throughout his writings, Nietzsche affirms a dark, tragic truth of becoming, in that conditions of becoming must be accepted as a baseline notion that renders all forms and conditions ultimately groundless." (131) And more affirmatively and with more gusto, Hatab proclaims:

> Nietzsche does have a global position, namely perspectivism, in the sense that the life-world is a field of perspectives, each willing its own life interests; as perspectives in the field of becoming, however, none can pose as the "truth. (136-137).

Again, what justification can Nietzsche submit for the belief that there is, in fact, a field of perspectives that emerge from the tragic flow of becoming? Is it not the case that Hatab's "tragic field of becoming" might not be just another perspective within this field? If so, is the position not inconsistently proclaiming to represent the "truth" that there are only perspectives? If, on the other hand, agonic becoming is not a perspective, then there is a "truth" beyond this field of perspectives. Then the field itself, however, is but mere phenomenal appearance when compared to the noumenal, yet dynamic field of pure becoming.

Turning to the second claim, namely that "no perspective is exclusively correct" or as stated immediately above, "none can pose as the "truth" examine the following simplistically crude position: "Christians, Muslims, and Jews have different perspectives on the same God." Although each religion has a different perspective on the same object, it is entirely possible that one perspective is correct. It is possible that one religion has the correct view. However, naive perspectivism inexplicably and unjustifiably claims that neither one of these perspectives is "exclusively correct" because they are "mere explanations – attempts to will something, anything," Hatab's Nietzsche would surely declare in that each of the above religions requires the postulation of a divine creator, differently conceived according to each culture, in order to cope with the one absolute truth: the tragedy of becoming. Yet, this explanation, uttered as it is by a Hatabian Nietzsche, is an attempt to narrate and reintegrate unique perspectives according to one meta-narrative that itself requires a unargued for postulate.

To be fair, Hatab glimpses some of the difficulties raised above and explicitly acknowledges the merit of the question: "Why should we accept his perspectivism? His judgments and his perspectivism would themselves only amount to a certain perspective." (135) But Hatab's perplexing answer to this straightforward query fails to satisfy: "Nietzsche considers all knowledge and value to be perspectival, he advocates commitment to one's own perspective over others;" and yet Hatab also holds that, "perspectivism is not equivalent to radical skepticism or to the relativistic notion that differing viewpoints are equally valid." (137) These two claims are easily refuted. Firstly, in Essay III: 12, Nietzsche clearly argues for the adoption of a plurality of perspectives and more controversially, that such perspectives must be embodied: "…the more affects we allow to speak about one thing, the more eyes, different eyes, we can use to observe one thing, the more complete will our "concept" of this thing, our 'objectivity' be." Secondly, if there are no facts because facts are indexed to an interpretation then how can differing viewpoints be compared and weighed according to an independent metric that would compare, objectively, the epistemic and veridical merits of each perspective? Again, while this point does not contradict Hatab's claim that Nietzsche is not a relativist, this apparent inconsistency needs to be explained by Hatab and not explained away.

Hatab affirms an immanent logic: a line of reasoning that says that understanding "life" (as a chaotic plenum of becoming incapable of direct understanding) requires that we affirm and examine all narratives which emerge from it. The problem with this view is twofold: 1) that it is just that, a view; immanent logic is but a mere perspective so what justification could one provide to believe it either dogmatically or existentially? Second, immanent logic is too vague to perform any real substantive work toward the comprehension of life itself. Hatab's own definition of immanence is confusing and vacuous because, presumably, it includes every possible force that I believe may be causally efficacious: "Nativistic immanence mandates that we accept as given all forces that we can honestly recognize at work in our lives, from instinct to reason, from war to peace, from nature to culture and so on." (16) But does this mean that immanent logic refers to all forms of reasoning that do not presuppose a divine, transcendent source? If so then it would seem to be just another iteration of some naturalistic position. But what is naturalism? On the other hand, if immanent logic simply denotes the set of all possible forces (physical, social, mental, etc.) that emerge from the agonic tension that is life, or more correctly that I recognize from my perspective as being causally efficacious then such a logic is tautologous and incomprehensible for we are being asked to understand some object by understanding it as an integration of incompatible, overdetermined forces.

Unlike Hatab, David Owen's *Nietzsche's Genealogy of Morality*, focuses more on the emancipatory power of perspectivism than, say, the ontological or epistemic underpinnings of the position. Specifically, Owen concentrates on showing how perspectivism helps to liberate individuals from forms of life that are not necessarily false but limiting in some fashion. There are two steps to revealing how perspectivism is successful in this regard. Firstly, Owen shows how Nietzsche uses perspectivism to demonstrate that alternative narratives are possible in regard to how we have been duped by poisoned belief systems. His account is etiological. Owen wishes to explore the "how" of this account by asking about the mechanics that allowed individuals to be duped into believing life-denying and false forms of life. The second aspect of Owen's account explains how genealogy functions to alleviate us from these very systems of poisoned belief. In brief, Owen argues that the cure is already infused in the diagnosis: because the reader of a genealogy recognizes that an alternative account of some feeling is possible, this recognition leads one to the realization that the narrative from which one understood a particular issue is not absolute.

The cause of moral degeneracy or perhaps more aptly put life degeneracy is an interesting question in the Nietzschean secondary literature. It is a curious question, because genealogy if we recall is both diagnostic and curative: the genealogist is responsible for diagnosing the conditions that led to the rise of herd values or as

Brian Leiter has referred to them, "Morality in a Pejorative Sense," so that such values may be treated, cured. *On the Genealogy of Morals*, it is then supposed, possess curative properties: each paragraph of the work helps to cure its' readers of the negative effects of 'Morality in a Pejorative Sense.' But how is the cure effected?

Once more perspectivism is the key to answering this question. Owen argues that in Nietzsche's mature work he "…is committed to the view that one can have beliefs, make statements and so forth, that are true or false." (30) Moreover, Owen is again in agreement with many Nietzschean scholars (including Conway, Leiter and Janaway) when he defines genealogy as a type of naturalized epistemology. However, where Owen differs from most scholars who work on these issues is concerning the status of truth or more aptly put 'truthfulness' in Nietzsche's corpus. For example, Brian Leiter in his work *Nietzsche's Morality* seems to hold that truth is only of instrumental value for genealogy, as genealogy is a tool used for the higher-types (the intended audience of Nietzsche's genealogy according to Leiter) to overcome 'Morality in a Pejorative Sense.

Owen, however, persuasively demonstrates that truth and more perspicuously put Nietzsche's commitment to truthfulness, is intrinsically valuable both for Nietzsche and for the genealogical method. In this manner, any reader (and not just Leiter's higher-type) who is committed to truth will be so affected by *On the Genealogy of Morals* that he or she will come to reconsider the reasons he or she has for believing in both the origin and value of Christian morality. As Owen explains:

> Nietzsche's genealogy of morality aims to show that those who hold this outlook (Christian morality) can only do so by ignoring or falsifying the historical story of how its various elements have emerged and the synthesis of these elements has developed. He does this by constructing what he takes to be a psychologically realistic and historically truthful account of this process and showing that this account cannot be accepted by those who hold the outlook in question in so far as holding this outlook requires that they have beliefs about the origins of the outlook that are incompatible with Nietzsche's account. (150-151).

On this point, I am in complete agreement with Owen. Nietzsche's three genealogies are successful because: 1) Nietzsche's genealogies have a higher commitment to truthfulness than more traditional methods of historiography; and 2) they force the reader to revise his or her views precisely because the account of morality that the reader once accepted is no longer capable of presenting a truthful explanation of morality. In fact, genealogy places such a premium on truthfulness that it freely admits it is polemical: it does not pretend to be objective.

A second important aspect of Owen's conception of the genealogical method has to do with the distinction he makes between ideology critique and genealogy. In an earlier article, Owen articulates the main differences between critical theory and genealogy by showing how each theory diverges with reference "to self-imposed, non-physical constraint on our capacity to self-govern." In the present book, Owen continues to explore the similarities and differences between Frankfurt school philosophers like Habermas, and genealogists like Nietzsche. He shows that where ideology critique is concerned with the self-recognition of agents to understand that they suffer from false consciousness, genealogical critique forces individuals to realize that they suffer from restricted conscious. The differences between false consciousness and restricted consciousness may be summarily stated as follows: individuals are said to suffer from false consciousness when: i) They have false beliefs which legitimize oppressive social institutions, and ii) are also blocked in some way from recognizing the false beliefs they hold (through the media, the educational system, repressive sexual laws, etc). Possessing restricted consciousness, on the other hand, simply entails that the individual is captured by a picture of reality which is neither true nor false in itself, but is taken to be the only frame of reference in which questions regarding the truth and falsity of various issues may be legitimately asked. Put another way, being held captive by a picture involves the agent failing to recognize a second-order belief concerning one's first order belief of a picture, namely, that it may indeed be false. (149) In this sense, being held captive by a picture is more of an active form of self-imposed constraint to self-government because it is a result of the subject accepting (and failing to interrogate) the ways of construing the world that are put to her. Ideology critique, on the other hand, involves a passive element concerning self-imposed immaturity because there is something or someone actively imposing an ideology on the subject. Ideology critique is more focused on revealing the real causal engines for the current stupefaction of the masses. It is assumed that once these conditions are removed that the individual would be cured; they would have access to the truth, and their false consciousness is thereby altered.

Owen is not claiming that the mere removal of the conditions for falsification is sufficient for the individual to arrive at the truth; additional work is required for the individual. The individual would still need to seek out the truth for herself, but notice that there is still a truth to seek. This is not the case for genealogy, or so Owen argues. Genealogy is inherently perspectival. What genealogy does is to show that in entertaining different and perhaps competing perspectives on some notion, such as the origin of Christianity, we are acting virtuously, epistemically speaking. (22-23) We are acknowledging that different perspectives on some notion are possible and this acknowledgment or so claims Owen, paves the way to emancipating us from poisoned belief systems.

As Owen explains further, a genealogy's liberating powers can be attributed to four aspects:

1) It identifies a picture which holds us captive, whereby this captivity obstructs our capacity to make sense of ourselves as agents in ways that matter to us;

2) This account involves a re-description of this picture which contrasts it with another way of seeing the issue to free us from captivity to this picture;

3) It provides an account of how we have become held captive by this picture which enables us to make sense of ourselves as agents and, more particularly, to make sense of how we have failed to make sense of ourselves as agents in ways that matter to us;

4) And in so far as this account engages with our cares and commitments, it motivates us to engage in the practical working out of this re-orientation of ourselves as agents. (149)

One of the chief ways the genealogist uses to jar a reader into re-thinking her understanding and subsequent valuation she gives to some idea is to employ the reader's affects. It is our emotions that cause us to shift our evaluations. "If Nietzsche is (eventually) to bring his readers to take morality as an object of critical reflection and assessment," Owen charges,

a necessary first step in this process is to demonstrate that "morality" is not the only form of ethical reflection and, further, to engage his readers' affects with the form of ethical reflection that he contrasts to morality so as to loosen and account in part for their captivation by this moral perspective. (85)

Owen is at his best when showing how Nietzsche employs rhetoric to render this "loosening" effect on his reader's moral commitments. In chapter five, Owen demonstrates how Nietzsche utilizes a constructed interlocutor, Mr. Daredevil Curiosity, as a tool to engage his reader's affects regarding the true underlying feelings that motivate modern subjects as the inheritors of slave morality. In using this figure, Nietzsche's can stir the emotions of his readers in a way that pure, rational, reflective analysis would fall short and thus provoke them to see slave morality in a very different light. Owen writes: "...Nietzsche's position is placed in the position of acknowledging, through the representative figure of Daredevil Curiosity, the mendacity of slave morality that was not possible for the slaves." (88)

By having the reader trade places with Nietzsche's constructed interlocutor, Owen surmises, the reader comes to realize, that when the slaves call for justice, they call for revenge, among other things. This recognition would not have been available to readers without the use of this literary device.

I think Owen captures the curative powers of genealogical inquiry in this remarkable work. Moreover, I agree with Owen where he states that there is an important difference between genealogy and ideology critique in that the latter has to do with being held captive by an ideology while the former has to do with being held captive by a perspective. With that said, the main problem with Owen's understanding of genealogy is that he believes that ideology critique and genealogical inquiry are not different in kind. Owen construes aspectival captivity as a cerebral, although affectively attenuated, reflective mode of non-physical constraint. Yet, even to claim that both ideology and aspectival captivity are two species within the genus of non-physical forms of constraint to self-government, is to misunderstand how particular values, questions, and truths came to be recognized as the only values, questions and truths considered valid in contemporary society. Herd valuation, Nietzsche is at pains to remind us, invades the body as well as the head. Nietzsche goes to great lengths to remind readers that torture, as a consequence of failing to pay off one's debt, played a pivotal role in the formation of memory which made guilt and Christian morality possible. Having a mistaken picture (aspectival captivity) is not just a form of non-physical constraint which impedes our abilities for self-government a la Marx, but is, in fact, a manifestation of a very real physical production which manufactures – at the very least – parts of the self.

More to the point, Owen fails to acknowledge how exactly the body is affected by power and how, once affected, causes one to close off potential life-affirming viewpoints. Michel Foucault, one of Nietzsche's most insightful commentators, emphasized the importance of the body in relation to genealogical inquiry when he wrote: "Descent (*Entstehung* or the markings of power) attaches itself to the body. It inscribes itself in the nervous system, in temperament, in the digestive apparatus..." While Owen seems to realize this objection in only implicit fashion in his recent book, where he acknowledges that, "Nietzsche's genealogy, in particular, is designed to mobilize our existing affective dispositions against morality" (131), it is difficult to see how this may be accomplished on a purely, reflective level even if one's affects provide a measure of tonality and charge to said reflection.

Part of the problem has to do with Owen's construal of perspectivism and more precisely aspectival captivity. How, we may wonder, does the process of unmooring ourselves from such mistaken pictures occur given Nietzsche's gripping portrayal of the genealogy of the ascetic ideal? Our tremendous capacity to torture ourselves is not something we can "will away" no matter how well we reflect on, and engage with, our emotional propensity to feel shame and guilt (especially when we realize that we are "unproductive" or "wasting time") and that such notions are genealogically, but not conceptually tethered to older emotions.

While Owen is correct in asserting that a successful genealogy does, in fact, mobilize the affects by using a variety of tools such as rhetoric, vivid portrayals of torture and shifting points of view, he has failed to pinpoint the precise manner how this mobilization occurs. (143) In sum, Owen seems to assume that a careful, historical and warranted investigation, albeit one affectively informed, regarding the origins of a Western, Christian moral outlook is sufficient in accounting for the agent's future enlightenment and emancipation. As I will argue, however, mere critical reflection is not enough; a genealogy is successful only insofar as it engages the very affects and physical movements of the body.

One solution to Owen's problem interestingly enough may be gleaned from one of his most astute followers, Cressida Heyes. Heyes in her work *Self-transformations: Foucault, Ethics and Normalized Bodies*, discusses Owen's writings at length and recognizes the difficulties in changing perspectives, both mentally, emotionally and, in some sense, physically, from a merely cerebral stance. She notes, inspired as she is by Foucault, that if genealogy is really about unmasking how the body has been coercively trained and that it is this disciplining of the body that allows for the infusion of power within a body, therefore making it more docile, then one must engage one's embodiment for the sake of emancipation. Heyes then shows convincingly, the benefits of esoteric forms of yoga as a way of unlearning ingrained, somatic disciplinary practices as well as learning new bodily movements that exist beyond the carceral regime.

Although there are problems with Hatab's and Owen's respective solutions to the perennial problems that emerge with the adoption of a perspectivist position, this is no way detracts from their respective books. Scholars actively engaged in the Nietzschean secondary literature, as well as graduate students who are writing dissertations on Nietzsche, would do well to purchase these texts. The intellectual dividends each book affords will be felt for years to come.

Brian Lightbody

Brock University

Bevis E. McNeil, *Nietzsche and Eternal Recurrence*. New York: Palgrave Macmillan, 2021. Pp. xvi; 278.

Professor McNeil has written about the eternal recurrence from the perspective that it is objective cosmology for Nietzsche (1.5). That position is vulnerable to the criticism that we do not find a proof of the Eternal Recurrence in the published works but mostly in the notebooks. The exceptions are two passages from *The Gay Science* (§109 and §341) but they are couched in metaphor. McNeil thus turns to *Thus Spoke Zarathustra* and states that there, in "Vision and Riddle" the metaphor of eternal recurrence is "strengthened and developed into a deductive proof" (99f). McNeil accepts Paul Loeb's reading that together, "Vision and Riddle" and "The Convalescent" contain a prospective memory. Zarathustra has a dying prospective memory of the shepherd and the snake that amounts and it shows up in fact in "The Convalescent" and this shows recurrence-awareness and so is a fictional presentation of evidence that the eternal recurrence is objective cosmology. But McNeil's attempt to establish that Nietzsche intended a deductive proof of the eternal recurrence as objective cosmology in "Vision and Riddle" fails because the context strongly suggests otherwise, and he does not address it. He does not address Laurence Lampert's commentary on this section in *Nietzsche's Teaching* that sharply calls the thesis he advances into question, stating: "this chapter seems to go out of its way to mock syllogistic or formal argument as a way of dealing with fundamental questions" (166). It is a scholarly lapse that McNeil does not engage this context, nor Lampert's development of the foregoing critique to which the context of the deduction gives rise. Also in "Vision and Riddle" and "The Convalescent" in following Paul Loeb, McNeil would seem to assuming that, having left metaphor behind, there is only *one* literal reading possible and that is the reading of recurrence-awareness. I will challenge that inference with a different, likewise literal reading of recurrence awareness in "Vision and Riddle" and "the Convalescent" from an evolutionary biology perspective as epigenetic evolution of novel mental life, to raise the question of what "is true" might then mean in the statement "the eternal recurrence is true."

Along these same lines of establishing that Nietzsche believed that the eternal recurrence was objective cosmology, McNeil presents the idea in Chapter 2 that Nietzsche found a precedent of his idea of the eternal recurrence as objective cosmology in the Stoics and Heraclitus, and in that chapter he relies on Nietzsche's notebooks to make his case that the eternal recurrence for Nietzsche was a cosmological project as it was for the Stoics. Although there is interesting material in Greg Whitlock's translation of Nietzsche's *Pre-Platonic Philosophers* lectures, they are very early in Nietzsche career, before the crisis of 1879 that is the starting point for his tragic wisdom in *Ecce Homo*, that date specifically cited there for its importance in his self-discovery of the meaning of his inheritance from his father as the same year of life as his father's death. He says the decline in 1879 set off his will to health out of which he made his philosophy, which would seem be an identification of origins. McNeil develops this connection from Heraclitus to the eternal recurrence, stating that in the fragments of Heraclitus "we find the originating core of Nietzsche's philosophy of the eternal recurrence" based on the lectures (234f). It becomes his main criticism of

Heidegger's interpretation in section 4.5 that he overlooks the Heraclitean element of play in Nietzsche's cosmology, so the connection of the Eternal Recurrence to Heraclitus it a key connection for different arguments. But in his section 2.4.1 in his introduction to *Greek Philosophy and the Eternal Recurrence*, almost all the relevant citations of Nietzsche's idea of the eternal recurrence that could link it to the Stoa are from the unpublished notebooks, and as I take it, Professor McNeil felt that by this point in his book he had established that Nietzsche thought the eternal recurrence was objective cosmology in the published writings in 2.3.4, as the metaphorical trappings of *The Gay Science* were not to be found in the literal presentation in "Vision and Riddle" where, putatively, a deduction of eternal recurrence is given, so that the notebooks can now come into use.

The one exception of note in this chapter, and it is cited here and in 1.6 on "Eternal Recurrence and Ancient Greek Philosophy," and also cited as the text on which Heidegger relies for his connection of the Eternal Recurrence to Greek cosmology (159, n. 7), is a citation in EH, *Birth of Tragedy*, §3 where Nietzsche writes that the eternal recurrence could have been taught by Heraclitus – the word "could" is important. In this passage, Nietzsche's tracing to the Greeks goes back to the myth of Dionysus and the idea of rejoicing in the inexhaustibility of life even though the highest types are sacrificed, which he, Nietzsche, says was a tragic wisdom and that he was, likely, the first philosopher to have tragic wisdom, and so, likely, first tragic philosopher. The tragic pathos of joy in destruction, which is the "Yes" saying *pathos*, became the Philosophy of Eternal Recurrence (EH, Z §1). Maybe he is the first, he says, but traces of eternal recurrence are in Stoic cosmology and they received all their main ideas from Heraclitus. Nietzsche mentions Heraclitus twice in EH, BT §3, and in both cases the mention is that perhaps the tragic pathos of joy in destruction is what he, Heraclitus, was getting at, that Heraclitus may have been a tragic philosopher too. That is what would be hard to ascertain, whether the philosophy of Heraclitus is a transposition of tragic wisdom. But reading *Ecce Homo* from the beginning, by the time we reach this text in EH, "Why I Write Such Good Books," we have been already introduced to Nietzsche's Dionysian tragic wisdom from chapter one, "Why I am So Wise," and a glance at that chapter shows that Nietzsche's tragic wisdom is what he learned by his experience of his inheritance of the condition from his father of death in life, that it was a "stimulus to *Mehrleben*." He was thrown a bad curve ball by his inheritance, he devised techniques of affirmative psychology to address renunciation, and he developed life in himself to *Mehrleben*, evolution beyond necessary survival adaptations. The subject matter of EH, "Why I am so Wise" is Nietzsche's evolution. "Why I am so Wise" is also heuristic in revealing that the starting point of his development was the "highest opposition" life can face (at the variant to the epigraph at KSA 13, 614) and yet the ending turned out so well in *Mehrleben*, and so he has very great confidence in life's inexhaustibility and indestructibility no matter how deeply it is cut into. This is his *ethos* appeal. So, reading *Ecce Homo* from the beginning, by the time we reach EH, BT §3, we recognize that in his statement there that his doctrine of the eternal recurrence is a philosophical transposition of tragic wisdom, the wisdom referred to is in EH, "Why I am so Wise," that the will to power in life needs resistance to bring itself up to the next level and brings resistance upon itself that it may do so, and did so in him to the point setting before him the highest opposition it had, but instead of being destroyed by it, he reached the highest rung on the ladder of life – and this is testimony to how the will to power works in us. The takeaway from the reference to tragic wisdom in EH, BT §3 is that the tragic wisdom he acquired by his experience of the inheritance of death in life from his father but that led to *Mehrleben* in EH, "Why I am so Wise" is his autobiographical introduction to the idea of the eternal recurrence, of why he is in a position to speak so confidently in this matter. Heuristically, the message of the Eternal Recurrence is that we should discipline ourselves against renunciation and a philosophy of pessimism, opposing it instead with a philosophical form of thinking that disciplines us to accept that there will be no remission of destruction, that destruction will be unconditional always, that it is not going to ease up for us, thus to embrace destruction as the law of evolution. To fully defeat philosophical pessimism we should think of the developmental character of life as being in a closed circle from which we cannot escape, that the circle keeps going on forever – not that that thought makes literal sense as life cannot keep evolving to *Mehrleben* if it is going in a circle. But none of his wisdom, which makes an *ethos* appeal, is relevant to cosmology as an *a priori* project. The only mention of the eternal recurrence in EH, "Wise" is in §3 (final draft) about how he cannot will the eternal recurrence out of an objection to the recurrence of his mother and sister; besides the gloss in EH, BT §3, there are 2 other mentions in *Ecce Homo*, in EH, Z §1 and §6.

McNeil quotes the text from EH, BT §3 in two sections 1.6 and 2.4.1 connecting the eternal recurrence to the Stoics and Heraclitus, but the connection is not direct and cannot support McNeil's reading that Nietzsche's idea of the eternal recurrence had its origin in Heraclitus's cosmology. The text in EH, BT §3 says that the eternal recurrence has is origin in Nietzsche's tragic wisdom, and so connects it to EH, "Wise," yet, in section 4.6 on Dionysus and the Eternal Recurrence, McNeil associates Dionysian *Übermütigkeit*, prankishness, with Heraclitean play (240) without consulting "Why I am so Wise." But Nietzsche's fractured mind split into a second *Döppelgänger* self ("Wise" §3, superseded draft) is just in the context of this Dionysian "prankishness," and that is a context of evolution and the context we should be using to test whether Heraclitean cosmic play is in this thought, which, after all, is before the idea of evolution. One might also consult KSA 11, 212-213 on Dionysian Wisdom. In that notebook text, will to power in life chooses for destructive paths as worthy of eternal recurrence because they are recognized as part of the process of evolution, why else? Finally, in EH, BT §3, Nietzsche refers us to *Twilight of the Idols*, the section, "What I Owe the Ancients," §5, and again Nietzsche identifies himself as the philosopher of Dionysus and as the teacher of the eternal recurrence. There is no mention of Heraclitus in this chapter on the topic of what he owes to the ancients. When the text of EH, BT §3 is studied in relation to texts relevant to it, it cannot bear the argumentative weight Professor McNeil puts on it. Both of McNeil's attempts to read the eternal recurrence as objective cosmology in the two published works cited, here and in "Vision and Riddle" that do not couch it in the metaphorical language of the *Gay Science* that has caused others to reject it as cosmology, fail. The idea that the originating thought of the eternal recurrence appeared for Nietzsche in his reading of Heraclitus fails as its actual origin is Nietzsche's own original tragic wisdom of gratitude for death in life, as he states in *Ecce Homo*, and the Eternal Recurrence bears similarity to Heraclitus only if he too somehow possessed tragic wisdom and turned it into Philosophy as he, Nietzsche, did. That makes the chapter on the Stoics incidental and makes the criticism of Heidegger for missing the Heraclitean element of play in the eternal recurrence cosmology a discussion *entre eux*. *Ecce Homo*, "Wise" tells us about Nietzsche's tragic wisdom. We learn that it is wisdom about the role of destructiveness to life in the workings of evolution in ourselves. Life seeks to develop itself to become more in and by power over a resistance which cuts into it. He survived the worst of it and that is his ethos appeal why he can set the heuristic of the Eternal Recurrence before us. The tragic wisdom that he transposed into the Philosophy of the Eternal Recurrence is a set of empirical statements.

EH, "Wise" §4 and §5 contain affirmation psychology in the setting of Nietzsche's development from the highest opposition to life to *Mehrleben*. There is use of recurring time in both sections. The central activity in each is how affirmative psychology elides the vengeful constructions of the art of the ill will. *Mehrleben* is the result because vengefulness is avoidance of will to power and affirmativeness lines us up with it: we become rich in life as we are not vengeful (Ibid., §6). It is clear that Nietzsche evolved acquired characteristics per these psychologically affirmative exercises; he designated these as being privileges explained by his having had the father he had but he does not say that he owes them to him in the meaning that his father had them before him and now he has them as an inheritence from him. That would be absurd. On the other hand life and the great "Yes" to life, or in the formula from §2, "life and *Mehr-leben*" is not explained by his having the father he did. This latter is an important thought for the interpretation of §3, final because, there again, we encounter opacity in understanding, and the opacity is referred to his second *Herkunft* designated in §1 and §3 identified as "collecting, saving and hoarding up." It is an opacity about the seience of the evolution of will to power. So, must we not ask whether the affirmative psychology of willing the eternal recurrence presented in *Thus Spoke Zarathustra* performs an evolutionary role, just as do the affirmative psychological exercises in §4 and §5 presented in the work that was to autobiographically introduce affirmative thinking of the Eternal Recurrence in AW IV.

Ecce Homo is a work of introduction in which N revealed his psychology and it was to be the autobiographical introduction to his four volume *Hauptwerk, Umwertung aller Werte*. Although not completed, all six plans for it culminate in the announcement of the *Philosophy of Dionysus*, the *Philosophy of Eternal Recurrence of the Same,* in book IV. A onetime subtitle for *Ecce Homo* was: "*Ecce Homo, oder ein Psychologen-Problem: Warum ich Einiges mehr weiss,*" (KSA 14, 465), and the final subtitle of Nietzsche contra Wagner is "*Aktenstücke eines Psychologen*" although it is cited with the same subtitle as the early subtitle for *Ecce Homo* in his letter to Naumann of December, 17 1888 (KSB 8: 1193) to bring it more into line with *The Case of Wagner*'s final subtitle – so persistent was Nietzsche on getting us to understand his psychology, hoping to piggyback on the popularity of *The Case of Wagner* and communicate his psychology by way of being the antithesis of Wagner in *Nietzsche Contra Wagner*. "Why I am So Wise," where the psychological problem is stated, stands out in *Ecce Homo* as the only chapter that would have been expressly picked up on in one of the plans for a book from Nietzsche's critical philosophy that was to be titled "*der Misosoph*" (KSA 13, 194). *Ecce Homo*, "Wise" is very important for the study of the Eternal Recurrence. In his letter to Naumann of November 6, 1888, (KSB 8: 1139) Nietzsche says that because *AntiChrist* will have the benefit of the introduction of *Ecce Homo*, the situation he faced five years earlier with *Thus Spoke Zarathustra*, presumably the broad misunderstanding of *Zarathustra*, will be averted, which suggests that *Ecce Homo* can be read as introductory to *Zarathustra* as well. And, in EH, "Wise" §3, superseded draft, the last line states that to understand anything at all of Zarathustra one must have, like him, a "foot beyond life," which phrase ties to his inheritance from his father. The precondition is in evolution: he enters a world of lofty things as a privilege explained, indirectly, obviously, by his having had the father he had, and that is the world of Zarathustra: the implication is that that world came to be as evolutionary from the inheritance of death in life, as his evolution. Finally, and most relevantly, in the case of a text crucial for McNeil's and Heidegger's project of connecting the Eternal Recurrence to Heraclitus's cosmology, in EH, BT §3, Nietzsche says that the psychology of joy in destruction, which is the psychology of the tragic poets, lies behind the idea of the Eternal Recurrence. That psychology is in evidence in *Ecce Homo*: it is the psychological problem of gratitude for death in life, which is his tragic wisdom. These texts, together with the letter to Naumann, are the basis for my use of EH, "Wise," §4 and §5 on affirmation psychology for my exegesis of the Eternal Recurrence in "On Redemption," that shows it does not document the McNeil (Heidegger) thesis that the Eternal Recurrence was objective cosmology for Nietzsche. To sum up: the plan for a book, *The Will to Power*, was superseded by the work Nietzsche stated to be his *Hauptwerk*, and we do not know that a deductive proof of the eternal recurrence would have appeared in Book IV. Furthermore, Nietzsche's introductory autobiography of tragic wisdom that he transposed into the "Philosophy of Dionysus of the Eternal Recurrence," as he states in EH, BT §3, is a narrative of his evolution to *Mehrleben*. EH, "Wise" §4 and §5 with their disciplines of affirmative psychology, are autobiography of evolution and do not suggest that the intended follow up was to be the Eternal Recurrence as objective cosmology. Also, although by the time of "Wise" §3 final draft, Nietzsche had dropped the plan for a four volume work, that text contains the one explicit mention of the Eternal Recurrence in "Wise," and we should note that the context in which it is mentioned there is the context of evolution, (KSA 6, 268). But McNeil accepts Heidegger's view of the *Will to Power* note-books as reliable in telling us what Nietzsche thought about the Eternal Recurrence although the project was superseded as a literary project.

In EH, "Wise" §4 and §5, Nietzsche presents autobiographical narratives of his affirmative psychology. Both open with a statement of beginnings in his inheritance from his father of death in life and have a *terminus ad quem* in *Mehrleben*. In a variant to the epigraph we read about how he created *ein Mehr* of life in himself "*als Schöpfung, eine wirkliche Zuthat*," which is the highest prize life can get, KSA 13, 614) although it has come of facing its highest opposition, now revaluated, and this is a narrative of evolution.

In EH, "Wise" §4, Nietzsche tells how he does not know the art of making others take and hold things against him, that no one has born him ill will. He adds the words "this too" in reference to this as being a privilege for which he is grateful to his "incomparable father" – so named lest we wonder how he could trace so much back to him, but it is because it is a negative debt and his father is incomparable in being the source of so consuming a negative effect. The referent of "too" is to the superseded draft of "Wise" §3 (KSA 14, 473), in which he says that having the father he did explains all his privileges, but not life or the affirmation of life, and this now also includes the privilege that no one bore him ill will in §4 and of not living among his equals (hard to do!) in "Wise" §5 as explained by having had the father he did. Nietzsche neglected to make the correction when he sent in the final version of §3 in which that line is not to be found. §5 also opens with a reference to his father and also identifies a privilege, namely, of never living among his equals. The section also explains his privilege to be the bearer of heavy guilt per the wrongdoing of others to him, as it is identified as being a privilege in §4. This is part of the §5 privilege of not living among his equals, the privilege of not regarding himself as equally entitled not to be wronged. By relinquishing entitlement not to be wronged he open to blaming himself for the wrongdoing, and this is explained by having had the father he had. But privilege of controlling asserting equal rights not to be wronged belongs to life and the affirmation of life, which did not come to him as inheritance from his father, he says as much, nor, obviously, as inheritance from him after life and the affirmation of life is excluded. The privileges have their origin in his "foot beyond life," which is the negative inheritance from his father, but then how did they come to him from that? It is in this line also that Nietzsche says his privilege of entering a world of lofty and delicate things is explained by having had the father he had, and that one cannot understand a word of Zarathustra who does not have something like his foot beyond life. The world of lofty and delicate things he is privileged to be in is the world of *Thus Spoke Zarathustra*, explained indirectly by having had the father he did from the negative inheritance from him. So the privileges are explained by indirection, but then, to ask again, how did the privileges come from the negative inheritance? After the statement of privilege, the narrative of EH, "Wise" §4 shifts from others as not having ill will against him to his having no ill will against others, even in cases in which he would be upholding a great value by having ill will. Nor does he have ill will against himself, and this (revaluation) marks him as an anti-Christian, he says. It is because he does not have ill will against others that others never had ill will against him. What he did was affirmative – not having ill will towards others is affirmative, ditto in §5, not blaming the wrongdoer for his wrongdoing as deserving punishment is affirmative. If he did not inherit the privilege of others not having ill will against him from his father but it is still explained by the inheritence he did receive from him, it must be have been derived indirectly, and what he inherited directly that it connects to must be whatever he was designating in the phrase above about having a foot beyond life together with its related expressions in the chapter, and of these most importantly in the riddle of §1 of having already died as his father while still living and becoming old as his mother. His privilege of no one having ill will against him was by reason of his having no ill will against others, which leaves the only way the privilege can be traceable to his father to be if the ill will came from him. That means that his trait of bearing others no ill will was the reversal of that inherited ill will and was autogenetic with Nietzsche, and on the path of *Mehrleben*, and that is clearly a phenomenon of evolution. His privileges were acquired characteristics, and this is the way Nietzsche was an *Anfang*, as he tells us about himself in §1, half of his *doppelte Herkunft*. One *Herkunft* is the trajectory of declining life that reached its lowest point in his father, the other *Herkunft* is his creation of life in himself from that lowest point, and in this evolution he is an *Anfang* contra the long developing decline to the lowest rung. He acquired the trait of not disprizing others in ill will and, in §5, the trait of not being aggrieved when he is wrongfully treated and is in the right. There, the privilege is not asserting the equal right not to be wronged, not living among his equals. Relinquishing the equal right not to be wronged opens on to blaming himself for the wrongdoing, even up to the point of bearing the "heavy guilt" identified as a privilege as the opposite of blaming in §4. This too, clearly, is not something his father did before him, so the direct inheritance from him by virtue of which it is explained must have been the ill will disposed to moral aggrievement at being wronged, and the privilege of the heavy guilt then traced to him by indirection could only have come autogenetically by mastering the disposition to aggrievement. These are privileges because they came by mastery of wanting to retaliate, which resists the development of life because retaliation is weakening, and the mastery means evolution of *Mehrleben* to the highest rung of life. He states his privilege of bearing guilt as being a heavy guilt because a heavy guilt is the counterbalance to being severely morally aggrieved, so to bear the heavy guilt means reaching the privilege of the highest richness in life needed to becoming equal to that degree of severity. This is epigenetics, starting with an inheritance of an epigenetic variation from his father and ending with the privileges as acquired characteristics evolved by reprogramming his epigenome by creating a stressful opposing mental environment of affirmative psychology. The acquired characteristics are epigenetic evolution and each is associated with a revaluation.

In EH, "Wise" §4's affirmative psychology Nietzsche tells us that, in his encounters with buffoons, bears and lazy students, he tames every bear, that the buffoons mind their manners around him and the that the lazy students were industrious with him and, to anticipate the theme of §5, that he never gave out a punishment to them. These changes are not realized in reality. The starting point is his inclination to take and hold against, which is an artistic construction by the ill will. Of this inclination, he says, he must remain master: "bear" "buffoon" and "lazy" are the work of the disprizing art of the ill will and contain vengeful, abusive thinking, and he must master the ill will in himself that makes these constructions he says, that is, master a first-order psychology of a disprizing and abusive ill will that otherwise runs out of control. The same pattern may be found in §5: the privilege is that he does not assert his equal entitlement not to be wronged, he does not "live among his equals," which then becomes the privilege to bear the "heavy guilt" as he says in §4 and is in §5 in the ideal of the god who blames himself in some ultimate way. The affirmative psychology that leads to the privilege of a heavy guilt is to blame his own innocence for the wronging – blaming innocence for its liability to wronging – instead of finding turpitude in the wrongdoer, to thus master moral aggrievement and elide the wrongdoer and sometimes even the wrongdoing. Note that the text is progressive on this point, "equal to" the wrongdoing is harder than to the wrongdoer, which implies evolution. What comes from his father is the ill will to be morally aggrieved and he masters aggrievement by the psychological exercise of bearing the guilt for the wrongdoing himself, with *Mehrleben* as the result associated to that acquired characteristic. It is by this indirection of evolution that the privilege is explained. His acquired privileges are his evolution of himself and his revaluations are associated with evolving them.

Affirmative psychological exercises were the key. In §4, Nietzsche masters his ill will to disprize by the discipline of remaining unprepared. He does not permit himself to have negative expectations against which he must brace himself against what is to happen. Instead, by his unpreparedness, what happens is in his experience just as chance would have it and not per his negative forecasting thoughts that would construct it otherwise. He says that he is the equal of any chance event, by which I take him to mean that, in those days at least, nothing like "still a buffoon, but not as bad as I expected he would be" – which would seem to be equal standing against something – is any longer happening, and that, at this point in time at which he is in the position to write *Ecce Homo* to lead us in the Revaluation, he is capable of full equality to chance. But less-than-full-out equality is implied. Importantly for the study of the meaning of eternality in the idea of the eternal recurrence, he says that he is always equal to chance in "Wise" §4, that is, he never arouses ill will in others, and in §5 that he never lives among his equals. These tense universals point to how we should be reading eternality in eternal recurrence. Plainly, they are not literal statements but declamations of love of life enough to do this in that it is very painful, and they make his ethos appeal to lead in the Revaluation. My takeaway from these sections of EH, "Wise" to the Eternal Recurrence is that the Eternal Recurrence too is affirmative psychology that facilitates evolutionary development.

As acquired characteristics, Nietzsche's privileges could have made changes to his germ-line cells as the variation from his father he was trying to sort was very possibly carried in the germ-line. Weismann's infamous barrier that would prevent this has been shown to be false. After all, why would N bother with the evolution of acquired characteristics unless he was thinking that acquired characteristics could consolidate into a common inheritance channel going forward as *"eins dichte und zusammentrage,"* as he might have been formulating the idea of the Overhuman in "On Redemption?" Note that the acquired characteristics of unpreparedness and relinquishing equal entitlement not to be wronged are also revaluations, revaluation psychology here is evolutionary. Also, the revaluation takes us from a lie to the truth: in §4, the moral lie is that what is merely chance can be bearish, etc. and in §5 the moral lie is that I am equally entitled not to be wronged and so there is wronging. If anything is being set up by this for his planned *Hauptwerk*, it would be to look for how the affirmative thinking of the Eternal Recurrence is a revaluation that brings into being a kind of general acquired characteristic, so it is about evolution, not cosmology, and truth as opposed to mendacity.

The central doctrines of Nietzsche's ideas about of evolution are that all living things seek to become more, that they seek out resistances to do so, that a resistance must be equal, not above or below (see EH, "Wise" §7 also, which perhaps was written intending to autobiographically introduce these ideas), and that the will to power in life interprets the overall resistance it faces to make it to be its equal, that is, it scopes the resistance down to an aspect it can face as equal and progresses up the chain of stronger resistance (KSA 12, 2[148], and 2[151]). In EH, "Wise" §4 equality is to the compulsion to disprize is full-out, and that means being equal to pure chance: the affirming discipline of unpreparedness has elided from imagination all there is to disprize as bearish, and for any value presented it is just chance. We find the same idea in §5, which repeats *Zarathustra* I, *The Adder's Bite* on the point, where he neutralizes the wrongdoing to himself by the revaluation that he does not have an equal right not to be wronged although innocent, so he is always equal to not living among his equals, always relinquishing equal entitlement not to be wronged when wronged. He is equal, as equal in will to power, to the wrongdoer's innocence contra his compulsion to blame. So, equality is full out in these sections, making his ethos appeal. He masters aggrievement at his innocence wronged by the psychological exercise of foregoing that he has an equal right not to be wronged, and thus the ill will's imagining of wrongdoing and the wrongdoer cathected with vengefulness and the idea of deserved punishment are elided. The psychology of the ill will in §5 is in the thought: "But I am his equal, equal-in-rights equal, and it is as his equal-in-rights that I am wronged," and he says that he never asserts his equal right not to be wronged. We find the same critique of asserting equal rights (AC §57). Always equal to chance, so not in ill will of expectations for others, and always equal (in will to power) to not living among his equal-in-rights equals so not falling to aggrievement, are declamations, not literal statements. They declare love of life. While the exercises lead to *Mehrleben* and imply the tragic psychology of joy in destruction, they are very painful at the level at which we have to live them and take a lot of courage to do. Both are psychological exercises to control vengefulness and clearly, they had lesser results early on as he applied them, and chance and moral guiltlessness are just neutralities left after the ill will has run itself out. Applying the psychological exercise elides an intentional object of the ill will cathected with vengefulness and replaces it with a neutral *an sich*.

Nietzsche's wisdom, possessing it or not, is at the heart of the statement at EH, BT §3 that Zarathustra's idea of eternal recurrence might be traceable to Heraclitus. It an important text for McNeil and Heidegger. Nietzsche asks the question whether his idea of the eternal recurrence is distinctive in Philosophy, that he has transposed Dionysianism into a tragic philosophy. In Dionysianism we find that in face of the fact that life sacrifices its highest expressions, Dionysianism responds by rejoicing in life's inexhaustibility. This become the bridge to the psychology of the tragic poets of joy in destruction. The point of the section that stands out is the statement that Nietzsche alone was in the position to transpose Dionysianism into Philosophy, tragic *pathos* into philosophical *pathos*, because before him, tragic wisdom was lacking among philosophers, but he is not sure if completely so. He then asks whether there were antecedents of his tragic wisdom and he thinks that maybe it may be found in Heraclitus. If Heraclitus possessed tragic wisdom, his cosmology might be a philosophical transposition of the Dionysian, just as is Nietzsche's. Clearly, if his thought of being the first philosopher to have tragic wisdom is so in play in this history of the Eternal Recurrence in EH, BT §3, before drawing any conclusions we should ask what it was that he presented as his wisdom in the first chapter "Wise," and the least glance at the chapter shows that its subject is evolution. The tragic wisdom here is that destruction is resistance for the will to power, and that otherwise we will not evolve. But then how can the Eternal Recurrence be *a priori* cosmology if it transposes a biological law of our evolution which is empirical? It is heuristic that the Eternal Recurrence is a declamation of resolve to commit to develop life under this law, the resolution that, so to speak, overcomes itself as resolve to make resolve a binding necessity and to so identify with it. What is left is Eternal Recurrence's truth content, but it is just what coincides with the empirical law of our evolution: that will to power needs resistance to develop life and so resistance will keep happening because evolution keeps happening. Combined, these become "Nietzsche's Philosophy of Dionysus: The Philosophy of Eternal Recurrence," but this combination would seem not to be literal cosmology. He may well have first encountered the idea of eternal recurrence in his early studies of Greek Philosophy but that does not mean that he later took it over as cosmology and was writing about it as such in *Thus Spoke Zarathustra*, and there is much to suggest that he had not.

In EH, "Wise" we find that the starting point for Nietzsche is in his inheritance from his father. Next there is a change by means of self-imposed psychological disciplines that address vengefulness against life as cathected in the disprizing constructions of the ill will, and then the creation of life to *Mehrleben*. This is evolution. From what we know about epigenetics, Nietzsche's affirming psychological exercises functioned to create an artificial environment of psychological stress against a first-order psychology that induced change in his inherited epigenetic profile from his father by working against its associated mood disorder. The affirming psychology results in *Mehrleben* because it clears up vengefulness and turns us towards the will to power. But it must be asked why is Nietzsche telling us all this about himself, how can the revaluation pass through him? Perhaps Nietzsche's epigenetic evolution went beyond the idiosyncratic because by reversing what was sui generis in his inheritance from his father he was reversing something wider that was also in that inheritance from him, namely, the socio-biology behind Christian socialization. From my research, which is limited, it is within theoretical possibility that because of his progressive brain disease, Karl Ludwig Nietzsche experienced trauma that induced further regulation of the epigenetic code in him already associated with the mood disorder of revenge that is a single identity in the socialization of Christianity. That further regulation of that identity then affected Friedrich Nietzsche so that in dealing with his father the personal and the universal became indistinguishable for him. Nietzsche's evolution then becomes all our evolution.

Professor McNeil cites "Vision and Riddle" and "The Convalescent" as containing documentation that the eternal recurrence was objective cosmology for Nietzsche, stating that there is a deduction of the Eternal Recurrence in "Vision and Riddle" that is free from the metaphorical presentation of it in *The Gay Science*, and that Paul Loeb has shown that in this text Zarathustra dies and has a prospective memory of his struggle with disgust at humanity that he picks up again reborn in his next life in "The Convalescent" thus to give evidence of recurrence awareness. McNeil writes that in "Vision and Riddle": "the cosmological metaphor of eternal recurrence in GS §109 and §341 is strengthened and developed into a deductive proof" (99). Laurence Lampert argued, and at length, in *Nietzsche's Teaching* that it cannot be judged with confidence what Nietzsche's intention was in presenting the deduction in "Vision and Riddle," (160-171). Zarathustra tells his vision of eternal return to the sailors whom he praises for choosing not to "grope along a thread with a cowardly hand" the thread of argument, hating to deduce a truth they should be courageously guessing at instead. They are identified as the true audience for the riddle in EH, "Why I Write Such Excellent Books," §3. It is not a guess at a possible deductive outcome, not like: 'Gödel guessed at formal undecidability before proving it,'but as an alternative that hates to deduce. They must already know it is true. And, per Loeb's interpretation, I will offer an alternative literal reading of recurrence awareness in "Vision and Riddle" that does not require us to conclude that Nietzsche believed in the objectivity of eternal return cosmology.

If Zarathustra is not deducing the Eternal Recurrence, what otherwise is going on? I suggest that during the presentation of the deduction of the Eternal Recurrence, his evolution to *Mehrleben* by its affirmative psychology is also occurring. Willing the Eternal Recurrence is evolutionary just as are the psychological exercises of EH, "Wise" §§4 and 5. In that case, the deduction is double-signifying: for the dwarf, it is a deduction – and a bad one as it is an enthymeme – and he becomes estranged as it takes on its true identity as evolutionary and he vanishes. He vanishes when the task of evolution is accomplished, his discouraging message, perhaps that the Spirit who bears the fatality [*Verhängniss*] of a task bears the heaviest fate [*Schicksal*] (EH, Z §6), overcome by Zarathustra's courage. Zarathustra's unfolding of the thought of the Eternal Recurrence is accompanied by his awareness of life developing in himself. He recognizes willing the Eternal Recurrence as the principle of *Mehrleben* and runs with it. He hears the dog howling and remembers that he heard a dog howl in his distant childhood and that is his past life and he has died and been reborn. Perhaps what has happened is that given the causal connection between willing the eternal recurrence and the evolution of *Mehrleben*, he identifies with willing the eternal recurrence as the principle of *Mehrleben* up to its literal idea of death and rebirth. Zarathustra temporarily identifies with the idea of the objectivity the *Eternal Recurrence*, the logical "must," of the deduction, as the principle of the evolution of *Mehrleben* to the point of believing he has a memory that the dog barking in his present life happened in his past life, and so believing he has awareness of his present life as a recurrence. Recurrence-awareness would then be the evolution of novel mental life that Zarathustra creates in himself on the spot as willing the Eternal Recurrence is pushed to its literal outcomes.

The point about the sailors guessing is that they do not take the coward's way in following the Eternal Recurrence as deduction but by it, they courageously face their own weakness of vengeful retreat from the law of evolution. The truth they guess is that willing Eternal Recurrence is evolutionary, and it must be that they can guess it because they already know it, an *anagnorisis* of tragic knowledge. So what shall we say "is true" means here? In this reading, recurrence-awareness is not veridical, and the deduction of the Eternal Recurrence is not logically sound, but it can be said that as long as I am achieving *Mehrleben* by believing in eternal recurrence I entirely cease to care about its literal falsehood. That is the reason for believing it although false. However, outside the human life-world, it might mean nothing. Would believing in the eternal recurrence have been developmental for Neanderthals for instance? We do not know whether they needed it. As paleo-epigeneticists mapped out the Neanderthal epigenome and identified the zones of differentiated methylation in their bodies in contrast with ours, they found, as expected, that the zone of highest differentiation was the brain. But then they recognized that one-third of the differences in the human brain had already been traced to cognitive disorders and mental illness in us which Neanderthals, then, must not have had. To go beyond Nietzsche's speculations in *On the Genealogy of Morals* on the origins of morals, perhaps our moralized vengefullness against will to power in life is traceable to gene regulation in this third of the differences, maybe because we had a different history from Neanderthals, or maybe we came out of the same history differently, or maybe because of the traumatic event that brought about their extinction but which we survived – they vanished about 40,000 years ago when the magnetic poles of the earth reversed, and maybe also because of it – all are ways pathologically weakened life that became so vengeful against the will to power that evolution stalled out could have appeared in us but not in them. Just to develop the point a bit, how otherwise could it have happened that we became vengeful against the will to power in ourselves in the weakness of vengefulness to thus make ourselves even weaker in life and slipping backwards? This would seem not to be possible being selected for as an adaptation except in the case in which it appeared in an environment of a cataclysmic and near extinction event that left a traumatic imprint on the epigenome of the remnant population, and not as in the gradualist Darwinian scenario of point mutations selected for. In this case, we can think about recurrence- awareness as novel mental life that we cause to evolve in ourselves as epigenetic evolution as we reverse the effect of our traumatic past, pushing ourselves to assent to the Eternal Recurrence reserved for literal belief. But matters may have stood otherwise with our Neanderthal cousins, and that means that there is a theoretical range in which this statement does not have meaning. So our assent to recurrence-awareness can be stronger than *als ob* assent and can create epigenetic evolution, but it still can be false outside the human life-world. So I agree with the Loeb/McNeil thesis that we can read recurrence-awareness in "Vision and Riddle," but I think only within this evolutionary framework of novel mental life.

The thought of the Eternal Recurrence is first introduced in *Thus Spoke Zarathustra*, on "On Redemption," and Professor McNeil writes a section on it, 1.9, but he does not address the leading idea of the section, and that is that we are vengeful against the will to power in life in ourselves and in others and we exculpate ourselves in the thought of the past's pastness being punishment to be in good conscience about why we are suffering. The line that bears this reading is: "'punishment' is what revenge calls itself, with a lying word it creates a good conscience for itself." As we unravel this line, it becomes clear that willing the Eternal Recurrence is the fix for an empirical a bottleneck in our evolution and not cosmology.

The psychological affirming exercises in EH,"Wise" §4 and §5 work by creating a psychological inconsistency: it is psychologically impossible both to be unprepared and also to construct the other in disprizing constructions (in §4) and, just the same in §5, it is psychologically impossible both to construct the wrongdoer as deserving punishment and also blame oneself for the wronging. Similarly, in willing the Eternal Recurrence, we cannot continue to treat the past's pastness as a punishment since willing the Eternal Recurrence locks out a different past as unavailable to imagination in the recurrence of the same past, so we cannot will both that the actual past recur as the same and also imagine the different past. The imagined different past is cathected with vengefulness against the actual past in which I suffered on account of will to power's development of life. Life will sacrifice itself for power, as Nietzsche tells us in *Zarathustra* II, "On Self-Overcoming."

Mastering vengefulness against the past means becoming equal in will to power to "same past" for any past that I want difference to, where "equal" in "equal to the same past" is an interpretation by the will to power and not the entire actual past all at once, just what I can handle, and then later "equal to" moves up. The end goal is to replace the thought of the past as punishing by its pastness with the thought of neutral time in which the actual past's pastness is elided by the recurrence of sameness, as with it also the imagined different past as it cannot be imagined.

We learn from EH, BT §3 that the Eternal Recurrence is a philosophical transposition of tragic wisdom into Philosophy. Nietzsche can make this transposition into tragic philosophy because, he is, likely, the first philosopher to have tragic wisdom. In "Wise" we learn that his catastrophic inheritance of death in life from his father was a stimulus to evolution, to *Mehrleben*. He discovered in himself a track of non-Darwinian evolution to life beyond life necessary for survival. His tragic fate was death in life and he experienced it as the highest opposition to life as how life became *Mehrleben* in him as power over this tendency. He is grateful to it, to his father "I thank my father," as the highest opposition, and his gratitude is the psychology of the tragic poet. His wisdom is that, like it or not, it is the nature of the will to power in life to sacrifice itself for power over a resistance, power that becomes realized in and by the life of *Mehrleben*, that his inheritance had this meaning. We have tragic fates, but deep within them lie the workings of evolution to develop life in our species. Nietzsche fused his new interpretation of evolution to the tragic psychology of the poets, and this became the Philosophy of Eternal Recurrence.

In all our lives then, and at all times, is the backdrop of will to power sacrificing life to engage a resistance, chunking the resistance into equal bits little by little, to grow in power over it in and by *Mehrleben*. But we are not aligned with this tragic law of our evolution and we become vengeful on account of the sacrifice of life will to power has required. We do not acknowledge it as resistence set by will to power we must face to evolve. Instead, in vengeance against it, I shun will to power for doing this to me, and in others, I actively seek to cripple it. I am vengeful against this resistance to life that has set me back, vengeful against the will to power, and, in vengeance, I construct the resistance in ill will as a historical event. In my ill will, I form up the idea of the different past in my imagination and cathect it with vengefulness against the actual past that pastness has locked up in opposing sameness. I have constructed the resistance set by will to power in the ill will and I forego *Mehrleben*, and so I suffer more. This suffering of which now I myself am the cause has to be hidden, it is telltale, it should not be happening after all, this weakness, and others will wonder. And, of course, I look for the company of those like myself. I lie to myself and to others and hide the trail connecting my suffering to vengefulness against the will to power from my not engaging with it. Were my suffering truthfully exposed and tracked as of my own doing, we would not be allowed to get away with it, as this becomes culture, and – this is the worry – an opposing culture might arise that would force me to stop doing it. So, I reconfigure these events to make my suffering come out as punishment and not my own doing, pastness is punishing me, and I disguise myself in good conscience. N used the phrase, "the Machiavellianism of the good and the just," and it would seem apt to this maneuver. The art of the ill will disprizingly reconstructs in imagination the resistance set by will to power to more power as *Mehrleben* as an event in the historical past with its law of pastness, and imaginatively constructs the different past opposed to it and locked out by pastness cathected with revenge. The true object of revenge is the will to power, revenge that life develops as it does as power, but the vengeful art of the ill will constructs will to power's setting of the resistance in its imagination as an event in the historical past that cannot be different. That thought against it – sameness that cannot be different – is full of suffering and revenge and, as this is all about powerlessness, the ill will assigns its suffering to the past's pastness by the further imaginative vengeful construct that the past's pastness is punishment for its suffering, to create the good conscience. My suffering is actually due to my vengefulness against will to power, but I have lied to claim that my suffering is punishment by the past's pastness and that I am good, that is what good is. All things that happen become punishment, the historical itself becomes punishment. I create the good conscience and face others aggressively in good conscience to counter reproach against myself. I do not want to face having to strengthen myself against the resistance set by will to power as I am, of course, weak at that point, otherwise there is no benefit to life to facing it, and so facing it is painful. Behind us all then, with few exceptions, is failure to square up with the process of will to power to evolve life in us as it does by its law of setting a resistance against us to master in *Mehrleben*. We are always backward looking on our failure because we are vengeful on account of it because more weakened, and remain so in a permanent state. In this way, the culture of Christianity is generated ongoingly. The more I fail, the more will to power tries to build up life by setting resistances for me, and so the more I fail as it is now harder. It is a downward spiral, and soon human beings will appear in whom there is so much weakness that they will not be able to square off with anything the will to power sets as resistance, and that will be the beginning of the end of *Mehrleben* as a potential for our species. Beyond heuristic, the idea of the eternal recurrence unravels the Machiavellian lie about our suffering that the past's pastness is the cause of suffering as punishment, and not that it is failing off engaging with the will to power. It effects an *anagnorisis* and turns us to engagement with how life evolves in us. Willing the Eternal Recurrence destroys the disprizing construction of the historical, destroying the past's pastness and the imagined different past in the recurrence of the same actual past, and so opens on to neutral time, turning us towards engaging with how life evolves itself. Willing the Eternal Recurrence is "beond humanity and beyond time," (EH, Z §1).

The will redeems its suffering foolishly by avenging itself on others. The foolish redemption of the suffering will is by avenging itself on "all who can suffer," that is, all who do not yet suffer and do not just on account of their being in line with the development of life by will to power, and so who can suffer still. This is what Nietzsche was reporting in saying pity had destructively intruded on him as he was growing in *Mehrleben* in all of three cases, (EH, "Wise," §4). We, Christians at any rate, destructively intrude on others in vengefulness against will to power in the development of life working in them. We vengefully seek to create the suffering of weakness in others to get them to fail off trying to master the resistance set before them by will to power, doing so as vengefulness against the will to power ensuring its failure and spreading vengefulness against it. Then life does not evolve anywhere or in anyone, and we are avenged – the mission of Christianity. This point from "On Redemption" relates by contrast to EH, "Wise" §4 and §5 where Nietzsche discloses that this is himself, he is the Christian, but then he shows us how he dealt with it. His ill will is set destructively against the stronger will to power in those he encountered. As he is on the lowest rung on the ladder of life, a case of extreme weakness in life, his first order compulsion is to vengefully attack life in others as vengefulness against stronger will to power. The bears and buffoons and lazy students of §4 and the wrongdoer of §5 are his own disprizing constructions in ill will cathected with vengefulness, as they are always anders. But he masters vengefully striking back by using psychological exercises to create new mental life that replaces the moralizing vengeful ill will of old mental life. In §4, vengeful moralizing has appeared as disprizing others as "bears" and "buffoons" and "lazy." He is inclined by his first-order psychology to want to punish his "lazy" students, but by the psychological exercise of being unprepared, he rethinks them as industrious. He has evolved new mental life as unpreparedness and, in §5 new mental life as not living among his equals to rethink the wrongdoer and wrongdoing as not opprobrious. It is the same with willing the eternal recurrence: it evolves new mental life forcing us out of vengefully interpreting suffering (of weakness) as a punishment by the historical and its pastness to face that we do it to ourselves; "punishment" is the *Lügenwort*. Willing the Eternal Recurrence is on the border line between the foolish redemption of suffering (of weakness) as beings of raging vengefulness on the one side and, on the other, authentic redemption in which I engage positively with the will to power as it works to develop life in myself On the one side is a culture in which we are turned in upon ourselves, abusive of others in their struggles to develop life in themselves, victimizing them in their vulnerability according as they can still suffer, in revenge against the will to power as revenge against the will to power in them. Destructively intruding pity belongs here, (see above). On the other side, I have turned outward away from society and compulsive intrusion on the other to engage alone with the will to power and become who it has set for me to be. Nietzsche's task as teacher of the Eternal Recurrence is to prepare this *Selbstbesinnung* in humankind.

McNeil has two chapters on Heidegger, 3 and 4. He writes in 3 that Heidegger's interpretation is "essential to any genuine understanding of [Nietzsche's] philosophical project" (p.157), a claim many would contest. Chapter 4 is "a full critical appraisal of [Heidegger]" (210), but in these days in which Heidegger has emerged as the central philosopher of a globalizing far right, it should at least be acknowledged that the question of the influence of National Socialism on Heidegger's interpretation of Nietzsche is on the minds of many.

My concern is with McNeil's scholarly lapses. The leading indicator line in "Vision and Riddle" is that the sailors "hate to deduce, and prefer to guess," but McNeil ignores the line and does not engage Lampert's lengthy discussion, based largely on this line, critical of a literal reading of a deduction. McNeil's decontextualization of the deduction from its complexifying context of deducing being hated versus guessing being preferred is a serious scholarly lapse.

In "On Redemption," the key indicator line is: "punishment is what revenge calls itself, it creates a good conscience for itself with its lying word" but McNeil does not address it. This line, together with the line that willing the Eternal Recurrence delivers us from the Spirit of Revenge, implies that willing the eternal recurrence disabuses us of a self-deception that hides not engaging the will to power to life in ourselves. McNeil should have acknowledged and engaged that line because its implication is that the Eternal Recurrence is not objective cosmology. He should have engaged Lampert's critique of Heidegger that ignoring the narrative structure of *Thus Spoke Zarathustra* in regard to this chapter set up his mishandling of "Vision and Riddle" and "The Convalescent" in Part III.

McNeil must also be faulted for uncritically following Heidegger in his use of the text of EH, BT §3 as documentation that Nietzsche believed that precedents of his idea of the eternal recurrence as objective cosmology are to be found in Heraclitus, on the grounds that there are many contextual factors involved in that section that do not allow for this straightforward tracing: that perhaps Heraclitus's cosmology is a transposition of the tragic wisdom, Nietzsche is unsure because he is unsure whether Heraclitus possessed tragic wisdom that he otherwise believes was lacking in philosophers before him but which he has achieved, which is philosophical autobiography, which then implies that the point of the comparison to Heraclitus is lost otherwise; that we learn from EH, "Wise" that the tragic wisdom required to transpose Dionysianism into the Philosophy of the Eternal Recurrence is a thesis about evolution that states a contingent truth about how evolution works, and so its carry over to the Eternal Recurrence makes its truth content also contingent and so knowable only *a posteriori*; that the heuristic involved in the Eternal Recurrence would seem set up by the declamatory tense universals in the affirmation psychology of EH, "Wise" §4 and §5 on the matter of Nietzsche's love of life in overcoming vengefulness against resistance set by will to power and engaging it, as it is painful, to make his ethos appeal, that thus suggests introduction to the idea that eternality in the Eternal Recurrence is declamatory of love of life despite its terrible law of evolution; that the opening quotation in that text to TI, "What I Owe the Ancients," §5 where Nietzsche also identifies himself as working on Dionysianism as transposed into the Philosophy of Eternal Recurrence and that he is the teacher of the eternal recurrence, makes no reference to Heraclitus, nor elsewhere in the chapter of ancients owed and ancients not owed, where one might expect it, in paragraph 4. Furthermore, Nietzsche cites the events of 1879 as the beginning of his philosophy and much of the study of Heraclitus cited by McNeil is earlier. All adds up to the conclusion that the linkage of Zarathustra's eternal recurrence to Heraclitus's cosmology at EH, BT §3 is weak and cannot support McNeil's strong claim about Heraclitus and the Stoa in Nietzsche's thinking about Eternal Recurrence as objective cosmology.

Thomas Steinbuch
Zhejiang University of Science and Technology, Hangzhou City (emeritus)
XiXi District, P.R. China

Jeffrey Church, *Nietzsche's Unfashionable Observations: A Critical Introduction and Guide*. Edinburgh: Edinburgh University Press, 2019. 239 pp.

There is no denying that Nietzsche felt a certain dissatisfaction with his *Unfashionable Observations*: he describes them as *"Jugendschriften"* and implies that his later works should be prioritized.[1] Yet Nietzsche also suggests the deep importance of the *Unfashionable Observations*. In an 1885 draft, he writes: "For me, my 'Unfashionable Ones' signify promises... Perhaps someone will yet discover that from *Human, All-Too-Human* on I have done nothing but fulfill my promises."

Church's *Nietzsche's Unfashionable Observations: A Critical Introduction and Guide* attempts to follow through on this discovery: it provides close analysis of the four essays and argues that the *Unfashionable Observations* comprise an important work of philosophy which helped lay the foundation for Nietzsche's later works. From the beginning of this text, Church emphasizes that there is a single argument underlying the *Unfashionable Observations*. He describes Nietzsche's argument as follows: modern life has become "dehumanizing" and a new form of "culture" is needed – one which will facilitate the production of "exemplary" human beings and thereby the realization of genuine "freedom" (1). Church observes that this argument is deeply influenced by Schopenhauer: Nietzsche follows Schopenhauer in arguing that modern culture is a false form of culture, an 'anti-culture'. Yet Church suggests that this argument is also deeply influenced by Kant: Nietzsche follows Kant in arguing that human existence is capable of acquiring value through the realization of "our distinctively human freedom" (3). Drawing on both Schopenhauer and Kant, Nietzsche attempts to envision a new form of culture which will make human beings freer, and his attempt to do this in the *Unfashionable Observations* laid a foundation for his later philosophical thinking.

---

1.   See Friedrich Nietzsche, *Sämtliche Briefe: Kritische Studienausgabe VI*, Giorgio Colli and Mazzino Montinari, eds. (Berlin: de Gruyter, 1986), 181. (KSB)

Church's reading of the *Unfashionable Observations* places strong emphasis on the influence of Kant and the Neo-Kantian movement[2] on Nietzsche. This is seen with one of his main claims of the book: that Nietzsche's *Unfashionable Observations* were never intended as a work of theoretical philosophy, but rather as a work of Kantian practical philosophy (15). Throughout the *Unfashionable Observations*, Church explains, Nietzsche concerns himself with the question of "the value of human existence" – a question that was fundamental to practical philosophy during the second half of the 19th century. Nietzsche accepts Schopenhauer's view that human existence is naturally without value. Yet Nietzsche goes beyond Schopenhauer at important moments in the *Unfashionable Observations* when he suggests that the lives of "higher individuals" (or "exemplars") give new value to human existence: higher individuals model different forms of human excellence within the cultural community, and thereby help to realize a distinctively human freedom. This concept of "higher individuals", Church suggests, is an appropriation of Kant's concept of the "genius" or "exemplar" (17-18). Just as Kant had characterized the "genius" as a legislator of rules within an aesthetic community, Nietzsche describes the higher individual as a legislator of rules within a cultural community, i.e., a legislator of different ways of living. Given that Nietzsche describes the higher individual as a model of "self-determination" and "freedom", moreover, he appears to connect his concept of higher individuals with Kant's concept of "autonomy" (18). Nietzsche embraces Kant's view that the achievement of freedom confers value on human existence, and he represents the production of higher individuals-or "culture" – as the single way in which human beings are able to acquire such value. The result is a critique of modern culture which is tantamount to Kantian practical philosophy – this is the central claim of Church's reading of the *Unfashionable Observations*.

Church suggests that the structure of Nietzsche's *Unfashionable Observations* is meant to reflect the underlying argument of the text. The first essay, "David Strauss the Confessor and the Writer," represents the first step in Nietzsche's argument: an account of the dehumanized individual of modern society. Nietzsche's intention in this first essay, Church suggests, is to use the example of David Strauss to initiate a discussion about the nature of culture. Nietzsche wants to persuade his reader of the need for a new form of culture, and he does this by representing modern German culture as an example of "anti-culture" and David Strauss as an example of an "anti-genius" (26). In his analysis of this essay, Church suggests that Nietzsche's criticism of Strauss ultimately falls back on the Kantian

---

2.   Church includes Schopenhauer, Lange, and Helmholtz as mid-19th century Neo-Kantian thinkers.

roots of his view of culture. Against Strauss' attempt to establish culture on the foundations of science and reason, Nietzsche insists on the need to separate culture and science. In this way Nietzsche draws on Kant's distinction between theoretical and practical reason, and he represents the production of culture in connection with Kantian practical philosophy.

The second essay of the *Unfashionable Observations*, "On the Utility and Liability of History for Life," contains Nietzsche's criticism of the culture that has produced figures like David Strauss: a culture which oversaturates human beings with knowledge and science. Just as Kant described human beings as divided by the ends of freedom and happiness, Church observes, Nietzsche represents human existence as an unending conflict between the fundamental needs of life (61). This is seen in his descriptions of the imbalanced character of modern culture: our need for perfection in matters of knowledge (especially historical knowledge) continually undermines our need to achieve wholeness and happiness, and thereby threatens our capacity for action. Yet contrary to the standard interpretation of this essay, Church argues that Nietzsche wants to identify the utilities of modern historical knowledge as well as its liabilities. This is seen in Nietzsche's suggestion that modernity's need for perfection has produced an entirely new virtue: "great justice", i.e., the pursuit of truth beyond the perspective of one's own culture (100-104). Focusing in particular on Nietzsche's accounts of "great justice" and the "überhistorischen standpoint," Church argues that Nietzsche attributes value to modern culture's desire to overcome its own perspectival limitations insofar as he believes that this desire can be used to bring modern human beings' need for knowledge into balance with their need for wholeness and happiness (76). What is necessary is simply that our desire for knowledge be extended to the desire to understand what is universally good beyond knowledge. This, Church suggests, is Nietzsche's attempt "to synthesize the *überhistorischen* and historical perspectives": modern historical culture must be brought into a contact with a concern for what is universally good from the perspective of humanity as a whole.

The third essay, "Schopenhauer as Educator," marks a turn in Nietzsche's argument: a turn from the "anti-culture" of modern society to the possibility of a healthier culture. In this essay Nietzsche argues that modernity requires "true educators and cultivators" because true educators alone can help us become accountable for our own existences. For Nietzsche taking ownership for the value of one's existence is a distinctively human form of freedom, and insofar as we require educators to become capable of doing this, "education is liberation" and all true educators are "liberators" (142-143). Nietzsche identifies his own education by Schopenhauer as a model for such liberation. Yet Church emphasizes in his analysis that Nietzsche's goal is to initiate a broader discussion about the interdependence of the individual and the community. He explains that Nietzsche believes educators are capable of increasing the freedom of human beings because they are capable of bringing us back to the collective effort of redeeming human existence (170). Educators like Schopenhauer provide us with an ideal of human existence that entails certain obligations and duties, and we become free precisely by submitting ourselves to these obligations and duties, and striving to give value to human existence at a collective level. Church contends that this account is derived from Kant's account of autonomy: Nietzsche argues that the individual becomes an individual only by helping to create a culture which produces exemplary individuals, and thereby inflects Kant's view that the human being has a moral obligation to perfect themselves and promote the happiness of others (182). Both Kant and Nietzsche suggest to us that we become human beings only by committing ourselves to the realization of humanity – Nietzsche simply follows Schopenhauer in suggesting that our moral obligations are derived from the concrete lives of exemplary human beings.

The fourth essay, "Richard Wagner in Bayreuth," contains Nietzsche's example of an exemplary individual who can help us achieve a healthier form of culture. Nietzsche chooses Richard Wagner: an individual who, despite being shaped by a fragmented anti-culture, forged a unity of character and now presents us with an image of the ideal human being. What enabled Wagner to overcome the shortcomings of modernity, Nietzsche suggests, was his longing for "purification" (205-206). Although Wagner's character was divided by the conflicting drives of natural existence, he was compelled by his desire for purification to redirect these drives inward and "sacrifice" himself so that his drives might combine into a single drive. Nietzsche concludes from this that Wagner demonstrates "the tragic justification of existence": he sacrifices himself so that his audience (or better, those who attend the Bayreuth festival) will believe in the capacity of human beings to transcend their natural existence. Wagner presents us with a possible way forward for modern culture, although Nietzsche emphasizes (following Kant) that there is no historical necessity in this way forward: we must choose this way.

Church concludes the book by considering the influence of the *Unfashionable Observations* on Nietzsche's later writings.[3] Although Nietzsche came to revise some of the views he introduced in the this work (e.g., his view of Wagner as an exemplary individual), many of

---

3. Church discusses the importance of four *Unfashionable Observations* themes for Nietzsche's later writings: the concept of culture as a unity of style, the view that history can be used to promote culture, the concept of freedom as self-determination (or exemplarity), and the view that our drive for power has a self-reflexive dimension.

its themes proved to be deeply important for Nietzsche's philosophical development. Accordingly, Church concludes, the *Unfashionable Observations* should be attributed greater importance than readers have attributed in the past. Church is no doubt correct here, and I believe his analysis is instructive concerning the importance of the *Unfashionable Observations* for Nietzsche's later writings. Yet I question whether Church's reading adequately represents Nietzsche's efforts to challenge Kant and the Kantian tradition in the *Unfashionable Observations*. After all, we cannot ignore Nietzsche's explicit criticisms of Kant, both in Nietzsche's unpublished writings from this period and in the *Unfashionable Observations* themselves.[4] It is important that we take these criticisms seriously – not because Nietzsche saw little value in Kant, but because Nietzsche sought to think both with and against Kant.[5] Nietzsche's interest in challenging Kantian views about human nature and freedom represents an important motivation of the *Unfashionable Observations*, and if our reading of this text does not emphasize this motivation, we will risk losing the sense in which these observations are truly "unfashionable." (In this direction, I encourage the reader to refer to secondary literature that has considered Nietzsche's early critical distance from Kant (Allison (1985) and Ansell-Pearson (1987)).

These comments notwithstanding, Church's Nietzsche *Unfashionable Observations: A Critical Introduction and Guide* deserves recognition for its achievements. This book provides close analysis of a difficult text, and I believe readers will benefit from referring to it alongside the *Unfashionable Observations* themselves. Perhaps most important of this book's achievements is its account of the overall argument of the *Unfashionable Observations*. While Church gives close attention to Nietzsche's reasoning in individual passages and sections, he relates the more specific in Nietzsche's reasoning to the overarching structure of the whole, and the result is a new and insightful reading of the *Unfashionable Observations*. I believe scholars would do well to follow Church in viewing the *Unfashionable Observations* as a single whole.

Christopher Myers
Fordham University

---

4.   In particular, see Nietzsche's criticisms of Kant, KSA 1, 351 and 409-410.
5.   As scholars such as Christa Davis Acampora, *Contesting Nietzsche* (Chicago: University of Chicago Press, 2013) and Yunus Tuncel, *Agon in Nietzsche* (Milwaukee: Marquette University Press, 2013) have emphasized, Nietzsche's reflections on the Greek "agon" [contest] during the period of the *Untimely Observations* influenced the way he interpreted historical figures. For Nietzsche, interpreters are meant to struggle with and against the author. See KSA 7, 9 [327], 29 [169], [173].

Ulrich Baer, ed. and trans., *Nietzsche and Love*. New York: Warbler Press, 2020. 140 pp.

Nietzsche on Love is a collection of all the places in which Nietzsche discusses love or related matters (e.g., marriage). These are laid out one to a page; the book is 140 pages long, though it by no means transcribes all of the places where Nietzsche discusses love. The index to the English *The Gay Science*, for instance, has 28 entries, while this book cites only 8. Most are short, taking up but a portion of their page – a few are more extended.

The editor – profiting no doubt from the availability of indexes and an online, searchable Nietzsche text in German and English at the *nietzschechannel* [http://www.thenietzschechannel.com/] – has sought to structure them loosely, but without any intervening sub-titles indicating changes in focus or theme. There is no commentary, aside from a short biography. The source of each citation is not given, although there is a general list at the end, grouped as to source in a particular book. If you do not know what passage they come from, you will have trouble finding their actual origin.

The tone is set by the first, single page, entry (from *Human, All-too-human*): "*Wanting to be loved*. The demand to be loved is the greatest presumption of all." (1), and to some degree this sets a theme for much of the book, that of the human desire for love. This theme is, in my understanding, however, made more complex by Nietzsche's remark (cited Baer, 50) from *The Gay Science* (§334) that one must "learn to love." This entry is of general importance to an understanding of Nietzsche. It is not only our cognitive capacities that are learned but emotions are also. This means two things. First, as he says in *Schopenhauer as Educator*, humans are today by and large deficient in their ability to love – they have not learned how. Love here means the ability to respond to something that is not yet one's own but to which one finds affinity – such was his initial encounter with Schopenhauer. It also means, secondly, that regaining, or rather learning, this ability is absolutely essential to his cultural and (I might say) political project, the project of what he calls in a letter to Rohde, "a completely new culture." (12/21/1871)

The *object* of love (no page/entry for this) is what Nietzsche calls an "exemplar." Recognition of that which is an exemplar to oneself is something that happens only occasionally, when, as he writes, "the clouds are rent asunder, and we see how we in common with all nature press towards something that stands high over us…" Although this relation is explicitly said to be available, indeed required, of all, it is hard to attain because it is "impossible to teach love."[6]

Note that we can *learn* love, but we cannot be *taught* it. As I have said before (and not only once) – it is the case, if you will excuse me, that what the world needs is love: "Never was the world poorer in love ... The educated classes ... become day by day restless, thoughtless and loveless," as they keep themselves from having anything to love.[7]

On this level, the collection thus serves an important function: it reminds those who see in Nietzsche only the advocate of the Will to Power, of a forceful imprinting of oneself upon the unshaped metal of the world, that there is much more that is complicated in Nietzsche. So: this collection usefully reminds us of the extensive concerns that Nietzsche has with the actuality of love and its cognate matters.

However, one would hardly know from this collection, except with difficulty, that love is *itself* complicated. Christ, for instance, loves too much.[8] Love is a "word... so ambiguous and suggestive...."[9] And here, the collection seems to me also to do a significant disservice. The choice to place these citations each on their own page, without even explicit reference to their source, in effect is subject to all the criticisms that have been made of the book entitled *The Will to Power*. As is known, this volume is a compilation of various Nietzsche texts drawn from an over ten year period of his *Nachlass*, arranged into rubrics that the editors (Elizabeth Forster-Nietzsche and Peter Gast) deemed pertinent to Nietzsche's work.

There are two problems with this. The first is that of the status of the *Nachlass* itself. Much of that material consists of formulations that Nietzsche was working with and that were often abandoned or importantly reworked for eventual publication. Some of it is neither of these and we do not have a clear sense of what Nietzsche might eventually have made of it. This problem affects or infects *Nietzsche on Love* only slightly inasmuch as all but five of the citations are taken from material Nietzsche did publish.

The second and more serious problem is that this layout wrenches each entry from its context. It is simply not true,

---

6. SE §5, WKG 3-2, 374, 378; Appears on p. 123.
7. SE §6, ibid., 362.
8. The theme of the *Antichrist*, cited only once and not on this. See next footnote.
9. MM I, WKG 4-x, 50. See the discussion of these themes in my "Christ, Antichrist and Christianity" in Holger Zaborowski and Markus Enders, eds.. *Jahrbuch für Religionsphilosophie / Philosophy of Religion Annual*, Vol. 13, (2014): 98-118 and "Nietzsche and the Critique of Religion," in Dan Conway, ed. *Essays on the Antichrist* (London: Routledge, 2019), 141-158.

though Arthur Danto (and Richard Schacht) claimed it was, that one can start pretty much anywhere in Nietzsche.

There is a natural order – not that of logic but that of thought – to the sequences in each of Nietzsche's texts. In 1882, Nietzsche sends to Lou Salomé a set of ten teachings on how to write.[10] In them he makes clear that everything in what one writes must be consciously intended with relation to its audience. It is centrally important to realize, however, that his works are *worked* – the story (which he encouraged) that he wrote each of the books of *Zarathustra* in 10 days is simply untrue as the material which appears there occupies several years of notebooks.

However, they are not just (re-)worked and polished: they have a particular style. Take this passage:

> One learns from such an interrogation of oneself, from such a temptation of oneself, to reconsider with a sharper look all that had hitherto been philosophized: one guesses better than before the *four-voiements, the detours, the sorts of city developments, the corners of the sun of thought* to which, against their inclination, thinkers did not let themselves be led or seduced only because they were suffering; one knows from now one towards where, towards what, the sick *body*, in its need, unconsciously, draws, pushes, attracts the spirit – towards the *sun, calm, gentleness, patience, the remedy, in some sense a new comfort.*[11]

The italics are mine. The variations in the listing is a device that Nietzsche uses often in the 1880's. We know from the notebooks for this period that these paragraphs were worked and reworked to get the rhythm and variety of that which is named right. Nietzsche paid attention both to the rhythms and listings he presents here.

Why?

The first thing to realize is that each of these terms modifies slightly and develops the landscape that is being traversed. There are *different* kinds of places, he tells us (*fourvoiements*, detours, urban developments, corners of shadow left by the sun) not all of which thought has found the way to visit. No one word will suffice for what Nietzsche is telling us – as Beckett notes in *Endgame,* we never can (nor should) say "just one thing."

The prose therefore reflects the superfluity of what there is, of where we might find ourselves at any given time, of the reality that the world is always more than we can make of it in a single instance. Consider again: Speaking of the death of God and thus

---

10.   Nietzsche to Lou, *Nietzsche Samtliche Briefe,* 6: 243-245. See my "In Defense of Rhetoric *or* How to Take a Writer Seriously: Nietzsche and the Question of Rhetoric," *Political Theory*, Vol. 41, No. 4 (August 2013): 507-532 .

11.   FW, *Vorrede,* §2.

"European morality in its totality," he writes: "This long and fruitful succession of *breaks, destructions, declines, overturnings....*" and a bit later on, in the counterpoint of health, "Will we perhaps experience too strongly the effect of the immediate consequences of the event [the death of God] .. as a *light, a happiness, a release, a becoming happy, a new comfort, a dawn of a new sort* which is only with difficulty described....?" (GS §343) The passages in italics (mine) reject the possibility that there is a root category which might contain our experiences. The world lies as surface, not in depth. One can only fully understand a passage in Nietzsche with reference to its resonances, what Babette Babich has called its "concinnity."

Or still again: in *Gay Science* §345 that which is "weakened, thin, extinguished, self-denying, disavowing" is opposed to that which is "powerful, whole, assured, firm," in a situation where "destiny, distress, opportunity, torment, voluptuousness, personal passion," present themselves as "surprise, dissension, contradiction" at the end of which one can "rest, breathe, take up again."[12] When in the preface to the *Philosophical Investigations*, Wittgenstein refers to his work as a series of landscapes across which the mind travels, he is doing something much like what Nietzsche is doing in these passages. On the first level he is getting the world right – one never thinks only "of one thing." (To get an example in a mechanical way: look up "world" in a thesaurus. One gets "globe, orb, planet, mother earth, terrestrial sphere, spaceship earth, biosphere, cradle of humanity" – and pushing a bit further on: "place, area, locale, territory, vicinity" – and then onwards still: "domain, region, zone, sphere, province, kingdom, sovereignty..." and that is not half of it). What Nietzsche is concerned with in these constructions is all that any/each word calls to mind.

Take the famous passage in the third book of *the Gay Science* (§125) about "God is dead." Without beating a drum for numerology, it is the 15th entry into the book. The book starts (§108) with an entry on the Buddha. Fifteen entries after §125, there is yet another entry on the Buddha that marks a pause in this chain of thoughts. (We go to a short entry on "mystical explanations" that serves as a kind of introduction to a set of reflections on "religiosity," "prayer," God," and so forth. This means that this entire sequence develops what is necessary to grasp fully the claim that "God is dead."

Each entry is titled.

The first set goes like this: §108: *New struggles* (how the shadow of Buddha and God live on after their death); §109 *Let us beware* (warning when dealing with "new struggles"); §118: *Origins of knowledge* (the problem is that there are "nothing but errors");

---

12. Translation is mine.

§111: *Origin of the logical* (why these errors); 112: *cause and effect* (again); §113: *On the doctrine of poisons* (again; now the origin of science); §114: *How far the moral sphere extends* (again: "all experiences are moral experiences"); §115: *the four great errors* (Summary of preceding); 116: *The herd instinct* (Consequences on encountering morality); §117: *Herd remorse* (more consequences); ... §123: *Knowledge as more than a mere means* (Again: on the faith in science); §124: *In the horizon of the infinite* (So what is our condition?: no more reference points); §125: *The madman (death of God)*.. and so forth. The last, §142, is about clearing the air of "everything Christian," which is all part of what has been considered. Much as Wittgenstein wrote about his work, these entries follow each other in a "natural" way, as in a conversation, but not in a logical one. And this is true in all that Nietzsche published – see, for instance, Alexander Nehamas's reading of the natural sequencing in the first section of *Beyond Good and Evil*.[13]

Pleasing as it is to have all these interesting passages about love, the decision to present them in this isolated matter encourages a fallacious way of reading Nietzsche. One is likely to come away with a set of box-top or fortune cookie pronouncements – and that seriously undercuts, even denies that Nietzsche is a great thinker, a radical philosopher and philologist. Nietzsche was more than *bon mots*.

Tracy B. Strong
University of Southampton
UCSD, Distinguished Professor, emeritus

---

13. Alexander Nehamas, "Who Are the Philosophers of the Future?: A Reading of *Beyond Good and Evil*" in: Robert Solomon and Kathy Higgins, eds., *Reading Nietzsche* (Oxford: Oxford University Press, 1988), 46-67.

Earl R. Nitschke Postcard

Tracy B. Strong, *Friedrich Nietzsche and the Politics of Transfiguration* (1975). Black and White photocopy of the book cover, laminated to brown postcard stock, with a blue circled '70' stamped in red. This card was sent to Tracy Strong's office at the University of San Diego in California.

Nietzsche Images, after Warhol.

Babette Babich is Professor of Philosophy at Fordham University, NYC and Visiting Professor of Philosophy, Religion and Ethics at the University of Winchester, England. Books include *Günther Anders' Philosophy of Technology: From Phenomenology to Critical Theory* (2022); *Nietzsches Plastik. Ästhetische Phänomenologie im Spiegel des Lebens* (2021); *Nietzsches Antike. Beiträge zur Altphilologie und Musik* (2020). Recent edited volumes include *Reading David Hume's ‹ Of the Standard of Taste ›* (2019) and *Hermeneutic Philosophies of Social Science* (2018).

Marc de Launay is Researcher at the Archives Husserl de Paris (ENS-Ulm), specialising in neo-Kantian themes. He teaches at the l'École normale supérieure dans le cadre du Master de philosophie contemporaine de PSL. He is equally dedicated to the translation of German philosophers and poets (Kant, Schelling, Nietzsche, Husserl, Cohen, Rosenzweig, Scholem, Cassirer, Adorno, Habermas, Blumenberg, Rilke, Peter Handke). Currently he is the director of the works of Nietzsche in the prestigious Pléiade edition. He is author, among other works of *Nietzsche. Essais d'autocritique* (1999); *Néokantismes et théorie de la connaissance* (2000); *Nietzsche, Œuvres philosophiques, Vol. I La Pléiade* (2000); *Une Reconstruction rationnelle du judaïsme* (2002); *Qu'est-ce que traduire ?* (2006, also in Portuguese, 2020); *Lectures philosophiques de la Bible. Babel et logos* (2008); *Nietzsche. Correspondance choisie* (2008); [with Marc Crépon], *Configurations du nihilisme* (2012); [with Ch. Krijnen], *Der Begriff der Geschichte im Marburger und Südwestdeutschen Neukantianismus* (2013); *L'événement du texte* (2015); *Nietzsche, Œuvres, vol. II, La Pléiade* (2019); *Nietzsche et la race* (2020); and *Peinture et philosophie* (2021).

Justin Gottschalk has degrees from Yale and the University of California at San Diego. He lives outside Washington, DC with his wife and two daughters, and has research interests in Nietzsche, Heidegger, and Strauss (as well as Peter Sloterdijk, H. P. Lovecraft and Hunter S. Thompson). He is currently working on putting together the essays on Shakespeare by the late Paul Cantor. Originally, Justin is from the Catskills (Liberty) in upstate New York and has taught for Lewis & Clark College's Semester in DC program.

Brian Lightbody is Professor of Philosophy at Brock University. Among his recent books are *A Genealogical Analysis of Nietzschean Drive Theory* (2023) in addition to *Nietzsche's Will to Power Naturalized: Translating the Human into Nature and Nature into the Human* (2017) and *Dispersing the Clouds of Temptation: Turning Away from Weakness of Will and Turning Towards the Sun* (2015).

Heinrich Meier is emeritus Director of the Carl Friedrich von Siemens Foundation in Munich and Professor of Philosophy at the University of Munich, and permanent Visiting Professor in the Committee on Social Thought at the University of Chicago. His books include *Carl Schmitt and Leo Strauss: The Hidden Dialogue* (2006 [1995]); *The Lesson of Carl Schmitt: Four Chapters on the Distinction between Political Theology and Political Philosophy* (1998 [2011]); *Leo Strauss and the Theologico-Political Problem* (2007 [2006]); *On the Happiness of the Philosophic Life: Reflections on Rousseau's "Rêveries" in Two Books* (2016 [2011]); *Political Philosophy and the Challenge of Revealed Religion* (2018 [2017]); *Nietzsches Vermächtnis. "Ecce homo" und "Der Antichrist." Zwei Bücher über Natur und Politik* (2019); and *What Is Nietzsche's Zarathustra? A Philosophical Confrontation* (2021 [2017]).

Christopher R. Myers is a doctoral candidate in philosophy at Fordham University. His dissertation focuses on the hermeneutic motivations of Nietzsche's and Dilthey's philosophies and he has an article forthcoming on Nietzsche's relationship to modern philosophical hermeneutics.

Gary Shapiro is Tucker-Boatwright Professor of Humanities and Philosophy, Emeritus, University of Richmond. He has written five single-authored books, among them, *Nietzsche's Earth: Great Events, Great Politics* (2016); *Archaeologies of Vision: Foucault and Nietzsche on Seeing and Saying* (2003); *Earthwards: Robert Smithson and Art After Babel* (1995); *Alcyone: Nietzsche on Gifts, Noise, and Women* (1991) and *Nietzschean Narratives* (1989). He is completing a book on the philosophy of the novel.

Thomas Steinbuch received his PhD in Philosophy from the University of Massachusetts at Amherst under the directorship of Leonard Ehrlich, renowned scholar of the philosophy of Karl Jaspers. With the encouragement of Ernst Behler, Steinbuch wrote a commentary on chapter one of Nietzsche's *Ecce Homo* (1994). He is co-founder of the World Posthuman Society with Yunus Tuncel and Francesca Ferrando and co-editor with Professor Tuncel of *Infinity: A Journal for Posthumanists*. He maintains a video lecture series on Nietzsche's *Ecce Homo* on YouTube. He resides in China. Retired from full time teaching at Zhejiang University of Science and Technology in Hangzhou, he is active in the life of the university and the student community of Xiaoheshan.

Tracy Burr Strong (1943-2022) was Professor of Political Philosophy at the University of Southampton in the UK and Distinguished Professor of Political Science, *emeritus* at the University of California at San Diego. Strong authored numerous essays on Nietzsche, Hobbes, Rousseau, Schmitt in addition to Lenin and Marx and Heidegger but also Mark Twain, Hawthorne, Emerson and Shakespeare as well as reflections on film and political theory. His recent books include *Learning One's Native Tongue: Citizenship, Contestation, and Conflict in America* (2019) and *Politics Without Vision: Thinking Without a Bannister in the Twentieth Century* (2012) and he also wrote *Friedrich Nietzsche and the Politics of Transfiguration* (1975, 3rd ed., 2001) and the introduction, "The Sovereign and the Exception" to Carl Schmitt, *Political Theology* (2005). In addition to editing several collections on Nietzsche, Strong was also editor of the journal, *Political Theory* (1990-2000).

FRITZ SCHUMACHER. Entwurf zu einem
Nietzsche-Monument (1898)
Copyright 1984 by Walter de Gruyter

Earl Nitschke Postcard
Fritz Schumacher, *Entwurf zu einem Nietzsche Monument* (1898)
65# printed card stock, central image outlined in blue. Sent to the editor in Nitschke's hand-
addressed, trademark, mailing of his work.